THE SIX NATIONS OF NEW YORK

A volume in the series

DOCUMENTS IN AMERICAN SOCIAL HISTORY

Edited by NICK SALVATORE

This facsimile of *The Six Nations of New York: The 1892 United States Extra Census Bulletin*

was produced from an original in the collections of The New-York Historical Society.

The Society acknowledges generous funding from

the De Witt Wallace–Reader's Digest Fund,

the Samuel and May Rudin Foundation, and

the Geraldine R. Dodge Foundation.

The Six Nations of New York

The 1892 United States Extra Census Bulletin

with an Introduction by

ROBERT W. VENABLES

CORNELL UNIVERSITY PRESS

ITHACA AND LONDON

Library of Congress Cataloging-in-Publication Data

The Six Nations of New York: the 1892 United States extra Census bulletin / with an introduction by Robert W. Venables.
   p.   cm. — (Documents in American social history)
   Originally published: Washington : Dept. of the Interior, Census Office, 1892. With new intod.
   Includes bibliographic references.
   ISBN 0-8014-3226-X (cloth : alk. paper)
   1. Iroquois Indians—Census, 1890.   2. New York (State)—Census, 1890.   I. Venables, Robert W.   II. Census bulletin (Washington, D.C.)
III. Series.
E99.I7S55   1995
929' .3747—dc20
                                                                                                    95-31895

CONTENTS

INTRODUCTION

Robert W. Venables

The "Six Nations" described in this volume are the American Indian nations of the Iroquois Confederacy. Centuries ago, and long before the arrival of Europeans, the Confederacy was founded by the people of five nations—Mohawks, Oneidas, Onondagas, Cayugas, and Senecas. The Tuscaroras became the sixth nation by 1722, after fleeing colonial slave hunters in their North Carolina homelands and taking refuge under the protection of the Confederacy. The core of the Six Nations' ancestral homeland stretches across what is now New York State.[1]

Centuries before the Tuscaroras joined the Iroquois Confederacy, a spiritual leader named Deganawidah, known as The Peacemaker, inspired the Iroquois to create one nation that nevertheless remained multinational. Oren Lyons, a contemporary Onondaga chief, explains that

the Peacemaker's vision extended to all the peoples of the earth then known to him. He erected a symbolic tree that has come to be called the Great Tree of Peace. This tree was intended to symbolize the law and would be visible from a great distance to all nations. Under the great long leaves of this tree (the Great Law of Peace) people would find protection from arbitrary violence. . . .

The Peacemaker unified the nations of the Confederacy into one nation under an ideology that was complex but whose symbols were easy to grasp. The longhouse, which had been a dwelling in which extended families resided, became the symbol of a nation: the sky was compared to its roof; the earth was like its floor; and the fires burning inside were like the nations stretching east to west. The people of a nation hold fast to the idea of a united nation, and The Peacemaker introduced ideas to promote that sense of unity.[2]

The Six Nations was published in 1892 as part of the Eleventh Census of 1890. At that time the U.S. government was attempting to break up tribal land by dividing communally held reservations into smaller segments—allotments—which would then be distributed to individual Indians as private property. The legal instrument for this policy was the General Allotment Act (also known as the Dawes Act) of 1887. At the same time, the United States intended to force Indians to give up their own national identities and become full citizens of the United States. They would thus become taxable, for the official designation of American Indians on federally recognized reservations was "Indians not taxed."[3]

Because the legal status of the Six Nations was complex, the Iroquois Confederacy had been exempted from the act.

The Six Nations is in part an attempt to see if and how the principles of the Dawes Act could be applied to the Iroquois.

Superintendent of the Census Robert P. Porter was referring to the allotment policy when he spoke of "advancement" and "civilized methods" in *The Six Nations*: "This bulletin contains various statistics and interesting facts concerning the history, present condition, and outlook of the Six Nations of New York . . . and shows their capacity and promise for future advancement . . . and attitude toward a full adoption of civilized methods."[4] Thus *The Six Nations*, though on the surface simply a census, was conceived to advance U.S. policy. The government's intent was no secret. In 1894, a briefer version of *The Six Nations* appeared as a chapter in a massive census of all the American Indian nations, and that volume states directly:

Allotment became a policy after the [Dawes] act of February 8, 1887 (24 United States Statutes, 388), although allotments of specific holdings of lands to Indians had often been made by law before this date. This act did not apply to the lands of the Six Nations of New York, The Five Civilized Tribes, three tribes in Indian territory, and one tribe in Nebraska, adjoining the Pine Ridge reservation in South Dakota. . . .

The several policies of the United States in relation to the Indian prior to 1890 have resolved themselves into three specific features, as follows:

(1) Allotment of Indians on definite areas of land, thereby destroying the reservations.
(2) General education of Indians, whether citizens, self-supporting, dependent, reservation, or tribal.
(3) Enlistment of reservation Indians as soldiers in the regular army, both in the cavalry and infantry.[5]

The statistics and descriptions in *The Six Nations* provide a finely detailed portrait of the people of the Six Nations more than a century ago, but the tabulations of cows, horses, even pianos served a more calculated purpose. Such facts permitted officials to calculate whether the Six Nations were ready—in the opinion of the Great White Father in Washington, D.C.—to join the American mainstream. Thus the report tries to assess how many individuals among the Six Nations might be eager for assimilation and how many were still determined to maintain their tradition and religion. Statistics regarding Christian missionary churches, for example, served as barometers of assimilation. But ironically, this report also detailed the factors that ultimately would hinder the government's efforts to implement its policy: the Iroquois's treaty and other legal rights.

The allotment of communally owned ("tribal") lands among individual Iroquois would have made them homesteaders on their own land and citizens of someone else's country. The report's white male authors candidly stated their own bias in favor of assimilation, but they concluded that the Six Nations could not be forced into the U.S. mainstream because their treaty and legal rights were intact. Today the Six Nations defend their sovereignty and their legal rights by citing evidence presented in *The Six Nations*.

The Six Nations' Iroquois Confederacy: The Haudenosaunee

The people who are pictured in *The Six Nations* wear Victorian clothing. They are described as living in Victorian-era homes on Victorian-era farms. They are nevertheless confident that they are Haudenosaunee, as they call themselves. Their traditional religion, their languages, and their philosophy exist within this Victorian context. They are part of their era, but they are apart from the non-Indians who surround them. The political philosophies and events and cultural evidence discussed in *The Six Nations* indicate how the Haudenosaunee have survived: they neither totally reject nor totally absorb ideas and objects from outside. Instead, they balance their own traditions with current realities. They have made their share of mistakes along the way; as in all societies, there are factions and clear disagreements about how each generation of Haudenosaunee should step toward the future. But they have survived because they have always adapted.

The longhouses in which the Haudenosaunee once lived were multifamily dwellings constructed with a wood frame, rafters, and an arched roof, weatherproofed with large sheets of bark. Many longhouses were 100 feet long; ceremonial longhouses stretched over 300 feet. Even in the mid–eighteenth century, after repeated epidemics had reduced their populations, the Haudenosaunee were still building multifamily longhouses that were typically 80 feet long and 17 feet wide. The name Haudenosaunee evokes the multifamily, communal spirit of these homes: it means People of the Longhouse, and it also serves as a metaphor for the multinational confederacy that extended from east to west across what is now New York State. The Mohawk Nation is the Keeper of the Eastern Door of this longhouse; the Senecas are the Keepers of the Western Door; the Onondaga Nation is the central hearth and fire, where the Grand Council of the entire Confederacy meets.

The term "Six Nations" remains significant because it is one of the terms by which the United States has recognized the Haudenosaunee in various treaties and laws. "Iroquois" has become accepted usage in English and French. Today, when the Haudenosaunee use these languages, they often use both "Haudenosaunee" and "Iroquois," although increasingly they prefer "Haudenosaunee." "Iroquois" was originally a pejorative, probably a French adaptation of the Algonquin "Irinakhoiw," "real adders"—the Algonquins and French being habitually at war with the Haudenosaunee.[6]

Historically, the Confederacy's heartland has been within what are now the boundaries of the State of New York. But Haudenosaunee lands extended southward into northern Pennsylvania, eastward into western Vermont, and northeast into the St. Lawrence Valley; and through diplomacy, trade, and wars of conquest the Haudenosaunee exerted power and influence in lands far beyond the present borders of New York State.

In crafting the Iroquois Confederacy, The Peacemaker had an able associate in Haiyentwatha, known today as Hiawatha. The Haudenosaunee believe their confederacy could have been founded as early as the thirteenth century; certainly it preceded contact with the Europeans. Elisabeth Tooker has concluded that "although there is some disagreement [among non-Indian scholars], virtually all suggested dates for the founding of the League fall in the period from A.D. 1400 or slightly before to 1600 or slightly before."[7]

Iroquois towns were agricultural centers and trading centers long before the Europeans arrived, and these towns quickly adapted to the new arrivals. In 1634 a Dutch trader, Harmen Meyndertsz van den Bogaert, described a Mohawk town with longhouses and extensive storage of corn and other crops. He also noted that the Mohawks had already adapted a wide variety of iron utensils to their own uses. Bogaert believed the iron utensils he saw had been stolen, but it is more likely that they had been obtained in trade.

> We came into their first castle that stood on a high hill. There were only 36 houses, row on row in the manner of streets, so that we easily could pass through. These houses are constructed and covered with the bark of trees, and are mostly flat above. Some are 100, 90, or 80 steps long; 22 or 23 feet high. There were also some interior doors made of split planks furnished with iron hinges. In some houses we also saw ironwork: iron chains, bolts, harrow teeth, iron hoops, spikes, which they steal when they are away from here. Most of the people were out hunting for bear and deer. These houses were full of grain that they call ONESTI and we corn; indeed, some held 300 or 400 skipples. They make boats and barrels of tree-bark and sew with it. We ate here many baked and boiled pumpkins which they call ANONSIRA.[8]

Van den Bogaert also noted that smallpox, accidentally introduced by the Europeans, had broken out in the area. It was one early episode in a long series of epidemic diseases that would alter the course of all American Indian histories.

Van den Bogaert relates that, at another town, "three women came here from the Sinnekens [a Dutch term for any Haudenosaunee living west of the Mohawks, not just the Senecas] with some dried and fresh salmon. . . . They also brought much green tobacco to sell, and had been six days underway. They could not sell all their salmon here, but went with it" to another town.[9] These women traders had traveled for six days through Haudenosaunee country, evidently without male escort—an indication of how Haudenosaunee women were respected and how safe travel was for Haudenosaunee in their own country.

Trade between Haudenosaunee and Europeans transformed both cultures. European colonists thrived on the fur trade, and so did the Haudenosaunee. By the eighteenth century, the Haudenosaunee were receiving a wide range of goods in payment for furs. A letter from Sir William Johnson to Governor General Jeffrey Amherst, dated February 12, 1761, demonstrates that trade goods were not simply objects of commerce: they were sold at the fort–trading posts, but they were also given away to ensure friendship and to secure alliances. The letter also indicates that European traders were making a profit of 50 percent. And finally, it indicates how the Haudenosaunee were adapting new ideas and new technologies. Johnson notes that the British had traditionally provided a blacksmith at each fort to repair muskets and tools:

> Inclosed is a List of Such Goods as are usually wanted & bought by the Indians, and on which the Trade Should at least at Oswego have 50 per Cent profit. . . . I am certain at that rate the Indians will think themselves fairly dealt by. It has always been Customary; it is very necessary, and will always be Expected by the Indians that the Commanding Officer of Every Post have it in his power to supply them in Case of Necessity with a Little Cloathing, Some arms & ammunition to hunt with; also some provisions on their Journey homewards, as well as a [black]smith to repair their arms & working utencils &ca.[10]

Johnson then lists goods usually traded to Indians, ("the prices differs with the times"), including coarse woolen blankets of various colors, called strouds; "French Blankets . . . in great Demand being better than ours" (even though war with the French was in progress); English blankets; Welsh cottons; "Flowered Serges"; "Calicoes"; "Linnens & ready made Shirts, of all Sizes"; needles; awls; knives; "Jews Harps small & large"; "Stone & plain rings"; "Hawks bells"; blades; horn combs; "Brass Wire different Sizes"; "Scizars & Razors"; "Looking Glasses"; "Brass & tinn Kettles large & Small"; "Women & Childrens Worsted & Yarn Hose with [an ornamental pattern called] Clocks"; "Roll of Paper Tobacco. Also Leaf D[itt]o"; "[tobacco] Pipes long & Short"; "Red Leather trunks in Nests"; black and white wampum; "Silver Works or toys, which the Indians wear"; "Tomahawks or small hatchets well made"; "Pipe Hatchets"; "Tobacco, & Snuff boxes"; "Pewter Spoons"; "Gilt Gill [four-ounce] Cups"; gunpowder; flints; "Small bar lead of $1\frac{1}{2}$ lb each"; "Goose, Duck, & Pidgeon Shot"; fowling muskets; beaver and fox traps; iron spears for fishing and for killing beavers; and "New England, or [New] York rum."[11]

Just as a Dutch trader observed iron hinges on Iroquois doors in 1634 and Johnson itemized popular trade goods in 1761, so *The Six Nations* lists Victorian furnishings in Haudenosaunee homes and includes photographs of individuals dressed in the non-Indian styles of the 1890s. No matter what the century, the Haudenosaunee have always adopted those parts of the material culture of non-Indians which they have found useful.

The Haudenosaunee's political survival parallels their adaptation of non-Indian material culture. They have adapted to newcomers rather than totally rejecting them or wholeheartedly embracing them. The political instruments they have depended on are treaties. Treaties neither absorb nor reject. They provide links between two political entities; each party signs a treaty so that each can remain unique and separate. The Haudenosaunee made treaties with the Dutch and then with the English, forging peaceful trading relationships that became known as the Covenant Chain. The economic and political links of the Covenant Chain shaped more than a century and a half of relations with English-speaking peoples before the American Revolution tore the English colonies apart. Today the Haudenosaunee are still confident that their treaties with the United States are shaped by the Covenant Chain.

When an Onondaga speaker, Sadakanahtie, addressed Governor Benjamin Fletcher in 1694, he began by proclaiming trade and military unity with the English: "We assure you we will never separate from you, we still have one Head, one Blood, one Soul, and one Heart with you." Because this obligation was mutual, however, Sadakanahtie noted his confidence that the governor would not make a separate peace with the Haudenosaunee's enemies: "As to the Dewagunhas and Shawonons, we are confident Cayenguirago [Governor Fletcher] will not admit them into his Government, till they have made Peace with us, which we shall willingly grant." He then eloquently reviewed the Covenant Chain and its connections to other Haudenosaunee symbols:

1. A rope of bark fibers, representing a weak tie or trade alliance, which the Iroquois chose to replace because it was too weak.
2. An iron chain, a synthesis of Indian and European elements that captured the idea of interdependent trade and evoked both the imagery of linked arms often used by the Haudenosaunee and the iron and other goods brought by the Europeans.
3. The pine tree of peace, symbolic of the Iroquois concept of legal order as established by the Confederacy's founders.
4. Wampum, shell beads in strings or woven in great belts and used to convey the seriousness of business at hand or to commemorate a solemn pledge. (Wampum are discussed and illustrated on pp. 25 and 33–34.)

All these symbols are evident in an English translation of Sadakanahtie's 1694 speech.

> When the Christians first arrived in this Country, we received them kindly. When they were but a small People, we entered into a League with them, to guard them from all Enemies whatsoever. We were so fond of their Society, that we tied the great Canoe which brought them, not with a Rope made of Bark to a Tree, but with a strong iron Chain fastened to a great Mountain. Now before the Christians arrived, the General Council of the Five Nations was held at Onondaga, where there has, from the Beginning, a continual Fire been kept burning; it is made of two great Logs, whose Fire never extinguishes. As soon as the Hatchet-makers (their general Name for Christians) arrived, this Gen-

eral Council at Onondaga planted this [pine] Tree [of Peace] at Albany, whose Roots and Branches have since spread as far as New-England, Connecticut, Pensilvania, Maryland and Virginia; and under the Shade of this Tree all these English Colonies have frequently been sheltered. Then (giving seven Fathom of Wampum) he renewed the Chain, and promised, as they likewise expected, mutual Assistance, in Case of any Attack from any Enemy.

Clearly, Sadakanahtie believed that the Haudenosaunee did not owe their survival to the English during the furious frontier wars with the French and their Indian allies. Rather it was the English who were sheltered and allowed to grow under the Haudenosaunee Tree of Peace. Having reviewed the union of Haudenosaunee and various colonies in the Covenant Chain, Sadakanahtie told New York's governor that the Haudenosaunee might have to make a separate peace with the French: "Brother Cayenguirago [Governor Fletcher], speak from your Heart, are you resolved to prosecute the War vigorously against the French, and are your Neighbours of Virginia, Maryland, Pensilvania, Connecticut and New-England, resolved to assist us? . . . If our Neighbours [the colonies] will not assist, we must make Peace."[12]

The Haudenosaunee and the English spent much of the eighteenth century polishing the Covenant Chain. Both sides recognized that their political systems would remain separate even as their trade and military alliance linked them together. As the Haudenosaunee were a separate, independent people, the English continuously had to request, rather than require, their assistance.

The evolution of the Covenant Chain was explained in 1744 at Lancaster, Pennsylvania, by Canasatego, an Onondaga chief representing all of the Haudenosaunee. Canasatego's speech of June 26, 1744, was translated by Conrad Weiser. Canasatego eloquently reviewed the Chain's historic roots in trade, using imagery very similar to Sadakanahtie's fifty years before. This is the speech of a representative of an independent people who did not consider themselves to be subjects of the English Crown. On the contrary, the Haudenosaunee regarded themselves as "elder brethren" of the English, at one with them in spirit, on the same land.

Canasatego was about sixty years old in 1744, tall, vigorous, broad-chested. He describes how the Mohawks secured the first Dutch ship, symbolic of trade, to trees in the Mohawk country. Then they tied the rope so the Dutch could reach other nations of the Iroquois Confederacy. First, the rope was tied to the Mohawks' neighbors, the Oneidas, represented by a rock (the Oneidas are the People of the Stone, or O-na-yote-ka-o-no). Then the rope was tied to the "big mountain," the Onondagas (the People on the Hills, or O-nun-da-ga-o-no). Since Onondaga is the capital of the Confederacy, the entire confederacy, including the Onondagas' neighbors to the west, the Cayugas and the Senecas, was now involved in the trade. Canasatego describes how at Onondaga the rope is entwined with the Confederacy's wampum, the sacred shell beads by which solemn events and pledges were commemorated.

The Dutch asked for land, he says, and it was granted on the assumption that they would "enter into League and Covenant with us, and . . . become one People with us." Canasatego may be referring to the Haudenosaunee concept of being of "one mind"—that is, holding common views—rather than to assimilation of the Dutch population. But he may also be stating an original intention to adopt the Dutch into the protection of the Great Tree of Peace, following the Haudenosaunee tradition of permitting adopted nations to retain their separate identities and cultures while accepting Haudenosaunee authority in external (international) affairs. Whatever his exact meaning, Canasatego notes that when the English arrived, they asked that the Iroquois extend the same friendship, and it was done. The English then replaced the wampum-entwined rope with a silver chain, to which the ship of trade has since been attached.

In this vision the Dutch and the English are peoples on a ship, for the Haudenosaunee perceived Europeans as visitors and guests on Haudenosaunee lands. Moreover, Canasetego emphasizes that the admission of the Europeans was the result of Haudenosaunee action: "we tied their Ship." At the beginning and at the end of his speech, Canasetego stresses that the land belongs to the Haudenosaunee.

Canasetego addressed the governor of Maryland in these words:

WHEN you mentioned the Affair of the Land Yesterday, you went back to old Times, and told us, you had been in Possession of the Province of *Maryland* above One Hundred Years; but what is One Hundred Years in Comparison of the Length of Time since our Claim began? Since we came out of this Ground? For we must tell you, that long before One Hundred Years our Ancestors came out of this very Ground, and their Children have remained here ever since. You came out of the Ground in a Country that lies beyond the Seas, there you may have a just Claim, but here you must allow us to be your elder Brethren, and the Lands to belong to us long before you knew any thing of them. It is true, that above One Hundred Years ago the *Dutch* came here in a Ship, and brought with them several Goods; . . . and . . . we were so well pleased with them, that we tied their Ship to the Bushes on the Shore; and afterwards, liking them still better the longer they staid with us, and thinking the Bushes too slender, we removed the Rope, and tied it to the Trees; and as the Trees were liable to be blown down by high Winds, or to decay of themselves, we, from the Affection we bore them, again removed the Rope, and tied it to a strong and big Rock [*here the Interpreter said, They mean the* Oneido *Country*] and not content with this, for its further Security we removed the Rope to the big Mountain [*here the Interpreter says they mean the* Onondago *Country*] and there we tied it very fast, and rowll'd Wampum about it; and, to make it still more secure, we stood upon the Wampum, and sat down upon it, to defend it, and to prevent any Hurt coming to it, and did our best Endeavours that it might remain uninjured for ever.

During all this Time the New-comers, the *Dutch*, acknowledged our Right to the Lands, and sollicited us, from Time to Time, to grant them Parts of our Country, and to enter into League and Covenant with us, and to become one People with us.

AFTER this the *English* came into the Country, and, as we were told, became one People with the *Dutch*. About two Years after the Arrival of the *English*, an *English* Governor came to *Albany*, and finding what great Friendship subsisted between us and the *Dutch*, he approved it mightily, and desired to make as strong a League, and to be upon as good Terms with us as the *Dutch* were, with whom he was united, and to become one People with us: And . . . he found that the Rope which tied the Ship to the great Mountain was only fastened with Wampum, which was liable to break and rot, and to perish in a Course of Years; he therefore told us, he would give us a Silver Chain, which would be much stronger, and would last for ever. This we accepted, and fastened the Ship with it, and it has lasted ever since.[13]

Several days later, Canasatego delivered his concluding remarks to the colonial subjects of King George II, urging them to consider the example of the Haudenosaunee:

We heartily recommend Union and a good Agreement between you our Brethren. Never disagree, but preserve a strict Friendship for one another, and thereby you, as well as we, will become stronger.

OUR wise Forefathers established Union and Amity between the *Five Nations*; this has made us formidable; this has given us great Weight and Authority with our neighbouring Nations.

WE are a powerful Confederacy; and, by your observing the same Methods our wise Forefathers have taken, you will acquire fresh Strength and Power; therefore whatever befals you, never fall out one with another.[14]

Benjamin Franklin echoed Canasatego's sentiments when he wrote James Parker on March 20, 1750/51, irritated that the colonists had yet to form a union comparable to that of the Iroquois:

It would be a very strange Thing, if six Nations of ignorant Savages should be capable of forming a Scheme for such an Union, and be able to execute it in such a Manner, as that it has subsisted Ages, and appears indissoluble; and yet that a like Union should be impracticable for ten or a Dozen *English* Colonies, to whom it is more necessary, and must be more advantageous; and who cannot be supposed to want an equal Understanding of their Interests.[15]

During the French and Indian War, from 1754 to 1763, the Haudenosaunee played a major role as allies of the English. After the French in Canada were defeated and France signed the Treaty of Paris, the Haudenosaunee could no longer threaten an alliance with the French whenever they suffered at the hand of Britain's land-grabbing colonists. Nevertheless, the British needed the Haudenosaunee as an economic ally in the fur trade. The Haudenosaunee were also possible allies against Indian nations beyond their frontier. For these reasons, British diplomats knew they could not afford a war with the Confederacy, and all these circumstances ensured Haudenosaunee independence. General Thomas Gage, commander in chief of British forces in North America, was also in charge of relations with the Indians. On October 7, 1772, Gage wrote to Sir William Johnson, superintendent of Indian affairs:

As for the Six Nations having acknowledged themselves Subjects of the English, that I conclude must be a very gross Mistake and am well satisfied were they [the Haudenosaunee] told so, they would not be well pleased. I know I would not venture to treat them as Subjects, unless there was a Resolution to make War upon them, which is not very likely to happen, but I believe they would on such an attempt, very soon resolve to cut our Throats.[16]

The British were unable to control their own colonists, however, and during the 1760s and early 1770s, corrupt British officials joined colonists in land speculation and frontier expansion. When the American Revolution broke out, the Patriot side could not control supporters who wanted Haudenosaunee lands, and by the end of the Revolution the new government was dominated by these people. The revolutionaries ended the war in debt, especially to veteran soldiers, and the government decided to pay these debts in Indian land, whether particular Indian nations had been neutral, pro-British, or even allies. The Indian treaties signed after the Revolution, then, were excuses for land seizures.

The American Revolution disrupted the historical relationship between the Haudenosaunee and the English-speaking peoples and threatened the treaties of the Covenant Chain. Both the British and the Patriots called upon the Haudenosaunee for support. Internally, factions within the Confederacy mirrored the factions within the British colonies: some were neutral, some were pro-Patriot, some were pro-British.

The Haudenosaunee realized that civil war is evidence that no one person or group can exert leadership. The Confederacy was and is a government that works by consensus, mediating among its separate parts rather than dictating to them. When consensus disintegrated, the Confederacy's Grand Council covered the council fire and thus was "neutral" during the war. The Haudenosaunee believed this disruption was temporary: once people had done what they believed they must do, the Confederacy and its spiritual ideas would once again rally the Haudenosaunee.

During the war, however, individual Haudenosaunee men fought on both sides, and their mothers, wives, and sisters supplied them with clothing and food. Though there were neutrals throughout the Confederacy, Oneidas and

THE SIX NATIONS OF NEW YORK

Tuscaroras were associated primarily with the Patriot side whereas Mohawks, Onondagas, Cayugas, and Senecas were associated primarily with the British. The war dealt cruelly with Indians, whites, and blacks throughout the rebellious colonies and on all the frontiers. It destroyed intricate trade networks that the Haudenosaunee had been building for nearly two centuries. During the summer and fall campaigns of 1777, at Oriskany and at Saratoga, Haudenosaunee warriors killed one another in battle, breaking The Peacemaker's direction at the founding of the Confederacy that no Haudenosaunee should spill the blood of another. The white civil war was mirrored in this Haudenosaunee civil war. During the summer and fall of 1779, Patriot armies guided by Oneida scouts destroyed Onondaga, Cayuga, and Seneca towns and all their cornfields and orchards. The devastation was a severe blow to the economic and political interests of Haudenosaunee women, because agriculture was under their control.[17]

Most Iroquois towns, no matter what political stance their residents took, were destroyed. Ferocious frontier warfare created thousands of Iroquois refugees. Most of them eventually reconstructed their lives in their original homelands, but about two thousand, from all six nations, fled to Canada. Accompanying them were people from nations adopted by the Iroquois, such as Tutelos and Nanticokes, as well as some Iroquois allies, such as the Delawares. Under the direction of two Mohawk leaders, Joseph Brant and John Deseronto, they established two major settlements in Ontario: near present-day Brantford, in the Grand River valley, and near present-day Deseronto. Haudenosaunee who stayed south of the Canadian border saw their homelands limited by a series of treaties made with the United States between 1784 and 1857.[18]

Between 1783 and 1890 the policies of the United States reshaped the Iroquois landscape in ways the founders of the Confederacy could not have anticipated. The historian John Mohawk calls the treaties and other land transactions "a series of land swindles."[19] Thomas Donaldson, one of the authors of *The Six Nations*, came to a similar conclusion. His attitude is paternalistic and his language overly polite, but he is frank: "Envious Caucasians, hungering for the Indians' landed possessions in New York state, as elsewhere, have been active and earnest in efforts to absorb their substance. They have been kept from doing so thus far through the efforts of earnest and active fair-minded people, who have prevented their spoliation."[20]

Here are a few of the important events that occurred during this period:

1783. The Treaty of Paris ended the war between Great Britain and the United States, but it did not end warfare involving Indians. Ignoring the Indians' land rights, the treaty transferred all Indian lands to the jurisdiction (but not ownership) of the United States. The United States had the right of "preemption," and Britain would not interfere as the United States undertook to negotiate with individual Indian nations. No Indians were consulted in the negotiations, and no Indian nation ever ratified the agreement. The United States therefore sought separate treaties of peace with various Indian nations.

1784. Negotiations at Fort Stanwix (Rome, New York) were convened to end the American Revolutionary War between the Patriots and the various pro-English Haudenosaunee nations. Before negotiations began between the Haudenosaunee and the United States, the various Haudenosaunee nations divided by the war reconciled and reunited their confederacy in an elaborate ceremony. An observer recorded:

> We were witnesses of the reconciliation of the Oneidas with their [Haudenosaunee] enemies. Although both dwelt, for several days, near the fort, and in spite of the cessation of hostilities, communications had not been reestablished between them. The "Great Grasshopper" [an Oneida leader] . . . followed by five other savages . . . went to the cabins of the Senecas. They walked stiffly, and stopped from time to time. The chief of the Senecas came out and went to receive them at some distance. They sat on the grass and compliments were exchanged by the two chiefs. They smoked the pipe of peace and separated. The next day the visit was returned by the Senecas to the Oneidas with . . . the same formalities.[21]

The terms of the Treaty of Fort Stanwix basically transferred to the United States the Haudenosaunee's jurisdiction over their old "empire," consisting of trade alliances and outright conquests in the lands west of Pennsylvania. The treaty stipulated that the Haudenosaunee "shall be secured in the peaceful possession of the lands they inhabit east and north of the same [i.e., in present-day New York State west of Rome], reserving only six miles square round the fort of Oswego, to the United States, for the support of the same."[22] But because the terms were imposed under threats of force, the Haudenosaunee Grand Council refused to ratify the treaty during deliberations in 1786. The United States proceeded unilaterally, as if the treaty had been ratified.

1790. On December 1 the Seneca leader Cornplanter addressed President George Washington in Philadelphia. During the past half-dozen years, both the United States and the State of New York had made several treaties with the Haudenosaunee. The state's strategy was to make a separate treaty with each nation. American settlers streamed into what had been the Haudenosaunee homeland for thousands of years. Cornplanter went to Philadelphia hoping for federal intervention. He described the current circumstances of the Haudenosaunee:

> Father: The game which the Great Spirit sent into our country for us to eat, is going from among us. We thought he intended that we should till the ground with the plough, as the white people do, and we talked to one another about it. But before we speak to you concerning this, we must know from you whether you mean to leave us and our children any land to till. Speak plainly to us concerning this great business.
>
> All the lands we have been speaking of belonged to the Six Nations; no part of it ever belonged to the King of England, and he could not give it to you.
>
> The land we live on, our fathers received from God,

and they transmitted it to us, for our children, and we cannot part with it.[23]

1791. On March 8, Joseph Brant, the prominent Mohawk who led many Haudenosaunee into Canadian exile, wrote to Samuel Kirkland, an American missionary among the Oneida Iroquois. Kirkland had been instrumental in persuading the Oneida Iroquois to side with the Patriots during the American Revolution, even as Brant was leading Mohawks to fight on the side of the British. Nevertheless, the Oneidas were being pushed out of their lands as quickly as those Haudenosaunee who had been neutral or pro-British. In outlining a just policy toward the Indians, Brant pointed to the Americans' own situation before the Revolutionary War: "Treat with them as a free people, and abandon the Idea of conquest. Let the Americans look back and take a cursory view of their own affairs at the beginning of the late war. They say themselves that it was not the Amt. of the Tax, but the mode of laying it that gave disgust, because it was opening the door for extending it to posterity."[24]

1794. The United States, eager to keep the Haudenosaunee from joining the Indians in Ohio in a war to stop U.S. expansion, decided to recognize all of the six nations in one treaty that guaranteed them rights to their reservation lands and to self-government. The Treaty of Canandaigua (November 11, 1794) noted that "the United States would never claim" the land still in Haudenosaunee possession. These lands were to "remain theirs, until they choose to sell the same to the people of the United States, who have the right of purchase." The Treaty of Canandaigua also pledged that the United States would never "disturb . . . any of the Six Nations, or their Indian friends residing thereon and united with them, in the free use and enjoyment" of their lands. This article recognized the sovereign right of the Haudenosaunee to determine who could live within their borders, and it also recognized a long-established tradition among the Haudenosaunee to adopt other Indians into their midst.[25]

1799–1815. A Haudenosaunee teacher, Handsome Lake (Ganio dai io, 1735–1815), received messages from spiritual beings. The Code of Handsome Lake—the Gai wiio—was a synthesis of the old ways with the new messages. These messages reinforced the traditional moral positions of individuals and families, but they also provided spiritual assurances that the Haudenosaunee could survive in an area much smaller than their original extensive homeland. Cornplanter had noted in 1790 that the Haudenosaunee were already discussing one alternative: the men would take up the plow. Haudenosaunee hunting lands had so far diminished that the men's traditional occupation of hunting could no longer be the principal business of their lives. But agriculture was traditionally the domain of Haudenosaunee women. Spiritual messengers instructed Handsome Lake to tell his followers that men could now farm the fields that the women once controlled. Though this message certainly deprived women of one of their roles, it did not diminish their status: the Code of Handsome Lake maintained cultural balance by preserving women's traditional political right to elect the male chiefs. The spiritual messengers told Handsome Lake:

Three things that our younger brethren (the white people) do are right to follow.

Now, the first. The white man works on a tract of cultivated ground and harvests food for his family. So if he should die they still have the ground for help. If any of your people have cultivated ground let them not be proud on that account. If one is proud there is sin within him but if there be no pride there is no sin.

Now, the second thing. It is the way a white man builds a house. He builds one warm and fine appearing so if he dies the family has the house for help. Whoso among you does this does right, always providing there is no pride. If there is pride it is evil but if there is none, it is well.

Now the third. The white man keeps horses and cattle. Now there is no evil in this for they are a help to his family. So if he dies his family has the stock for help. Now all this is right if there is no pride. No evil will follow this practice if the animals are well fed, treated kindly and not overworked. Tell this to your people.[26]

1812–1815. In the War of 1812 Haudenosaunee again fought on both sides. Haudenosaunee living in Canada fought on the side of the British; although Handsome Lake urged his followers to stay out of the war, many Haudenosaunee in New York chose to fight with the Americans. Their brave service did not stop the United States or New York from continuing their pressure on Haudenosaunee lands.

1821–1845. Despite the assistance the Oneidas had rendered during the Revolution, the United States removed most of them from their homelands. The removal of the Oneidas was only one part of a policy to remove Indians from the eastern woodlands. During the 1820s, 1830s, and 1840s, Indian nations east of the Mississippi were forced westward along the "Trail of Tears." Most of the Haudenosaunee successfully resisted removal by asserting their treaty rights and by recruiting political allies among non-Indians. Between 1821 and 1842, however, most of the Oneidas were forced from New York to Wisconsin. Between 1839 and 1845, several hundred Oneidas also moved to Ontario, leaving only a small remnant behind in their traditional homeland.[27]

1838. The Treaty of Buffalo Creek, an outright fraud committed by the United States, intended to take all Haudenosaunee lands and remove the Haudenosaunee to Kansas. The treaty intended to suppress any Haudenosaunee claims of sovereignty within New York State. Thus, except for some lands still possessed by Long Island Indians, all land in the State of New York would clearly be under the jurisdiction of the state and under the sovereignty of the federal U.S. government. Although the other Haudenosaunee were involved, the treaty focused on the Senecas. Back in 1826, the Senecas had sold land to the Ogden Land Company, which had obtained the exclusive right to buy land from the Senecas. The firm expected to get the remaining Seneca lands under the 1838 treaty. None of the Onondagas at the reservation near Syracuse signed the treaty, but some Mohawks, Oneidas, and Cayugas did. The treaty implied that the lands of the Mohawks and Oneidas, after they had removed, would be publicly sold under the supervision of the United States and the State of New York. The Cayugas had already sold their lands in New York between 1789 and 1807 (except for a small grant of land that was finally sold in 1841). Because many Cayugas had moved to other Haudenosaunee reservations, the treaty promised the Cayugas funding to help them resettle in Kansas. In fact, the treaty made provisions for each of the Haudenosaunee populations.[28]

Some legitimate Haudenosaunee leaders signed the treaty. Some were gullible and others could be bribed—a scandal among their own people. But many signers had no positions of leadership and were merely fronts bribed by the United States, the State of New York, the Ogden company, and other land speculators. Many U.S. citizens rallied to oppose the treaty, especially the Quakers, who focused on the Senecas, because they had the most land to lose. In 1840 the Quakers published *The Case of the Seneca Indians in the State of New York. Illustrated by Facts.* This 256-page report was "Printed for the information of the Society of Friends, By Direction of the Joint Committee on Indian Affairs, of the Four Yearly Meetings of Friends of Genesee [New York], New York [City], Philadelphia, and Baltimore." Among the many documents reprinted in the report was "The memorial of the chiefs and sachems of the Seneca nation" to President Martin Van Buren, dated December 10, 1839, which complained that

> the Government agent, Mr. James Stryker, placed here, as we have supposed, to protect our interests, has engaged in unfair and corrupt means to obtain signatures. Bribes have been offered by him to chiefs, to induce them to sign; in proof of which, we refer to the affadavits. . . .
>
> We have been defrauded in so many ways. . . . You have prospered and increased in numbers and in wealth, by the protection of the Great Spirit, who watches alike over the destinies of the red man and the white. We hope and trust that we shall not be driven by force and against our wishes from our peaceable possessions. We ask to be permitted to remain, and live and die on the ground given us by God, and bequeathed by our fathers; and may the Great Spirit make you a great, a just, and a happy nation.[29]

1842. The U.S. government did not simply give up. Instead, it followed a great fraud with a lesser fraud. U.S. officials charged with Haudenosaunee affairs left the Mohawks, Oneidas, and Onondagas alone for the moment and forced upon the Senecas a second treaty at Buffalo Creek, signed on May 20, 1842. The Senecas who signed it believed the treaty included the best terms they could obtain for their people, and so it was politely termed the "compromise" treaty. The compromise, however, was all on one side. The Senecas retained their lands in New York except the reservation land along Buffalo Creek, near Buffalo, and the lands of the Tonawanda band of Senecas. The Tonawanda band immediately protested because none of their chiefs had signed the treaty.[30]

1848. On the Seneca reservations of Allegany and Cattaraugus, a strong faction of Senecas overthrew the traditional chiefs and installed a new government based on direct election and male suffrage. They thus overthrew the power of the clan mothers. Each clan mother had traditionally consulted the other women in her clan, and the women resolved whom their clan mother should appoint as a chief. The Seneca Revolution was encouraged by Quaker supporters. The traditional chiefs later fielded candidates for president of what was reconstituted as the "Seneca Nation," but the momentum at Allegany and Cattaraugus favored assimilation to non-Indian ways. The State of New York incorporated this new Seneca Nation and absorbed it within its legal system.

1857. The Tonawanda band of Senecas finally secured a land base. They had always opposed the provisions of the 1842 treaty, which gave up their lands to the Ogden Land Company, and in 1848 they rejected the Seneca Revolution, because they were determined to maintain the traditional election of chiefs by the women of the clans. After a long legal battle, they used U.S. money to buy back some of the land ceded against their will in 1842. Prominent among Seneca leaders who worked to reestablish their reservation were Jimmy Johnson, a grandson of Handsome Lake, and Ely S. Parker.

1861–1865. During the American Civil War, 162 Haudenosaunee from within New York reservations served in the Union army and navy. Several dozen Oneidas whose families had been removed to Wisconsin also served. Many were killed or wounded, and two Senecas, William Kennedy and John B. Williams, died in the notorious Andersonville prison in Georgia. Ely S. Parker, who had served his Tonawanda people so courageously in the battle to retain a homeland, served as the aide of an old friend, Ulysses S. Grant. At Appomattox, Parker—whose handwriting was far superior to Grant's — penned the surrender terms Grant dictated to the Confederate army of Robert E. Lee. When Grant became president, Parker became the first American Indian to serve as commissioner of Indian affairs.[31]

1876. *The United States* v. *Abraham Elm* was a federal case brought against an Oneida veteran of the Civil War. Elm, born in 1842, had served in the Fifth Vermont Volunteer Infantry. As the court noted, Elm "voted for representative in Congress at the election of 1876, claiming to be a citizen of the United States. He was indicted for illegal voting . . . and the question is now presented whether or not the Oneida Indians [in New York] are citizens of the United States, and as such, entitled to vote." The court declared that because the tribe's communal lands had been alloted to its members as separate, individually owned plots of land,

> the tribal government has ceased as to those who remained in this State. It is true, those remaining here have continued to designate one of their number as chief, but his sole authority consists in representing them in the receipt of an annuity which he distributes among the survivors. The twenty families which constituted the remnant of the Oneidas . . . do not constitute a community by themselves, but their dwellings [on allotted lands] are interspersed with the habitations of the whites. In religion [the Oneidas remaining in New York were Christians], in customs, in language, in everything but the color of their skins, they are identified with the rest of the population.

Elm had "abandoned his tribal relations" and was indeed a citizen of the United States.[32]

The thirty-four-year-old veteran had won his right to vote but had inadvertently given the State of New York cause to regard the Oneidas as having ceased to exist as a people. This situation would not be reversed until 1920 when another federal court found in *United States* v. *Boylan* that Oneidas still living on a thirty-two-acre plot of land were still a federally recognized Indian nation.

The *Elm* case focused on two major themes, allotment and assimilation. From the perspective of the United States, allotment and private property could lead to citizenship and taxation, especially if particular Indians no longer retained a substantial Indian identity, as indicated by such factors as religion and customs. The *Elm* case thus led to the investigations reported in *The Six Nations*, with its examinations of how Haudenosaunee lived, how they worked, how they worshiped, and the extent of their material possessions.

Allotment and an End to the Reservations: Political Issues

Could the Iroquois be transformed into all-American homesteaders? This question lies behind the comprehensive report *The Six Nations*.

"Homesteader" has a wholesome American ring to it, conjuring up the Jeffersonian ideal of the yeoman citizen-farmer. The word reflects the U.S. government's encouragement of individual citizens to take up a plot of land and a plow. But the Iroquois had been farmers long before 1492, planting corn, beans, squash, and other crops on lands held in common. Iroquois philosophy set the principle for a relationship with the soil: the land did not belong to individuals. The United States opposed this principle, and in the late nineteenth century launched a political assault against the Six Nations of the Iroquois Confederacy.

In fact U.S. policy was aimed primarily at Indian nations west of the Mississippi, where most lands still in Indian's possession were located. The United States was determined to impose individual landownership on the various western nations. Virtually all American Indians maintained that land could not be owned by individuals. The U.S. army, for all its wars of conquest, had not destroyed this premise. So the United States set out to subdue the Indians with legislative mandates, committee reports, and proclamations from well-intentioned Christian reform organizations. And although the communal reservation lands of the Haudenosaunee were not the prime target of the United States, they were the prime target of the State of New York.

The Six Nations is only one part of a more extensive study issued by the Census Office in 1894 as *Report on Indians Taxed and Indians Not Taxed in the United States (Except Alaska) at the Eleventh Census: 1890*. Both colonial and U.S. officials had made estimates of Indian populations, but the first U.S. census to include Indians was the seventh, of 1850. One clear purpose of the 1890 census was to determine the number of "Indians living within the jurisdiction of the United States."[33] This seemingly bland statement is highly charged in legal terms, for it assumes that Native American nations had relinquished their sovereignty. In practice, many Indian nations maintain that they are still sovereign. The sovereignty issue is addressed in *The Six Nations*, and the debate goes on today.[34]

The Six Nations is a summary of issues as perceived by three U.S. investigators: Thomas Donaldson, Henry B. Carrington, and Timothy W. Jackson. Most of the data were gathered by Carrington in 1890 and 1891, and the report was published in 1892. The census outlines Haudenosaunee history, details current conditions of Iroquois communities, and defines the legal and treaty obligations between the United States and the Iroquois.[35]

In the 1880s, official U.S. government policy was to make American Indians "homesteaders" on their own reservations. Eventually, each individual Indian would become a U.S. citizen rather than a citizen of an Indian nation. In 1887 Congress passed the General Allotment Act, also known as the Dawes Severalty Act, as we noted earlier. The act proposed to divide up the reservations, providing 160-acre homesteads to heads of families, 80 acres to single Indians, and 40 acres to minors. Any acreage left over would be sold as "surplus" to non-Indians. Moreover, the land allotted to individual Indians would not be in their full possession: the United States would hold these plots "in trust" for at least twenty-five years. It could then transfer ownership to the individual Indians, who could thereafter sell the land.[36]

In 1890 the act's principal sponsor, Senator Henry L. Dawes of Massachusetts, addressed the eighth annual Lake Mohonk Conference of the Friends of the Indian, a reform group that had helped design the Dawes Act. Revealing his attitude toward race as he summarized the goals of allotment, Dawes referred to data currently being gathered across the continent for the 1890 census:

> The census will, I think, reveal some startling facts in regard to the Indians. We have been under the impression for the last twenty-five years that the Indian has been increasing. That, I think, will appear not to be true for the last ten years. The aggregate will fall, I am informed, considerably short of what it was in 1880. The loss is mostly confined to the full bloods. Mixed

bloods hold their own better, and are increasing in this land.

The Indian people will not remain as a separate race among us, as the black race must. These figures show where he is going. He is to disappear in the midst of our population, be absorbed in it, and be one of us and fade out of sight as an Indian. So you must administer the Indian Bureau with that in mind. You must give up the idea of keeping Indians together. You must, as soon as possible, spread them out into the community among the people. . . . Their blood, their sinew, their strength, are needed, and will help us.[37]

Because the Haudenosaunee's treaty and other legal relationships with New York State and the United States were already complex, the Dawes Act specifically exempted the Senecas of New York from its provisions. But treaty and legal obligations notwithstanding, the Dawes Act implied that other Haudenosaunee reservations—as well as the lands of the Shinnecock, Poosepatuck, and Montauk Indians on eastern Long Island—could be divided into individually owned plots. In fact the provisions of the Dawes Act were impractical, because reservations in the Northeast did not include enough land to make viable family farms. If reservation lands on Long Island were divided equally among all Indians living on them, for example, each Indian would receive only about four acres.

Despite the evident unfeasibility of the scheme, New York representatives could not resist the prospect of assimilating American Indians and opening up still more of their land to occupation by non-Indians. Thus the state assembly decided in 1888 to investigate whether the state could impose the principles of the Dawes Act on all of New York's Iroquois, including the Senecas, and on the Long Island Indians. A committee under the chairmanship of J. S. Whipple published its report in 1889. The Whipple Report concluded that "the Dawes bill, while apparently applying in terms to all the reservations of this State, except those of the Senecas, is not, at least in many important and essential respects, well adapted to the needs and circumstances of the New York Indians."[38] It also asserted, however, that the state could impose allotment within its borders, dividing up the Indian reservations. The report provoked vigorous protest. In 1890, both houses of the legislature passed the Whipple Bill, but the governor, responding to protests, refused to sign it.[39]

Supporters of the Dawes Act and the Whipple Bill were a diverse group. The Dawes Act received majority support in Congress because it allowed land speculators to profit from Indian lands, but it also attracted support from well-intentioned reformers who believed that Indians would be absorbed into the American mainstream when their communal landholdings were broken up. The act was a typical product of American democracy and congressional action: a compromise that made concessions to the greedy in exchange for a favored reform. U.S. Commissioner of Indian Affairs J. D. C. Atkins noted in 1885:

When the [individual] farm and the school have become familiar institutions among the Indians, and reason-

able time has intervened for the transition from barbarism or a semi-civilized state to one of civilization, then will the Indian be prepared to take upon himself the higher and more responsible duties and privileges which appertain to American citizenship. . . . It is confidently believed, that among the next generation of Indians the English language will be sufficiently spoken and used to enable them to become acquainted with the laws, customs, and institutions of our country, and to regulate their conduct in obedience to its authority.[40]

Obedience to U.S. authority—sovereignty—was what both the self-interested and the reform-minded members of Congress shared as a premise for Indian policy. The Eleventh Census of 1890 counted about 280 Indian "tribes" in the United States, not including Alaska.[41] Each of these nations had a separate government that followed a distinct cultural tradition and religion. The U.S. government had no intention of sharing the continent with 280 other nations.

New York State's Whipple Report echoed these sentiments. It concluded, for example, that the Onondaga Nation's "present condition is infamously vile and destestable, and just so long as they are permitted to remain in this condition, just so long will there remain upon the fair name of the Empire State a stain of no small magnitude." The report concluded that the state could unilaterally impose something like a Dawes Act in New York State.

It cannot be determined what proportion of these people would favor change. They cling to the old order of things with much tenacity. The chiefs and head men and office-holders and those with political ambitions will vigorously resist any change, any attempt or suggestion looking toward interference with their authority or to a limitation of their prerogatives. However this fact may be, it ought not to be allowed to stand in the way. If the State or nation must support and protect the Indians, it should also have control over them. If they still remain "wards," their guardians ought to know what is for their welfare and supply it. Their rights should be protected and preserved with the most exact justice, but whenever any conditions of existing treaties stand in the way of their welfare and progress, such conditions should be set aside; neither should the State or nation be longer embarrassed by the refusal of the Indian to receive what is for his own good. Plainly and bluntly, his consent to any measures manifestly and clearly tending to benefit and improve him should no longer be asked. . . .

Pity is of no account. Sentiment or fine words will not save the Indian. The business ideas of business men must be applied to his case. . . .

Their lands should be divided in severalty [i.e., allotment]. . . .

These Indian people have been kept as "wards" or children long enough. They should now be educated to be men, not Indians, and it is the earnest belief of the committee that when the suggestions made, or at least the more important of them are accomplished facts, and the Indians of the State are absorbed into the great mass of the American people, then, and not before, will the "Indian problem" be solved.[42]

In some ways, *The Six Nations* refutes the state's claim. Its authors concluded that no unilateral action could be taken by either the state or the federal government; the consent of the Haudenosaunee was necessary. Thomas Donaldson noted: "If the Iroquois, native or foreign [i.e., Canadian] born, want to become citizens of the United States they must renounce allegiance to their own people. . . . [N]either the state of New York nor the United States can break them [the reservations] up without the Indians' consent, or through conditions analogous to those of war. They have always been recognized as nations." And Henry Carrington noted that "the alleged absurdity of the Six Nations of New York being a 'nation within a nation' does not change the fact or nullify the sequence of actual history." With regard to Iroquois communities, Carrington concluded that "the percentage of the relative grades of acquisition or waste of large or medium accumulations, of bare support or of scant support, is almost identical with the average of communities wholly white, and the percentage of absolute suffering from want much less than in very many settlements of white people."[43]

However pro-Iroquois Carrington and Donaldson may sound, their conclusions were politically drawn. *The Six Nations* reaffirmed the contention that the federal government was sovereign and would be the final arbiter regarding the rights of the Haudenosaunee and the future status of their lands. In a two-page report that appears at the end of *The Six Nations*, Timothy W. Jackson, the U.S. Indian agent for the Six Nations, expressed the federal view as he admitted the existence of Iroquois rights: "In my opinion, the proper way to civilize the Indians of New York is to secure a division of their lands in severalty, and place them in full citizenship; but there are many questions and difficulties to be overcome before this can be done without injury to the rights of the Indians."[44]

Since the 1890s the Haudenosaunee and their supporters have managed to block all efforts to terminate their reservations. And many politicians at both the state and national levels still entertain notions of eliminating Indian reservations in New York.

The 1892 report makes it clear why Iroquois leaders at the turn of the century believed it was possible to maintain their worldview: the report presents ample evidence of the Iroquois's success in balancing their heritage with contemporary challenges and opportunities. It is also easy to see how non-Indians misperceived the Iroquois's willingness to balance tradition with the technology and ideas of non-Indians. These misperceptions reinforced the notion that the Iroquois could be eased—or forced—into the mainstream.

The 1892 report contains information about housing, occupations, diseases, personal morals, education, and the Haudenosaunee "national game," lacrosse. The bulletin often compares social behaviors inside Iroquois communities with those in neighboring white communities—to the whites' disadvantage. The census workers even counted the sewing machines in Haudenosaunee houses. Though one must reserve a healthy skepticism about the completeness of any census, the array of facts is amazing. The data also makes clear the intrusiveness of the census takers' inquiries. The *Syracuse Herald* for February 8, 1891, describes General Carrington's visit to Onondaga:

The General has been accompanied by his son, R. C. Carrington, as his clerk, and they have been conducting their census office in the parlor of Chief Daniel La Fort, the head of the Onondaga nation. The two "pale faces" have eaten and slept in Chief La Fort's house, and have personally experienced what Indian life is with the better class of the Onondagas, their quarters being hardly more than a stone's throw from the Council House of the Six Nations. . . .

General Carrington has already spent seven months among the New York Indians, making minute inquiries as to their condition, and one old Indian remarked that he had to tell everything he had, even to his chickens. Every house is visited and located upon a map which gives roads, lanes, by-paths and makes a real directory if any stranger should wish to make a personal visit afterward. Educational, social, agricultural, religious, and even traditional elements, are made subjects of inquiry and record. "Why," said the Indian, "he even asked me how many wives I had and how many I ever had, and what had become of all my children. He just got everything I knew."

The special census was part of the national enumeration of 1890, one of the more famous in North American history because it marked the official closing of the frontier. Census takers counted so many non-Indians within the territories claimed by the United States that the government no longer regarded the term "frontier" as applicable. Far into the west, the end of the frontier was marked by literal death throes: on December 29, 1890, while General Carrington was still gathering data among the Haudenosaunee, more than three hundred Lakota people were mercilessly slaughtered by U.S. forces at Wounded Knee, South Dakota. This massacre marks the end of the American frontier more precisely than any mere census statistic.

Conditions in the East, as *The Six Nations* demonstrates, were substantially different. On the Great Plains, American Indians were adversaries, yet Haudenosaunee men had fought alongside their non-Indian neighbors throughout the nineteenth century. *The Six Nations* lists Iroquois veterans who had served during the Civil War (some of them in "Colored" units). It even lists three Iroquois veterans of the War of 1812–15 who were still alive in 1890.

The Six Nations gives a significant political portrait of the Haudenosaunee. A considerable amount of the text relates to Haudenosaunee sovereignty, government, and land claims. When data for *The Six Nations* were being collected, sovereignty, treaty rights, land rights, and human rights were major issues, just as they are today. The conclusions of this official document are used today in court cases reviewing treaty rights and in negotiations between the Haudenosaunee, the United States, and New York State.

Haudenosaunee Views in the Late Nineteenth Century

The most complete single source of evidence for Haudenosaunee views in the late nineteenth century survives in the Whipple Report, published in 1889. Just two years before the census takers visited the Haudenosaunee, the Whipple committee sought their opinions and published more than eight hundred pages of testimony.[45] The transcripts record the tension felt by some Haudenosaunee witnesses, and even their reluctance to speak frankly. The accuracy of the transcripts is important, and fortunately a brief description of actual methods survives. Andrew S. Draper, an advocate of the Whipple Report who was superintendent of public instruction for the State of New York, stressed how thorough the committee had been, using "all the modern improvements and appliances,—stenographers, counsel, and power to subpoena witnesses and administer oaths."[46]

The Whipple Report includes important if constrained interviews with some of the Iroquois leaders on whom Henry B. Carrington would depend. It also provides insights into attitudes held by some white New York State leaders in the 1880s. For example, J. S. Whipple, the chairman of the committee, had especially strong interests in seeing the Haudenosaunee assimilated. He was the assemblyman who represented the city of Salamanca, built on lands leased from the Senecas. The quotations given here include a few from the Haudenosaunee whose photographs appear or whose actions are described in *The Six Nations*. Whenever a person interviewed also appears in *The Six Nations*, I have supplied a page reference to guide the reader to the photograph or description in the census.

At the Tuscarora reservation north of Buffalo, near Lewiston in Niagara County, the Whipple Committee questioned Luther Jack (before p. 39) regarding the political structure of the Tuscarora Nation and the Confederacy as a whole. The counsel for the committee, Judge O. S. Vreeland, began:

Q. What is your age?
A. Twenty-nine.
Q. You are a Tuscarora Indian?
A. Tuscarora Indian.
Q. Born on this reservation, were you?
A. Yes, sir.
Q. Have you a family?
A. Yes, sir.
Q. Wife and children?
A. No wife.
Q. No children?
A. No children.
Q. You are one of the chiefs of the nation?
A. Yes, sir.
. . . *Q.* What are the duties of the chiefs, what do they do?
A. They regulate the nation?
Q. They are the government of the nation?
A. Yes, sir; they are the government of the nation.
Q. To which clan do you belong?

A. Wolf.
Q. How long have you been a chief?
A. Fifteen years.
Q. Then you were how old when you were chosen chief?
A. About thirteen.
Q. About thirteen when you were chosen chief?
A. Yes, sir.
Q. You don't have to be 21 years of age, or 18 to be a chief?
A. No; but I never acted until I was 21.
Q. Until you were 21?
A. No; until after, until the last five years or so off and on, the last two winters regular.
Q. When did you have a right to act, when you were 21; what is the age of the majority [that is, no longer a minor] of your nation, 18 or 21?
A. Well, we have no regulation about that, but it is by the chiefs, if they see fit to have a man under 21 act, they let him act.
Q. The chiefs have control of that?
A. The chiefs have the control of that.
Q. You began to act when the chiefs allowed you to?
A. No; I began to act when I thought I was fit for it.
Q. How did you get to be a chief?
A. Well, they choose by my clan, by the women of my clan.
Q. The women of your clan chose you?
A. Yes, sir.
Q. How many women belong to your clan?
A. Well, at the time they chose me, I could not recollect; I don't remember.
Mr. [Barnet H.] Davis [committee member]: Don't the men choose the chiefs?
A. No.
Judge Vreeland: The women choose the chiefs?
A. Yes, the women choose the chiefs; the women of my clan.
Q. Do they meet together somewhere, these ladies?
A. Yes, sir; they meet together.
Q. And vote?
A. Yes, sir; they vote.
Q. And they chose you?
A. Yes, sir; and after they chose me they referred to the chiefs in council for adoption, for approval.
Q. After they appointed you then it was referred to the chiefs?
A. To the chiefs for approval.
Q. And they approved it?
A. They approved it.
Q. Would they have a right to disapprove it?
A. Yes, sir.
Q. If the chiefs didn't want you they could say so, and then you could not be a chief?
A. Yes, sir.
Q. Then someone would have to be picked out, somebody else?
A. Yes, sir; then it would be referred back to the women to reconsider about it.
Q. When you were chosen, was there somebody else that wanted to be chief besides you?

A. I don't know; I was not there.

. . . *Mr. Davis:* Wouldn't you like to be a citizen?

A. I am a citizen now of the nation here [that is, the Tuscarora Nation].

Q. Wouldn't you like to vote?

A. No, I wouldn't like to vote.

Mr. Whipple: Would you like to become a citizen, if it was so fixed that you would not be taxed, and you could not alienate your land—could not get rid of it, and then have the right to vote?

A. No, I don't think that—

Q. Don't think that would be a good thing?

A. No; there will be some scheme in regard to it, and in a few years we would be compelled to pay taxes.

. . . *Judge Vreeland:* Is your objection to becoming a [U.S.] citizen, for fear of some scheme by which you will be taxed or your land sold or something of that kind?

A. Well, as soon as we become citizens the land will be divided, and by so doing I think there is a curse to the nation.

Q. You don't think the land ought to be divided?

A. No; I don't think it ought to.

Q. What objection would you have to dividing the land, giving every man his fair share, and fix it so he could not sell it?

A. Well, the nation, it seems to me, is contented as they are, and then I was to say about dividing the lands; I don't think it would be fair for us; it will amount to about twelve acres apiece; divided up into twelve-acre lots, about 408 shares, and we have got to have outlets to it, and there will roads all over it; it will be all roads.[47]

Another Tuscarora interviewed by the Whipple Committee, Elias Johnson (pp. 39, 67), had once been a chief but had been deposed, as Judge Vreeland noted:

Q. You are not a chief?

A. No, sir; not now, I am one of the has-beens.

Q. When were you a chief, Mr. Johnson?

A. I was deposed last February [Johnson's testimony was given on July 27, 1888].

Q. Were you unruly?

A. No, sir; I don't claim I was, I claim I was deposed on account of being just; I am not ashamed of the reason that I was deposed.

Q. By whom was this done?

A. I was deposed by the Onondagas, suggested by the warriors of the tribe.

Q. The Onondagas have the power to depose?

A. Yes, sir; to install and depose.

Mr. [George F.] Roesch [committee member]: You say this was suggested by the warriors of your tribe?

A. Yes, sir.

Mr. Davis: For what reason?

A. That I was removed?

Q. Yes, sir.

A. On account of taking an interest in a case that was presented before the council, Dr. David Hewitt, in a case of land that he claims to be his.

Q. Who was Dr. Hewett [sic]?

A. He is a member of the tribe.

Q. How long ago was that?

A. Last winter.

Mr. Roesch: You were deposed by a vote of the Onondagas?

A. The way to depose my office is that a council be called by the [clan] relations in the tribe, of the whole tribe.

Q. Of which you are chief?

A. Yes, sir; and they take a vote asking our congress, as it was termed [at Onondaga, the Grand Council of the Confederacy], the Onondagas being the head of our government, asking them to have me deposed, and they in the meantime had sent a delegate here by the name of Baptist Thomas, an Onondaga, and his character, I suppose, need not be mentioned, and he reported the desire of the relations here to the Onondaga council, and they accepted of it; that I should be deposed, and that was the way I was deposed.

Q. Are we to understand then that the Onondagas are the law-givers and law-makers for the Six Nations?

A. No, sir, they are not the law-makers, but they are the giver [the agent] of the law; they were made from time immemorial.

Q. Then you are governed by the laws of the Onondagas, are you?

A. Yes, sir; that is, concerning the authority of the chiefs; they are to install and depose, that is all; and all cases or matters in our council here they have nothing to do with.

Q. When you have a council of the Six Nations [the Grand Council at Onondaga] the presiding officer is an Onondaga?

A. Yes, sir.

Mr. Davis: Who is the presiding officer of the Onondagas now?

A. La Fort.

Mr. Roesch: When you are deposed from your chiefship, does that disqualify you forever from holding office?

A. No, sir; they can be elected at other times if they choose.

Q. Are the chiefs at present elected for life?

A. Yes, sir, or good conduct, they are supposed to be elected for life; there are certain laws which, if they violate, will cause them to be deposed.

Mr. Davis: Can a deposed chief be reinstalled again?

A. Yes, sir, by being first reelected [by the women of his clan], and then have him go through the same ceremonies, just as if he never had been a chief. . . .

Mr. Roesch: Is the head chief selected by the other chiefs?

A. [No.] By their clan, Turtle clan, the women of the Turtle clan.

Q. Then you have women suffrage in your tribe?

A. Yes, sir; we are ahead of the white folks, they are just agitating it. . . .[48]

The Whipple Committee also heard testimony at the Onondaga reservation, just south of Syracuse. There, at the capital of the Confederacy, Daniel La Fort (pp. 5, 42) was acting as the presiding chief of the Grand Council of Iroquois chiefs. (Frank Logan, the actual presiding chief or *Tadodaho*, was too aged to undertake most of the duties of his office.) The committee met in a schoolhouse constructed with state money. Chief La Fort was fifty-six when Judge O. S. Vreeland began the questioning. No interpreter was necessary.

Q. Are you one of the chiefs?
A. Yes, sir; one of the chiefs.
Q. You were the presiding officer of the last council of the Six Nations?
A. Where?
Q. At Cold Spring?
A. Yes, sir.
Q. Does the presiding officer of the Six Nations always come from the Onondagas?
A. Yes, sir.
Q. They have the right to that position, have they, from a long time ago?
A. Yes, sir. . . .
Q. Do you own the land or the chiefs of the nation?
A. Well, they call it common land, it belongs to the tribe.
Q. All belongs to the tribe?
A. Yes, sir. . . .
Q. How many cows have you?
A. Three.
Q. How many horses?
A. Two.

Vreeland then referred to the Senecas on the Cattaraugus and Allegany reservations, where in 1848 a strong faction of Senecas had overthrown the traditional chiefs. After 1848, the traditionals, rather than try to reestablish the old system entirely, decided to participate in the elections. The Old Party of traditionals (also known as the Old Chiefs Party) had rallied their supporters and in 1852 won the presidency of the Seneca Nation. Struggles for power ensued. But a struggle for power during an election was a system Judge Vreeland preferred, whereas the system of clan mothers and chiefs at Onondaga clearly was not. Thus Vreeland queried:

Q. Do you know about the way the Cattaraugus and Alleghany Indians elect their council and president?
A. Yes, sir.
Q. What do you think about that plan, do you think that would work here?
A. I don't know; I guess not very good.
Q. You think the chiefs are the best?
A. I think the best, a good deal. . . .
Vreeland turned to a different subject:
Q. Is there much timber on the reservation?
A. No; not much.
Q. What has become of the timber?
A. Sold it.
Q. Who sold it?
A. Some of our boys sold it.
Q. What kind of timber grew?
A. Any kind; maple, beech, hemlock, bass-wood, white-wood, iron-wood. . . .

Q. Do your people generally encourage the school and like to have their children go to school?
A. Yes, sir; some of them.
Q. Not all?
A. Not all.
Q. What portion of them don't like the school?
A. I don't know; I guess they don't want to learn. . . .
Q. Is there much intemperance among your people?
A. Yes, sir.
Q. Some drunkenness?
A. Yes; some drunkenness, some temperance men.
Q. You are a temperance man?
A. Yes, sir; prohibition.

Assemblyman George H. Frost continued the questioning:
Q. . . . What religions have they on the reservation?
A. Some different kinds?
Q. Name one of them.
A. One is Methodist, one is Episcopalian; some old party.
Q. There is what they call the pagans?
A. I suppose so.
Judge Vreeland: You are the old party?
A. Yes, sir; we believe just as anybody else.
Mr. Davis: Do they believe in a God?
A. Yes, sir; we believe in a God, just as well as you do.
Mr. Frost: All the Indians?
A. Yes, sir.
Q. Are you one of the Christians or the pagans?
A. No; I am the old party.
Q. Which party patronizes the school?
A. Well, both parties; all parties, I guess. . . .
Mr. Roesch: Is the old party stronger than the new among your people?
A. Yes, sir; I guess so.
Q. More in the old party than in the new?
A. More people.
Q. . . . Do some of the old party get married before the minister?
A. Yes, sir.
Q. When they get married before the minister do they then profess religion?
A. Well, I don't know.
Q. Or do they go back among the old party to live?
A. Well, they go back when they are a mind to.
Mr. Whipple: They just have the minister say the words?
A. That is all.
Q. It don't change the religion?
A. Don't change the religion.
Q. Where do you bury the dead?
A. In the ground; dig it about five or six feet deep; don't make any difference whether they are Christians or not; two burying grounds.
Q. Have you any ceremonies at the burial of the dead?
A. Yes, sir; O, yes.
Q. If any Indian chief gives offense, is he ever punished by the nation?
A. We don't have any punishment by the nation; it goes out before the justice in the town; we ain't got any punishments here.

Judge Vreeland: Are your people healthy?

A. Yes, sir, just as healthy as you are.

Q. Are there any particular diseases that are prevalent here among you?

A. Well, we don't have anything but your diseases, you know; I suppose we didn't have them a great many years ago.

Q. You don't have any consumption?

A. Well, some small-pox; we don't have it, we get it from some of your people.

Q. Do any of your people have consumption?

A. Yes, sir, some of them have; yes, sir, we got diseases from you.

Q. You got them from us?

A. We got too much.

Q. You got them from us?

A. O, yes, sir.[49]

Some of the most interesting parts of *The Six Nations* deal with Iroquois wampum (illustrated opposite p. 33 and described on pp. 33–34). Wampum are white and purple shell beads, often woven into belts that symbolize major reference points in Iroquois history and culture. (Ironically for a book about "the Six Nations of New York," the fine group photograph "Reading the Wampums, 1890" facing p. 33 was taken in Brantford, Ontario, in 1871, and shows a gathering of Haudenosaunee chiefs from the Six Nations Reserve in Ontario. The implication on p. 33 that the photograph shows a wampum reading among the Mohawks at St. Regis (Akwesasne) is erroneous.)[50]

At Onondaga the committee questioned Thomas Webster (facing p. 5), keeper of the wampum for the Confederacy. Webster had been a chief since the age of twenty-one; in 1888 he was sixty-three. Judge Vreeland began the questioning; Jaris Pierce (facing p. 5) served as interpreter.

Q. Are you the wampum holder of the nation?

A. Yes, sir.

Q. Tell us what wampum is?

A. He thinks that it would take too much time for that.

Q. Tell us what it looks like, I mean?

A. He says the President of the United States [George Washington] when he understood the nature and character of this wampum, sanctioned it; he [President Washington] says he is very much pleased with the character of these laws that are used by the Indians, and says to them, to the Indians, you stand by the Roman [i.e., U.S.] laws faithfully, and I will never interfere with your business, and it shall remain so as long as the trees stand up straight, and when the trees fall down towards the other way, then it is time to overhaul; when they begin to grow down, then I will see about it; now you remain under it [the Iroquois Great Tree of Peace] and continue under it, and never set it aside; he [George Washington] says "Don't come in under our laws, because we are changing; keeps changing all the time; you can not come in under our laws and live under them; for that reason we [the Iroquois] are abiding under it [the Great Tree of Peace], hanging on to it, as long as we can."

Q. What does this wampum mean; what is it for?

A. He says it is nothing for a white man, it is all for the Indians; there is a tree set in the ground, and it touches the heavens, and under that tree sets this wampum; it sets on a log, and the fire, coals of fire, placed by the side of it, and this fire is unquenchable, and the Six Nations are all to this council fire, held by this tribe [i.e., the council is held at Onondaga].[51]

When Jaris Pierce was himself invited to testify, he was severely critical of Webster and the traditional chiefs. He felt that remaining under the guidance of the wampum and the treaty made by George Washington (the 1794 Treaty of Canandaigua) actually hindered the Iroquois. Yet immediately before his criticism, he told the committee a parable, demonstrating that he understood the view of more traditional Iroquois. Pierce's story captures the competing interests of traditional Iroquois and the State of New York:

A man is driving in a cold day, the wagon has to follow the ruts from one wagon to another; it is hard work for you to jump out of that with your team; you would almost fight; big load, you meet somebody else and had to turn out [of the rut]; that is the way with these Indians; that is the way, especially, they don't want to drive [to] one side; you [the State of New York] want to force them out.

The exchange continued between Judge Vreeland and Jaris Pierce:

Q. When they once get out they would be better?

A. When they once get out they would be better for it; most all these men [in the room] are chiefs, and they are all willing to come under the law, but there seems to be something hanging about them; they get started a little way and they fall right back into the old rut; if the State could get the best laws regulating these Indians I think they would go right to work right under their yoke.

Q. What can the State do to help them get out of these old ruts?

A. . . . we are held under by these chiefs; don't you see this old man [Thomas Webster] sitting in this chair with his wampum; nobody can read them; I would not give three cents to read them over, and I don't believe I could and I don't believe you could; it is just as he said, it would take a good while to understand it; we are held down by these wampums, by the treaty [of Canandaigua, 1794] with General Washington, which he sanctioned at the time; it is for you gentlemen to know what this is; if you find what a damage it is to the Indians, because there is no education, no work, because there is no business for us to do; educate an Indian; he is cast off to-day; says he is the friend of the white man; he is a treacherous man; we will not have anything to do with him; they put him in office; there is danger, danger right off; he is going to overturn the whole reservation; no confidence placed in him; they

place them just the same as the white men, treacherous and tricky.[52]

The Whipple Committee responded immediately to
Pierce's words. Later the same day, July 10, 1888, the committee convened what the report refers to as "a secret session on the Onondaga reservation, at the house of Jaris
Pierce." There, Pierce and another Onondaga, Albert Cusick
(facing p. 34), deplored what they perceived as the low morals of the Onondagas.[53]

No Haudenosaunee interviewed by the Whipple Committee was more eager to assimilate than John Jimeson, a
Seneca on the Cattaraugus reservation. When the committee visited Cattaraugus, Judge Vreeland asked Jimeson

Q. Would you like to own your land yourself?
A. I would desire that with all my heart. . . I had strong
talk to go to Albany myself with my own money and
see if I could not do something about it; my white friend
. . . says you go there alone, you are not strong enough,
the pagan councilors will go there and oppose you.
Q. Do you think a considerable number of your people
would like to do as you would?
A. A good majority.
Q. And you think the young pagans think some so, too?
A. Yes, sir; I do; I have talked with them.
Q. What suggestions have you got to make, Mr. Jimeson,
about the matter, as to what should be done to bring
this about; what should be done to help your nation?
A. I feel . . . the Ogden Land Company ought to be put
one side.
Q. You want to get rid of that claim?
A. Yes, sir. . . . After we get rid of that, be white folks;
citizens; finish up the whole business; go right along;
be protected; be somebody; be men; so I could vote . . . ;
if I go to vote now, they say, stand back, get behind me;
you should go down and see us; we are a good deal like
white folks; you would be astonished.
Q. More of your people would cultivate land if that was
done?
A. Why, man alive, it would put the courage right into
their heads to take good care of it, if we owned the property through and through . . . they would make good
citizens; you would find some smart, intelligent Indians among us, if they would become citizens.[54]

At the Akwesasne Mohawk reservation on the banks of
the St. Lawrence River, Judge Vreeland started an exchange
with Louis Gray (p. 76), a fifty-eight-year-old Mohawk
farmer who was Episcopalian. Gray's responses give us in-
sight into the Mohawks' agricultural practices and their
attitudes toward white-style education.

Q. How much land have you, Mr. Gray?
A. I cannot tell.
Q. About how much?
A. I don't know how many acres.
Q. About a hundred?
A. That is for me to know.
Q. How much?

A. One hundred and fifty acres.
Q. What crops do you raise?
A. Wheat, oats, peas, corn, potatoes.
Q. Raise any apples?
A. No.
Q. You never set out any apple trees?
A. Well, I tried once, but they all died; mice eat them;
they died. . . .
Q. So you give it up?
A. Yes, sir.
Q. Why don't you try again?
A. What is the use of throwing money away for noth-
ing; if I put out more maybe the mice eat more. . . .
Q. Do you have some stock?
A. Yes, sir; some.
Q. How many head of stock have you now?
A. Nine head of cattle.
Q. Cows?
A. Three cows; some young cattle.
Q. Do you send your milk to the factory?
A. No.
Q. Sell milk?
A. Yes, sir; make butter.
Q. Sell butter?
A. Yes, sir.
Q. Have you a team?
A. Yes, sir.
Q. Most all the Indian farmers have teams, have they?
A. I suppose most all have got teams. . . .
Q. How do your schools get along now?
A. Well, I think not much good.
Q. What is the trouble? . . .
A. They don't send their children to school; some folks,
who live about twenty rods away from the school-house,
got plenty of children and don't send them to school; I
don't know what the reason.

Vreeland then asked questions about allotment.

Q. Your people here own this land altogether, in com-
mon?
A. Yes, sir.
Q. As a tribe?
A. Yes, sir.
Q. How would you like to each own your land separate;
have it divided up into severalty so every man would
have his fair share?
A. Well, I will tell you, last spring, the Oneidas, they
divided up their land; good many I see got no land, no
houses, pretty poor; I guess I would rather be this way.
Q. You would rather have it as it is now?
A. Yes, sir.
Q. What was the trouble with the Oneidas?
A. They sold out.
Q. If the law had been made so he could not sell it, he
would have had it now, would he?
A. Yes, sir; I suppose so.
Q. Then your objection to dividing up would be because
you are afraid the Indians would sell the land [to
whites]?

A. I am afraid, you know, if they made the law they change it often, the law.
Q. Afraid they will change it?
A. Yes, sir.
Q. What you are afraid of is that the Indian would sell his land and get poor?
A. Yes, sir; I am afraid about one-fourth go right and sell as quick as they get the land.
Q. You think one-fourth would be ready to sell?
A. Yes, sir; sell it right off.
Q. You think they would sell the land and squander the money, and then they would go out into the road?
A. Yes, sir; sleep along side the road or make a camp.
Q. You probably don't want to be a citizen?
A. No, sir.
Q. Why not?
A. Because I don't want to.
Q. Could you give me some reason why not?
A. Yes, sir; I can not make citizen; I am not a white man; I am an Indian.
Q. Can not be made into a citizen?
A. Can not read nothing, can not write.
Q. You can not read?
A. No.
Q. The children here can read if they go to school; how would it do to have your children be citizens, but not have you be a citizen?
A. Maybe, by and by; maybe me under the ground.
Q. When you are gone somebody after you be a citizen?
A. Yes, sir.[55]

The relentless questioning often provoked answers of resignation, but the committee also encountered witnesses who attempted to educate them in the unique philosophy of the Haudenosaunee. Andrew John Jr. (pp. 38, 46) was the forty-one-year-old president of the Seneca Nation. (The Seneca Nation includes the Allegany and Cattaraugus reservations but not the more traditional group of Senecas gathered at Tonawanda.) When President John was sworn in before the Whipple Committee, he represented the traditionals' most recent victories in their ongoing struggle with the assimilationists. The committee, meeting at Salamanca on the Allegany Seneca reservation, was particularly concerned about the links between the Seneca Nation and the Grand Council of the Iroquois Confederacy, which met at Onondaga. Judge Vreeland again began the questioning:

Q. Do you belong to the old party or the new party?
A. The old party. . . .
Q. Have you ever been on any reservation except this one?
A. O, yes, sir.
Q. Besides the Cattaraugus?
A. Yes, sir.
Q. What others?
A. I have been to Tonawanda.
Q. Anywhere else?
A. Well, been to Tuscarora; I have been to the Onondaga reservation.

Q. Are you familiar with all of these Indians?
A. O, yes, sir.
Q. How recently have you been to Onondaga?
A. I was there yesterday. . . .
Q. Was there a council of the Six Nations there?
A. Well, they were holding a meeting there, the old party meeting. . . .
Q. What is commonly called the pagan party?
A. Yes, sir. . . .
Q. You belong to that party?
A. Yes, sir; I belong to the old party; they are not pagans.
Q. They are sometimes called pagans?
A. Well, they make a mistake.
Q. That term, then, is inappropriately applied?
A. Yes, sir.
Q. . . . Retain the old national customs?
A. Yes, sir.
Q. What was the purpose of this meeting of the old party?
A. Well, the purpose was for speaking it over of the old Indian doctrine; what they believe.
Q. Did you transact any business there?
A. No.
Q. Have any religious services?
A. Yes, sir; Indian way.[56]

On another day of testimony, John tried to explain the Haudenosaunee's traditional religious beliefs to Assemblyman George Roesch. The religion had been refocused by the Seneca teacher Handsome Lake between 1799 and 1815; Haudenosaunee tradition is still based on his teachings.

Q. Why did you say the other day that your party should not be called pagans?
A. They don't worship idols.
Q. Would you tell us what the general belief of the pagans is?
A. Well, the general belief is, one great spirit controls everything; God, he is called in English, he is a supreme power on earth, everything; and then they believe in temperance, that is the most part of their religion, is temperance; and they believe in thanking, mostly, to the Great Spirit, that is the most important thing; most everything they see they thank him; and it is their doctrine to be kind to one another, to be good, honest people; and they believe a man is to have only one woman to live with; and they are strict; their doctrine is against marry more than one woman; it commenced about eighty-eight years ago that way; before that we was wild; they would murder one another, and drinking just about that time; there was a good deal of whisky brought for the Indians; and they had terrible times; and then they got up this Indian doctrine; and Handsome Lake he preached to the Indians; . . . some good things he showed to the people, and everybody adopted right away; after that doctrine everybody was good; everybody was good; and all shaking hands and all feeling good; and that is the starting of this Indian religion; and along about that time a party of Indians went

to Washington, went to the President [Thomas Jefferson], and they showed their doctrine, and, in reply, he made—I was looking over some old papers, some old Indian things—it was all coming to pieces, and I just took a sketch [i.e., made a handwritten copy] of it, to tell us about the reply from the President through the Secretary of War [Henry Dearborn]; I took a sketch of it, and here is the sketch; it states the date [1802] right there.

The following is a copy of the paper referred to by witness:

To CONYODAREYAH (OR HANDSOME LAKE), *with his brethren and associates of the Seneca and Onondaga nations of Indians, now present at the seat of government of the United States:*

Brothers.—Your father and good friend, the President of the United States, has taken into consideration all that you communicated to him, when you took him by the hand three days ago, and he has authorized me to give you the following answer:

Brothers.— . . . If you and all the red people follow the advice of your friend and teacher, the Handsome Lake, and in future be sober, honest, industrious and good, there can be no doubt but the Great Spirit will take care of you and make you happy. . . .

Brothers.—Your Father, the President, will at all times be your friend, and he will protect you and all his red children from bad people who could do you or them any injury, and he will give you writing on paper to assure you that what land you hold can not be taken from you by any person except by your own consent and agreement.[57]

Through such testimony, the Haudenosaunee stated their own case in their own words, and they demonstrated that U.S. government documents supported their traditional rights. Today the Haudenosaunee use the same tactics. John Mohawk, a Seneca and a professor at the State University of New York at Buffalo, is confident that "as long as there are Iroquois Indians who are willing to place the good of the whole above the interests of the few, there will always be an Iroquois Confederacy."[58]

Suggested Readings

The Haudenosaunee have written extensively about their history and culture. Paul Wallace's 1946 history of the founding of the Confederacy has been reissued with a foreword by Chief Leon Shenandoah (Onondaga) and an epilogue by John Mohawk (Seneca): Paul Wallace, *White Roots of Peace* (Santa Fe: Clear Light, 1994). Oren Lyons (Onondaga) and John Mohawk have edited and contributed articles to *Exiled in the Land of the Free: Democracy, Indian Nations, and the United States Constitution* (Santa Fe: Clear Light, 1992). Many Haudenosaunee contributed to *Indian Roots of American Democracy*, a special issue of the *Northeast*

Indian Quarterly edited by José Barreiro (Ithaca, N.Y.: Akwe:kon Press, 1988). The Seneca scholar Arthur C. Parker wrote many works, including *The Constitution of the Five Nations* (1916), reprinted in *Parker on the Iroquois*, ed. William N. Fenton (Syracuse: Syracuse University Press, 1968). A fine Haudenosaunee autobiography is Clinton Rickard, *Fighting Tuscarora: The Autobiography of Chief Clinton Rickard*, ed. Barbara Graymont (Syracuse: Syracuse University Press, 1973).

Useful eighteenth-century insights into the Haudenosaunee can be found in Cadwallader Colden, *The History of the Five Nations Depending upon the Province of New-York in America , 1727 and 1747* (Ithaca: Cornell University Press, 1958). An 1851 classic has been reprinted: Lewis Henry Morgan, *League of the Iroquois* (Secaucus, N.J.: Citadel, 1962).

A well-written survey of Haudenosaunee history through the early 1990s can be found in three chapters of Ronald Wright's *Stolen Continents: The Americas through Indian Eyes since 1492* (Boston: Houghton Mifflin, 1992). Insights into current political and cultural tensions between the Haudenosaunee and non-Indian governments and within Haudenosaunee communities can be found in Bruce E. Johansen, *Life and Death in Mohawk Country* (Golden, Colo.: North American Press, 1993); and Geoffrey York and Loreen Pindera, *People of the Pines* (Toronto: Little, Brown, 1991).

Significant works on the twentieth-century Haudenosaunee include three thorough studies by Laurence M. Hauptman: *The Iroquois and the New Deal* (Syracuse: Syracuse University Press, 1981); *The Iroquois Struggle for Survival: World War II to Red Power* (Syracuse: Syracuse University Press, 1986); and *Formulating American Indian Policy in New York State, 1970-1986* (Albany: SUNY Press, 1988).

André Lopez, *Pagans in Our Midst* (Rooseveltown, N.Y.: Akwesasne Notes, 1980); and Fred R. Wolcott, *Onondaga: Portrait of a People* (Syracuse: Syracuse University Press, 1986), include photographs of Iroquois in the era described in *The Six Nations*.

Ongoing legal issues affecting the Haudenosaunee are discussed in Christopher Vecsey and William A. Starna, eds., *Iroquois Land Claims* (Syracuse: Syracuse University Press, 1988); Jack Campisi and Laurence M. Hauptman, eds., *The Oneida Indian Experience: Two Perspectives* (Syracuse: Syracuse University Press, 1988); Helen M. Upton, *The Everett Report in Historical Perspective: The Indians of New York* (Albany: American Revolution Bicentennial Commission, 1980); and several articles in Christopher Vecsey and Robert W. Venables, eds., *American Indian Environments: Ecological Issues in Native American History* (Syracuse: Syracuse University Press, 1980).

Detailed scholarly articles on the culture and history of each of the Six Nations appear in Bruce G. Trigger, ed., *Northeast*, volume 15 of *Handbook of North American Indians* (Washington, D.C.: Smithsonian Institution, 1978). Each article is accompanied by useful maps and illustrations.

Notes

1. Elisabeth Tooker, "The League of the Iroquois: Its History, Politics, and Ritual," in *Handbook of North American Indians,* ed. Bruce G. Trigger, vol 15, *Northeast* (Washington, D.C.: Smithsonian Institution, 1978), 424-426; Lewis Henry Morgan, *League of the Iroquois* (1851; Secaucus, N. J.: Citadel, 1962), 51–53.

2. Oren Lyons, "The American Indian in the Past," in *Exiled in the Land of the Free: Democracy, Indian Nations, and the United States Constitution,* ed. Oren Lyons and John Mohawk (Santa Fe: Clear Light, 1992), 37–38.

3. Robert P. Porter, "Letter of Transmittal," January 2, 1892, in U.S. Department of Commerce, Bureau of the Census, *Extra Census Bulletin. Indians. The Six Nations of New York*, by Thomas Donaldson [with Henry B. Carrington and Timothy W. Jackson] (Washington, D.C.: United States Census Printing Office, 1892), vii. See Census Office, *Report on Indians Taxed and Indians Not Taxed in the United States (Except Alaska) at the Eleventh Census: 1890* (Washington, D.C.: Government Printing Office, 1894), 131. For background on the Allotment Act, see Francis Paul Prucha, *The Great Father: The United States Government and the American Indians,* 2 vols. (Lincoln: University of Nebraska Press, 1984), 2:660–671.

4. Porter, "Letter of Transmittal," vii.

5. Census Office, *Report on Indians Taxed and Not Taxed,* 65.

6. J. N. B. Hewitt, a Tuscarora, defined "Iroquois" in *Handbook of American Indians North of Mexico,* ed. Frederick Webb Hodge, 2 vols., Bureau of American Ethnology Bulletin 30 (Washington, D.C.: Smithsonian Institution, 1907), 1:617. See also Gordon M. Day, "Iroquois: An Etymology," *Ethnohistory* 15, no. 4 (1968): 389–402.

7. Tooker, "League of the Iroquois," 420; see also 418–422. And see Daniel K. Richter, *The Ordeal of the Longhouse: The Peoples of the Iroquois League in the Era of European Colonization* (Chapel Hill: University of North Carolina Press, 1992), 30–49; and Matthew Dennis, *Cultivating a Landscape of Peace: Iroquois-European Encounters in Seventeenth-Century America* (Ithaca: Cornell University Press, 1993), 85.

8. Harmen Meyndertsz van den Bogaert, *A Journey into Mohawk and Oneida Country, 1634–1635,* trans. and ed. Charles T. Gehring and William A. Starna (Syracuse: Syracuse University Press, 1991), 3–4. Today one can only speculate about the social changes that may have come about when hinged doors were installed in a communal dwelling; such doors may have altered the sense of common space and increased a sense of individual space.

9. Ibid., 4, 6.

10. Sir William Johnson to Governor General Jeffrey Amherst, February 12, 1761, enclosure: "A List of Such Merchandise as is Usually sold to the Indians—the prices differs with the times—" in *The Papers of Sir William Johnson,* ed. James Sullivan et al., 14 vols. (Albany: SUNY Press, 1921–65), 3:331.

11. Ibid., 334–335.

12. Cadwallader Colden, *The History of the Five Nations Depending on the Province of New-York in America, 1727 and 1747*; (Ithaca: Cornell University Press, 1958), 149–150.

13. Speech of Canasatego, Lancaster, Pa., June 26, 1744, in *Indian Treaties Printed by Benjamin Franklin, 1736–1762,* (Philadelphia: Historical Society of Pennsylvania, 1938), xxxvii, 51–52. Canasatego's imagery is an elaboration of similar imagery used by an Onondaga in 1694 (Colden, *History of the Five Nations,* 149). See Francis Jennings, "Iroquois Alliances in American History," and "Glossary of Figures of Speech in Iroquois Political Rhetoric," both in *The History and Culture of Iroquois Diplomacy*, ed. Francis Jennings (Syracuse: Syracuse University Press, 1985), 38, 116–117; and Francis Jennings, "The Constitutional Evolution of the Covenant Chain," in *Proceedings of the American Philosophical Society* 115 (April 1971): 88–96.

14. Speech of Canasatego, Lancaster, Pa., July 4, 1744, in *Indian Treaties Printed by Benjamin Franklin,* 78.

15. Benjamin Franklin to James Parker, March 20, 1750/51, in *The Papers of Benjamin Franklin,* ed. Leonard W. Labaree, 26 vols. (New Haven: Yale University Press, 1959–87), 4:118–119. The number of copies of Canasatego's 1744 speech that Franklin sent to England is discussed in *Indian Treaties Printed by Benjamin Franklin*, vii, 304.

16. General Thomas Gage to Sir William Johnson, October 7, 1772, in *Papers of Sir William Johnson,* 12:995.

17. See Frederick Cook, ed., *Journals of the Military Expedition of Major General John Sullivan against the Six Nations of Indians in 1779 with Records of Centennial Celebrations* (Auburn, N.Y: Knapp, Peck & Thomson, 1887); and Barbara Graymont, *The Iroquois in the American Revolution* (Syracuse: Syracuse University Press, 1972).

18. See Anthony F. C. Wallace, *The Death and Rebirth of the Seneca* (New York: Knopf, 1970); and Charles M. Johnston, ed., *The Valley of the Six Nations: A Collection of Documents on the Indian Lands of the Grand River* (Toronto: University of Toronto Press, 1964).

19. John Mohawk, "Epilogue," in Paul Wallace, *The White Roots of Peace* (Santa Fe: Clear Light, 1994), 125.

20. Bureau of the Census, *Six Nations of New York,* 2.

21. Eugene Parker Chase, ed., *Our Revolutionary Forefathers: The Letters of François, Marquis de Barbe Marbois* (New York: Duffield, 1929), 205.

22. Treaty with the Six Nations, Fort Stanwix, October 22, 1784, in *Indian Treaties, 1778–1883: Indian Affairs: Laws and Treaties,* ed. Charles J. Kappler, vol. 2, *Treaties* (1904; New York: Interland, 1972), 6.

23. Cornplanter, "The speech of the Cornplanter, Half-Town, and the Great-Tree, Chiefs and Councillors of the Seneca nation, to the Great Councillor of the Thirteen Fires," December 1, 1790, in *American State Papers. Class II. Indian Affairs. Documents, Legislative and Executive, of the Congress of the United States, From the First Session of the First to the Third Session of the Thirteenth Congress, Inclusive: Commencing March 3, 1789, and Ending March 3, 1815,* ed. Walter Lowrie and Matthew S. Clair Clarke, vol. 4 (Washington, D.C.: Gales & Seaton, 1832), 141–142.

24. Joseph Brant to Samuel Kirkland, March 8, 1791, in Simcoe Papers, Toronto Archives, Toronto.

25. Treaty with the Six Nations, Canandaigua, November 11, 1794, in Kappler, *Indian Treaties,* 34–37.

26. Arthur C. Parker, *Parker on the Iroquois,* ed. William N. Fenton (Syracuse: Syracuse University Press, 1968), 38; see also 36. These excerpts are from a 1903–13 version by Edward Cornplanter (Seneca). As Cornplanter, a follower of Handsome Lake, recited the code in Seneca, it was translated into English by William Bluesky (a Seneca and a Baptist preacher) under the guidance of Parker (Seneca).

27. Robert W. Venables, "Victim versus Victim: The Irony of the New York Indians' Removal to Wisconsin," in *American Indian Environments: Ecological Issues in Native American History* , ed. Christopher Vecsey and Robert W. Venables (Syracuse: Syracuse University Press, 1980), 140–151.

28. Treaty with the New York Indians, Buffalo Creek, January 15, 1838, in Kappler, *Indian Treaties,* 2:502–516.

29. *The Case of the Seneca Indians in the State of New York. Illustrated by Facts.* (Philadelphia: Merrihew & Thompson,

1840), 179 and 183. Isa. 10:1–3 ("Woe unto them that decree unrighteous decrees . . .") is quoted on the title page.

30. Treaty with the Seneca, Buffalo Creek, May 20, 1842, in Kappler, *Indian Treaties,* 2:537–542.

31. Laurence M. Hauptman, *The Iroquois in the Civil War* (Syracuse: Syracuse University Press, 1993), 36, 47–58.

32. United States v. Abraham Elm (1876) in New York State Legislature, *Report of the Special Committee Appointed by the Assembly of 1888 to Investigate the "Indian Problem" of the State,* 2 vols., Assembly doc. 51 (Albany, 1889), 1:385–386, 389, 387; hereafter Whipple Report.

33. Census Office, *Report on Indians Taxed and Not Taxed,* 24.

34. See Howard R. Berhman, "Perspectives on American Indian Sovereignty and International Law, 1600 to 1776," in Lyons and Mohawk, *Exiled in the Land of the Free,* 125–188.

35. Henry Beebe Carrington, the primary author of *The Six Nations*, is related to Iroquois history in two other ways. First, in 1866 Carrington was the commander at Fort Phil Kearny in Wyoming when he ordered a subordinate, Captain William J. Fetterman, not to pursue Lakota, Cheyenne, and Arapaho warriors beyond a certain ridge. The impetuous Fetterman disobeyed orders and, with all eighty of his men, was wiped out. Until George Armstrong Custer was defeated at the Little Big Horn in 1876, the so-called Fetterman Massacre was the most controversial military debacle after the Civil War. Many government officials and the journalists blamed Colonel Carrington. Congress called for an investigation. One of the men General Ulysses S. Grant sent west to grill Carrington in 1867 was Grant's good friend Ely S. Parker, a Tonawanda Seneca who had served with Grant during the Civil War. Parker concluded that Fetterman had been destroyed because he disobeyed orders, but privately he was also critical of Carrington for not being more alert. The second "Iroquois connection" reflects a basic attitude Carrington brought to his census work among the Iroquois. His report is often sympathetic to the Iroquois; yet Carrington's own culture was at best paternalistic toward Indians, and Carrington was very much a part of his culture. Having gathered so much information among the Haudenosaunee, Carrington ultimately learned very little. While he was on the reservations gathering census data, he became fascinated and then obsessed by four wampum belts at Onondaga: the Hiawatha Belt, the Washington Covenant Belt, "the Wampum to Mark the First Sight of Pale Faces," and the Champlain Belt. He convinced an Onondaga, Thomas Webster, that he should be allowed to purchase them so that the Smithsonian Institution could preserve them for posterity. Carrington gave Webster $75, but the Smithsonian did not reimburse him, so he sold the belts to the Reverend Dr. Oliver Crane of Boston for $330. In 1893 Crane sold them for $500 to John Boyd Thatcher, the mayor of Albany. Thatcher had the four belts displayed at the 1893 World Columbian Exposition in Chicago, celebrating the 400th anniversary of Columbus's second voyage. In 1907 the Onondagas lost a lawsuit to regain possession of the belts. In 1927 Thatcher's widow willed them to the New York State Museum in Albany. There they remained, despite unceasing protest, until 1989, when the State officially returned them to the Haudenosaunee. See Dee Brown, *Fort Phil Kearny: An American Saga* (Lincoln: University of Nebraska Press, 1962); William H. Armstrong, *Warrior in Two Camps: Ely S. Parker, Union General and Seneca Chief* (Syracuse: Syracuse University Press, 1978), 123; Stephen Fadden, "Beaded History," in *Northeast Indian Quarterly* 4 (Fall 1987): 17–20; José Barreiro, "Return of the Wampum," *Northeast Indian Quarterly* 7 (Spring 1990): 8–20; and "The Wampum Issue," a collection of articles and documents reprinted in *The*

American Indian Reader: Education, ed. Jeannette Henry (San Francisco: Indian Historian Press, 1972), 198–232.

36. An excellent review of the history of the Dawes Act and its impact on American Indians is Frederick E. Hoxie, *A Final Promise: The Campaign to Assimilate the Indians, 1880–1920* (Lincoln: University of Nebraska Press, 1984).

37. Isabel C. Barrows, ed., *Proceedings of the Eighth Annual Meeting of the Lake Mohonk Conference of Friends of the Indian, 1890* (New Paltz, N.Y., 1890), 84–85. The impact of U.S. wars against the western Indian nations is reflected in the decline of the Indian population from 306,543 in 1880 to 248,253 in 1890 (both census figures exclude Alaska). See Census Office, *Report on Indians Taxed and Not Taxed,* 23, 24.

38. Whipple Report, 1:76. The report discusses the Shinnecocks, Poosepatucks, and Montauks on pp. 53–55. *The Six Nations* specifies the amount of land that would be assigned to each Iroquois in the last column of a table at the top of p.13.

39. *The Six Nations* discusses this bill on pp. 82–83. The Whipple Report of 1889 also called for resolution of a claim to Indian lands by white speculators involved in the Ogden Land Company. This firm, formed in 1810, bought out earlier speculators, so it could trace its claims back to 1786. The Ogden Land Company became involved with the federal government in the treaty-making process, and the Iroquois were increasingly pressured to remove to lands in the west, so the legal morass deepened with each decade of the company's existence. The company claimed it owned most of the Iroquois lands in western New York; the federal and New York State governments claimed that at best it had only the right of first purchase—that is, a preemptive right to buy any lands the Iroquois were willing to sell. The Whipple Committe, despairing of ever untangling the conflicting claims, reported that

> this at least seems true: either the Indians hold the title, and the Ogden Company has the first right to purchase, or the Ogden Company has the title and the Indians a right to perpetual occupancy; and since it must be conceded that both the Indians and the Ogden Company have an interest in these lands, which can only be terminated in either case by purchase; and since there is no present prospect that the Indians will, for any indefinite time to come, relinquish the possession to these lands, it seems of vastly more importance to the Indians that some plan be devised for the extinguishment of this Ogden claim than that the exact location of the fee [title] in these lands be ascertained and settled. (1:37)

40. J. D. C. Atkins, Commissioner of Indian Affairs, Report for 1885, in *The American Indian and the United States: A Documentary History*, ed. Wilcomb E. Washburn, 4 vols. (Westport, Conn.: Greenwood, 1973), 1:358.

41. Census Office, *Report on Indians Taxed and Not Taxed,* 36–37.

42. Whipple Report, 1:45, 73–75, 79.

43. *Six Nations of New York,* 3, 79, 82.

44. Ibid., 83.

45. The state published two editions of the Whipple Report, one in a single volume of 410 pages, the other in two volumes of 1,282 pages. The "Testimony" appears only in the two-volume edition.

46. Barrows, *Proceedings of the Lake Mohonk Conference,* 84.

47. Whipple Report, 1:583–591.

48. Ibid., 603–608. Judge Vreeland asked: "Have you any suggestions to make in reference to your people, Mr. Johnson?" Johnson replied:

I consider our government very much insufficient to serve our present condition; in the first place, it is because they have no redress; when the chiefs make a decision that is not satisfactory to any of the parties in the case they have no redress; it ends there . . . no appeal; and now I will tell you what I thought; I have considered the matter considerable; in the first place, I believe it would be a good thing if there was a law enacted by the Legislature giving us [a] chance to appeal our matters before the county court, if they are not satisfied with the decision of the council. . . . The present form of government appoints a chief and retains a chief for life; and as long as these chiefs will conform firmly to the Onondaga pagan party, they are upheld whether or no, and no chief, who has the spirit of progress, can stand long as a chief; . . . if we could have an appeal, why there would be a remedy; and if we could have a new form of government, if we got a bad man, a bad officer, why, if we wanted another . . . we could have him rejected and put in another man. . . . (608–611)

Johnson, of course, had just been "rejected" and replaced, but by the traditional system, not a "new form of government." And Johnson himself had noted that a deposed chief could be reinstated if he obtained his clan's support.

49. Ibid., 466–474.
50. The photograph is found also in *The Iroquois Book of Rites*, ed. Horatio Hale (Toronto: University of Toronto Press, 1963), facing p. 6. Hale wrote on the back of this photograph: "This picture represents the chiefs of the Six Nations, on their reserve near Brantford in Canada, explaining their wampum belts (Sept. 14, 1871). . . . The wampum belts were explained to me on the reserve, at the residence of Chief G. H. M. Johnson; and at my request the chiefs afterwards came with me to Brantford, where the original photograph . . . was taken." The mistaken explanation provided in *The Six Nations* raises the eternal question of the accuracy of any document in any era— especially a census.
51. Whipple Report, 1:497.
52. Ibid., 502–503.
53. Ibid., 505–506.
54. Ibid., 795–796. Jimeson may be the Jimerson referred to on p. 51.
55. Ibid., 2:899, 902–904.
56. Ibid., 1074, 1082–1083.
57. Ibid., 1104–1106.
58. Mohawk, Epilogue to Wallace, *White Roots of Peace,* 156.

ELEVENTH CENSUS OF THE UNITED STATES.

ROBERT P. PORTER,

SUPERINTENDENT.

EXTRA CENSUS BULLETIN.

INDIANS.

THE SIX NATIONS OF NEW YORK

CAYUGAS, MOHAWKS (SAINT REGIS), ONEIDAS, ONONDAGAS,

SENECAS, TUSCARORAS.

BY THOMAS DONALDSON,

EXPERT SPECIAL AGENT.

WASHINGTON, D. C.

UNITED STATES CENSUS PRINTING OFFICE.

1892.

CONTENTS.

LIST OF MAPS.

iv

LIST OF ILLUSTRATIONS.

LETTER OF TRANSMITTAL.

DEPARTMENT OF THE INTERIOR,
Census Office,
Washington, D. C., January 2, 1892.

Sir:

This bulletin contains various statistics and interesting facts concerning the history, present condition, and outlook of the Six Nations of New York, including an account of the Iroquois league, its territory, ancient and modern government, and social customs. It gives also a detailed description of the reservations, government, religion, industries, and social state of these Indians, and shows their capacity and promise for future advancement.

The data herein were obtained for the Eleventh Census, under the direction of Mr. Thomas Donaldson, expert special agent of the Census Office, by General Henry B. Carrington, United States army (retired), special agent for the collection of the statistics of the Six Nations. General Carrington spent many months among the Indians of the Six Nations, and made careful observations respecting their various political, religious, and social meetings, their homes, health, and habits. Becoming personally acquainted with many families and prominent individuals, he learned their histories and traditions, and ascertained their opinions and attitude toward a full adoption of civilized methods.

The bulletin has been prepared under the authority of the act of March 1, 1889, to provide for taking the Eleventh and subsequent censuses, viz: "The Superintendent of Census may employ special agents or other means to make an enumeration of all Indians living within the jurisdiction of the United States, with such information as to their condition as may be obtainable, classifying them as to Indians taxed and Indians not taxed".

Very respectfully,

ROBERT P. PORTER,
Superintendent of Census.

The Secretary of the Interior.

CONDITION OF THE SIX NATIONS IN 1890.

The special agent found no places on any of the reservations for the sale of intoxicating liquors. Such places are unlawful and unknown. He did find, however, that intoxicating liquors were sold to the Indians by white men or women living off the reservations. He found neither houses for immoral purposes nor gambling dens on any of the reservations. Houses for immorality are foreign to the social life and surroundings of these people, and gambling among the Six Nations is in the line of single risks, as opportunity offers.

The struggle now within the Six Nations for control of their government lies between the pagan and christian elements, and, in addition, they have to war with the wiles of the white man. Official corruption has been noted in the past among those high in authority, but this is now being rapidly remedied. The Six Nations are in most danger from without. The pagans, as used here (meaning the old party), are those holding to the faith of their fathers and opposing the white man and his methods. The christian element means those who accept christianity as a doctrine. As far as personal morals and the daily life of most of these people are concerned, the difference is merely technical, and consists in definition, the word of a pagan being considered as good as that of a christian, and, in the view that the state has nothing to do with one's profession of creed, among the Indians a self-reliant pagan is preferable to a dependent christian. In the league of the Iroquois the largest liberty of the person consistent with the safety of the league is permitted. From personal independence and sense of manhood many of the Iroquois have never departed. The reservation Indians of the west are the reverse of this. They look upon the nation and the great father as providers and dispensers of food and clothing, and lean heavily upon them and the public treasury. The Six Nations of New York have generally asked the great father, the Congress, and the New York legislature to let them severally alone. They have been in a measure let alone by the authorities, and the result is that they are self-sustaining and much further advanced in civilization than any other reservation Indians in the United States, and as much so as an average number of white people in many localities. They have borne the burdens of peace with equanimity, and met the demands of the war for the Union with patriotism and vigor. Envious Caucasians, hungering for the Indians' landed possessions in New York state, as elsewhere, have been active and earnest in efforts to absorb their substance. They have been kept from doing so thus far through the efforts of earnest and active fair-minded people, who have prevented their spoliation. The Six Nations have been charged with being pagans, heathens, and bad citizens generally, but investigation shows the latter charge to be false. In the matter of creed, among the Tuscaroras there is not a pagan family recognized as such. Among the Tonawandas and Onondagas very nearly two-thirds belong to the pagan party, several of the most influential men having recently left the christian party for personal and political reasons.

Of the Cattaraugus and Allegany Senecas, a majority belong to the pagan party, and of the Cornplanter Senecas and the Saint Regis Indians none are pagans.

In the battle for progress the christian party has taken the offensive or progressive side, and at an early day, if supported from without, may gain control. The difference between the pagan and christian is most marked in their material interests, the christian more readily grasping modern ideas and methods of life, with their educational incentives. As a rule, the pagan falls behind in the use of farm machinery, in advanced crop culture, in the education of his children, and matters of essential public spirit.

On all the reservations crimes are few, stealing is rare, and quarreling, resulting in personal assault, infrequent. Respecting the Saint Regis Indians, the only suits of a criminal nature for a long time grew out of resistance to the game laws, which stopped their netting on their own waters. The total local offenses during the year was 16 in an Indian population of 5,133.

As to whether or not the Six Nations are law-abiding, with the single exception of the matter of marriage and divorce, that is, with respect to the police laws, they are shown to be as law-abiding as the same number of average white people, and no communities elsewhere, white or otherwise, are known where person and property are more safe, or where male or female can walk unattended at night with greater security. Pauperism is unusual, and the tramp almost unknown. Still there is a select but small corps of loafers on each reservation.

Upon investigation, the Six Nations, as before stated, are shown to be further advanced in civilization than any other reservation Indians, western or otherwise. In this connection certain elements, perhaps heretofore ignored through lack of close inquiry, are striking.

The special agent calls attention to the gradual elimination of diseases resulting from white association in early times. This has reduced mortality and increased longevity. The growth of self-reliance is especially noticeable. This tends to greater diffusion of agricultural products, better homes and clothing, and the constant and growing conviction that their best interests lie in civilized methods.

The relation of poverty and property has already closely followed the relations of general society. There is scarcely any poverty among the Six Nations, but two paupers being noted on the schedules. The percentage of deaths under one year of age is low. The percentage of advanced ages without chronic impairment of faculties is beyond that of any like number of people in the United States. The family increase and surviving members of families, as at Saint Regis, preclude the possibility of general immorality in their homes.

The Six Nations Indians are not foreigners; they are Americans and persons within the meaning of the laws of the United States, and the school books used in their schools are printed in English.

Portions of the Bible, and especially hymns, have been translated into the Iroquois dialect, and at Saint Regis (Catholic) the Latin forms, psalter included, have been translated into Iroquois, the Mohawk dialect; but the Bible in many of the churches and the International Sunday-school lessons are in English. The adult Indians prefer to pray in their own language, their thoughts or desires flowing naturally without the mental abstraction necessary in finding the English word for their exact meaning.

LANGUAGE.

The total Indian population of the Six Nations, exclusive of the Oneidas not on a reservation, is 5,133. Of this number, 2,844 speak the English language and 1,985 do not. The remainder are infants, absentees, or persons who refused to answer the questions of the enumerator.

The great number of the Six Nations who can not speak or read the English language is a drawback to their advancement. Officials are sometimes elected who can not read the laws of New York or of the United States, and almost a majority of this people are cut off from the information and advantages obtained through the reading of newspapers and general literature. This seems to be one of the greatest evils afflicting the Six Nations. The young, however, are usually brought up to read and speak the English language; but, as with other Indians, there is not much hope of change in this respect with adults of middle or advanced age. A compulsory school law for these reservations would aid the growth of the English language. There is no such law in New York for white people.

THE LEGAL STATUS OF THE SIX NATIONS OF NEW YORK.

The total acreage of the reservations of the Six Nations is 87,327.73, with an Indian and adopted population of 5,203, or 16.78 acres for each person. The value of the whole is estimated at $1,810,699.60.

The law and facts show that the reservations of the Six Nations of New York are each independent, and in some particulars as much sovereignties, by treaty and obligation, as are the several states of the United States. The Saint Regis reservation, however, differs somewhat from the others. The lands within these reservations, of course, partake of and carry with them the conditions of the grant. These nations are anomalies, and, with the exception of the Five Civilized Tribes in Indian territory, who are each known by treaty as nations, are the only ones of like character in the United States. They are in fact almost nations within a nation. They were created and grew more out of fear of the Indian and the desire to get rid of and keep him at peace at any price than as an act of justice. In Indian territory they are embarrassing to the national government and an eyesore to the people who desire to live there. In New York they are a wonder to the curious and the expectant haven of hope to many speculators.

The end of the century will probably see the so-called nations in Indian territory absorbed or dispersed and a marked change in the present Indian nations in New York.

The incidents of the enumeration of the Seneca nation showed a strong desire on the part of the advanced portion to break away from old-time ideas and to keep abreast with their white neighbors. The entire reorganization of the Iroquois Agricultural Society was a step forward. A more important indication in the same direction was that of the spring election in May, 1891, when nearly every person elected was able to speak and read the English language, and embraced among their number men of property and progressive tendencies.

The members of the Six Nations of New York residing on reservations or living in tribal relations do not vote at county or state elections, nor do they pay taxes to the counties or the state. They are therefore Indians not taxed. They have a constitution, and the Senecas have a charter from New York as well as their own. They are amenable to national and state courts or laws only in respect of crimes, except the Saint Regis Indians, hereinafter noted (a).

If the Iroquois, native or foreign born, want to become citizens of the United States they must renounce allegiance to their own people; but if those of the Six Nations in New York become such citizens they can not carry their real property interest with them so that it will be subject to levy and sale for debt on contracts. This, in fact, is at present a practical inhibition in their way to citizenship. The several reservations belong to them (Saint Regis differs somewhat from the others), and neither the state of New York nor the United States can legally break them up without the Indians' consent, or through conditions analogous to those of war. They have always been recognized as nations.

The several tribes and bands of the Six Nations differ somewhat in respect to land holdings and titles on or within the several reservations. A lien or preference, in case of sale, called the "Ogden Land Company's rights" hangs over the Cattaraugus and Allegany Senecas, but the United States extinguished it as to the Tonawanda Senecas. The title to these reservations is in the nation, and the members are therefore at common law "tenants.

a There is no law for this, but by agreement and usage the Saint Regis Indians can sue and be sued in the inferior courts of the state of New York, and judgment is always enforced. They have no courts among themselves.

in common". Each owns his undivided share absolutely, independently of the United States or the state of New York. The individuals, however, only hold a fee equivalent to the ownership of the land they improve, with power to sell or devise among their own people, but not to strangers. It is a good title. The nation itself can not disturb it. Within the Six Nations each head of a family or a single adult has the right to enter upon unoccupied land, build upon it, and improve it, thereby acquiring a title, with authority to sell to another Indian or devise the same by will; but all these transactions must be between Indians.

The Cornplanters are Senecas of the Seneca nation, voting with them for officers annually, and having a representative in the nation's council. The band, although in Warren county, Pennsylvania, inherit a common interest in all the Seneca lands in New York, draw alike annuities, but do not vote in New York, except as Indians for their own officers, namely, officers of the Seneca nation. They are also heirs in Pennsylvania of Cornplanter, the probate court of Warren county, Pennsylvania, having partitioned the inheritance of Cornplanter (a special gift of gratitude from Pennsylvania) among them, inalienable except among themselves. They have been admitted to the privileges of citizenship in that state.

The conclusion is irresistible that the Six Nations are nations by treaty and law, and have long since been recognized as such by the United States and the state of New York, and an enlightened public will surely hesitate before proceeding to divest these people of long-established rights without their consent—rights recognized and confirmed in some cases by the immortal Washington and by more than a hundred years of precedents and legislation.

The Six Nations of New York Indian question can not be settled permanently without action on the Ogden company's claim by the Congress of the United States.

PEACEMAKER COURTS.

The peacemaker courts are peculiar to the Seneca Indians of New York. They exercise probate jurisdiction and jurisdiction over minor offenses. Appeal may be taken to the council of the Seneca nation proper on the Allegany and Cattaraugus reservations, and to the separate council of the Tonawanda Senecas. The term of office of a peacemaker is for three years, one being elected annually for each reservation, but those of the Tonawanda band, as with all its officers, have no official relation to the other bands of Senecas.

The president of the Seneca nation sits as judge upon the impeachment of a peacemaker. Among the grounds of impeachment is taking a bribe, or, by relationship or otherwise, having interest in a case.

Divorces, as well as probate matters, come before this court. Petitions, summonses, answers, all pleadings, returns of process, and record follow the forms prescribed for state courts of like jurisdiction. During 1889 a contested election among the Tonawanda band was, upon application, decided by the state court of New York, sitting at Batavia, Genesee county, in which county the Tonawanda reservation is in part situated. A record of their proceedings is duly kept.

UNITED STATES INDIAN AGENT.

The civic establishment of the United States Indian agency at Akron, New York, consists of an agent, Timothy W. Jackson, the incumbent in 1890, whose salary is $1,000 per year; J. E. Paxon, messenger, at $400 per year; J. G. Rugg, physician, at $200 per year, and Chester C. Lay, interpreter, at $150 per year.

The agency contains one frame building, the property of the United States, of the value of $250. As the office of the agent is usually at his residence, change in the incumbent removes the office. In July, 1891, the agent's office was at Salamanca, New York, A. W. Ferrin succeeding T. W. Jackson.

The United States Indian agent receives from the Commissioner of Indian Affairs annually and distributes, under bond, both cash annuities and goods, except for the Saint Regis Indians, who receive neither from the United States, and over whom the agent has no immediate charge.

The Indian agent is the official to whom is referred by the Commissioner of Indian Affairs all complaints by Indians preferred against each other or against the white people, and upon his investigation and report the Commissioner initiates relief or other action. He is especially charged with the investigation of all cases of trespass upon their lands or other rights, as also illegal sales of intoxicating liquors to the Iroquois, and, as their protector, places in the hands of the United States district attorney the proper evidence upon which to prosecute suits at law against offenders. It is also his duty to investigate and report upon all crimes of which the state courts of New York have jurisdiction; also to interest himself in local troubles between the Indians themselves, and to report annually to the Commissioner of Indian Affairs all births and deaths, as the basis of the annual distribution of goods or money.

The New York state agent and attorney have no official connection with the United States Indian agent. The former acts for the Onondaga Indians, and pays the state annuities to the Six Nations, while the latter, under special law, acts for the Saint Regis Indians. Each reservation has a state school commissioner.

OFFICERS OF THE LEAGUE OF THE IROQUOIS IN THE UNITED STATES.

Eleventh Census: 1890.   Six Nations of New York.

DANIEL La FORTE (Ha-You-Ws Esh), "Intestine Bruiser,"
Chairman of League, and Acting To-do-da-ho— Wolf Tribe.—Onondaga.

THOMAS WEBSTER (Ha-yah-du-gih-wah), "Bitter Body,"   JARIS PIERCE (Jah-dah-dieh), "Sailing Whale,"
Keeper of the Wampum—Snipe Tribe.—Onondaga.   Clerk of Six Nations—Onondaga.

THE LEAGUE OF THE IROQUOIS FROM 1660 TO 1890.

The Indians of the league of the Iroquois, both in the United States and Canada, have passed through almost all stages of savage life and a portion of the progressive Anglo-Saxon, and almost all the vicissitudes of war and peace. How civilized ways and methods affect a savage nation the league of the Iroquois best illustrates.

The vitality of this people and the tenacity with which they hold to their traditions, even while adopting or accepting changes, have no parallel in aboriginal life.

In 1890 the census of the United States and the official report of Canada not only show that the league of the Iroquois probably numbers more now than at any period for more than a hundred years past, or than it ever has since first met by Europeans, but that it is steadily increasing.

League of the Iroquois in the United States, 1890	7,387
League of the Iroquois in Canada, 1890	8,483
Total	15,870

LEAGUE OF THE IROQUOIS IN THE UNITED STATES IN 1890.

Six Nations of New York	5,239
Senecas and Onondagas in Warren county, Pennsylvania	98
Total in New York and Pennsylvania	5,337
Senecas and Cayugas at Quapaw agency, Indian territory	255
Members of the league enumerated, residing in Connecticut, Massachusetts, and New York	79
Oneidas in Wisconsin	1,716
Total in the United States	7,387

The following statement has been furnished through the kindness of Mr. E. D. Cameron, superintendent of Indian affairs at Brantford, Canada:

LEAGUE OF THE IROQUOIS IN CANADA IN 1890.

Oneidas of the Thames	715	Iroquois of Saint Regis (a)	1,190
Mohawks of Bay of Quinte	1,056	Iroquois of Gibson	137
Six Nations of Grand river, Brantford	3,288	Iroquois of the Lake of Two Mountains	375
Iroquois of Caughnawaga (a)	1,722	Total	8,483

a A few Algonquins, mixed.

The Iroquois of Grand river are in detail as follows:

Mohawks	1,344	Onondagas	325
Oneidas	244	Tuscaroras	327
Senecas	183		
Cayugas	865	Total	3,288

The following statement shows the total number of the league of the Iroquois, estimated and actual, at the several periods named:

1660	11,000	1736	7,350
1665	11,750	1738	8,825
1677	10,750	1763	11,650
1681	10,000	1768	12,600
1682	13,000	1770	10,000
1685	10,250	1773	12,500
1687	10,000	1779	a8,000
1689	12,850	1791	7,430
1698	6,150		

a Not including emigrants, Mohawks, Onondagas, etc.

There is no record given of the number of the league between 1791 and 1877.

The emigration to Canada of a large portion of the league left a smaller portion in the United States after 1790.

In 1868 the Iroquois in Canada (all of the league) were given at 5,881; in 1874, 6,845; in 1875, 6,893; in 1876, 6,953; in 1890, 8,483.

In 1877 the total number of the league of the Iroquois in Canada and the United States was estimated to be 13,668, and in 1890 it was 15,870. The rate of increase in Canada and the United States is now about the same.

The Cherokees of Indian territory and the Eastern Cherokees, along with the Wyandottes (Wyandot, Wendot) of Quapaw agency, Indian territory, are of Iroquoian stock, but are not included in the membership of the league. (See Extra Census Bulletins on Eastern Cherokees and Five Civilized Tribes, and final report on Statistics of Indians, Eleventh Census.)

STATISTICS OF INDIANS.

THE SIX NATIONS OF NEW YORK IN 1890.

TOTAL POPULATION OF THE SIX NATIONS OF NEW YORK AT SEVERAL PERIODS FROM 1796 TO 1890, INCLUSIVE.

1796, Morse	3,748	1865, United States Indian Office	3,956
1818, Parrish	4,575	1870, United States census	4,962
1819, New York legislature	4,538	1870, United States Indian Office	4,804
1821, Morse	4,056	1875, New York state census	4,672
1825, United States Secretary of War	5,061	1875, United States Indian Office	4,955
1829, General Porter, United States Secretary of War	5,100	1877, United States Indian Office	5,041
1845, United States Indian Office (a)	3,884	1880, United States Indian Office	5,139
1855, New York state census	3,774	1885, United States Indian Office	4,970
1855, United States Indian Office	4,149	1887, United States Indian Office	4,966
1860, United States Indian Office	3,945	1890, United States Indian Office	5,112
1865, New York state census	3,992	1890, United States census	b5,239

a Oneidas omitted (removed west).

b Not including the Cornplanter Senecas in Warren county, Pennsylvania, 98 in number, which would give a total of 5,337.

POPULATION OF THE SIX NATIONS RESERVATIONS IN NEW YORK AND CORNPLANTER SENECA RESERVATION IN PENNSYLVANIA.

TRIBES, ETC.	Total.	RESERVATIONS.						Oneidas off reservation.
		Onondaga.	Tonawanda.	Allegany.	Cattaraugus.	Tuscarora.	Saint Regis.	
Grand total	5,309	494	561	897	1,598	483	1,170	106
Onondaga	a470	341	4	67	17	41		
Oneida	212	86	13	1	4		2	106
Mohawk	18	6	2		1	2	7	
Cayuga	183	5	20	5	153			
Seneca	b2,680	6	517	792	1,355	10		
Tuscarora	408		1		7	400		
Saint Regis	1,129	34	3	2	1		1,089	
Abenaka	10			10				
Muncie	16		1		15			
Brothertown	1				1			
Delaware	3				3			
Stockbridge	7				1	6		
Caughnawaga	15	15						
Half blood	28	1		3	24			
Quarter blood	42						42	
Eighth blood	17						17	
Total—Indians by reservations and Oneidas	5,239	494	561	880	1,582	459	1,157	106
Additions by marriage:								
White	68			16	16	23	13	
Negro	1					1		
Mulatto	1			1				

a 11 Onondagas reside on the Cornplanter reservation in Warren county, Pennsylvania, making the total Onondagas of the Six Nations 481.

b 87 Senecas reside on the Cornplanter reservation in Warren county, Pennsylvania, making the total Senecas in New York and Pennsylvania 2,767.

The total population of the Cornplanter reservation, Warren county, Pennsylvania, and adjoining the Allegany Seneca reservation, New York, is as follows: Onondagas, 11; Senecas, 87, and 1 white man; total, 99.

The total population of the Six Nations reservations in New York and 106 Oneidas off reservation is 5,309. This includes 70 white and colored persons.

The total Indian population of the Six Nations reservations in New York and 106 Oneidas off reservation is 5,239.

VITAL STATISTICS.

The total Indian population of the Six Nations reservations in New York is 5,133. The births during the year were 181; deaths, 156; gain by births over deaths, 25. All reservations gained by births except Tuscarora, where the net loss by death was 6. The deaths by consumption were 39, or 7.6 to the 1,000 of population; the births 35.3 to the 1,000, and the deaths 30.4 to the 1,000.

The several causes of deaths are given in detail in the table on the following page. The deaths from June 30, 1889, to June 30, 1890, included 3 persons between the ages of 90 and 100, 4 persons between the ages of 80 and 90, 4 persons above 78 but less than 80, and 5 persons between the ages of 60 and 75, in a total Indian population of 5,133.

CAUSES OF DEATHS AMONG THE SIX NATIONS OF NEW YORK IN 1890, AS FAR AS KNOWN, AND TOTAL NUMBER OF BIRTHS.

RESERVATIONS.	Total Indian population.	Total deaths.	Consumption.	Heart disease.	Paralysis.	Suicide.	Typhoid fever.	Fever.	Lung fever.	Brain fever.	Blood poison.	Pneumonia.	Scrofula.	Old age.	Childbirth.
Total	5,133	156	39	1	1	1	1	8	1	1	1	3	2	4	1
Onondaga	494	10	2		1			2				1			
Tonawanda	561	22	7					4						1	
Allegany	880	34	7					2	1			1		3	
Cattaraugus	1,582	46	8			1				1					
Tuscarora	459	19	8				1						1		
Saint Regis	1,157	25	7	1							1	1	1		1

RESERVATIONS.	La grippe.	Croup.	Accident.	Smallpox.	Neuralgia.	Spinal complaint.	Kidney trouble.	Cholera morbus.	Measles.	Rheumatism.	Sudden death.	Unknown.	Deaths under one year of age.	Total births.	Excess of deaths over births.	Excess of births over deaths.
Total	11	1	1	1	1	1	1	1	12	1	1	22	38	181	6	31
Onondaga												3	1	19		9
Tonawanda	1											6	3	25		3
Allegany			1									5	14	43		9
Cattaraugus	6			1	1	1	1		12			6	8	56		10
Tuscarora	3							1				2	3	13	6	
Saint Regis	1	1								1	1		9	25		

At the Cornplanter reservation, Warren county, Pennsylvania, the births were 4 and the deaths were 5. Of the latter 3 were infants under 1 year of age and 2 were adults, 1 from pneumonia and 1 from consumption.

STATISTICS OF CRIPPLES, AND ACUTE, CHRONIC, AND OTHER DISEASES OF THE SIX NATIONS OF NEW YORK: 1890.

RESERVATIONS.	Total Indian population.	Total.	Cripples.	Deformed from birth.	Deformed from rheumatism.	Crippled by railroad accident.	Crippled from accident.	Defective hearing.	Defective speech.	Deaf.	Deaf and dumb.	Defective sight.	Blind in one eye.	Blind.	Defective mind.	Acute rheumatism.
Total	5,133	272	9	5	2	1	12	16	2	5	9	26	3	7	5	61
Onondaga	494	41		1		1		4		2	3	2	3			
Tonawanda	561	19	4					2						1		
Allegany	880	20	1	1				3			1	2			1	2
Cattaraugus	1,582	128		2	2		9	4	2	3	2	9		4	1	44
Tuscarora	459	48	3	1			3	3			1	10		1	1	13
Saint Regis	1,157	16	1								2	3		1	2	2

RESERVATIONS.	Consumption.	Scrofula.	Chronic rheumatism.	Heart trouble.	Neuralgia.	Ague.	Liver complaint.	Kidney disease.	Erysipelas.	Asthma.	Paralysis.	Spinal trouble.	Hip disease.	Rupture.	Old age.	Paupers.
Total	39	22	11	4	3	2	4	1	4	1	7	3	1	2	3	2
Onondaga	4	4	11	1		1	2	1	1							
Tonawanda	6	1		1			1			1						2
Allegany	5	2							1		1					
Cattaraugus	19	8		2	3	1	1		1		5	2		1	3	
Tuscarora	3	4							1		1	1	1	1		
Saint Regis	2	3														

The statistics of the Cornplanter Senecas in Warren county, Pennsylvania, show 1 person to be defective in sight, 1 defective in mind, and 1 afflicted with rheumatism.

LONGEVITY POPULATION ABOVE SIXTY YEARS OF AGE OF THE SIX NATIONS OF
NEW YORK FOR 1889 AND 1890.

RESERVATIONS.	Families.	Indian population.	Between 60 and 70 years.	Between 70 and 80 years.	Between 80 and 90 years.	Between 90 and 100 years.
Total............................	1,192	5,133	173	64	26	6
Onondaga........................	115	494	16	10	10	1
Tonawanda	139	561	30	14	7	1
Allegany............................	239	880	32	5	1	1
Cattaraugus........................	378	1,582	50	16	5	2
Tuscarora...........................	106	459	14	8	....	....
Saint Regis.........................	215	1,157	31	11	3	1

The age of 60 years, the ordinary limit of life assurance, is made the basis of comparison. By the American table of mortality adopted by the state of New York as the standard for valuation of policies, the " expectation " is, at 10 years of age, 48.7 years, or the age of 58.7. More than 5.2 per cent of the living persons given above have passed the age of 60 years.

At the Cornplanter reservation, Pennsylvania, 6 persons were above the age of 60 and none above 70 years.

MARRIAGES AND DIVORCES AMONG THE SIX NATIONS OF NEW YORK FOR 1890.

RESERVATIONS.	Married.	Nominally single.	Bigamists.	With two wives.	Separated.	Divorced.	Having two living wives.
Onondaga..............	199	278	2	4	20	....	....
Tonawanda	208	353	....	....	6	1	4
Allegany	360	416	....	....	42	....	2
Cattaraugus........................	552	956	....	....	9	4	1
Tuscarora...........................	152	305	....	....	....	1	....
Saint Regis.........................	443	726	....	....	....	....	2

The special agent in his report explains the difficulties of obtaining complete data and which also attended the recognition of Indian family ties as marriage ties. Many of the nominal marriages amount simply to cohabitation as man and wife during pleasure, without any form of legal union or separation, but an almost universal conviction is gaining ground that marriage must be held binding whatever its form unless a divorce be secured upon separation. The table headings given above are transcripts of the returns made by the enumerator. The several tribes have various ideas of the meaning of the word bigamy, which accounts for the apparent inconsistency in the headings.

Felonies committed by members of the Six Nations are cognizable under the laws of New York or the United States. No felonies were reported during the census year, and but few trivial offenses, except intoxication. The number of Indians in jail or prison for offenses against person or property during the year in an Indian population of 5,133 was as follows: Onondaga, 1; Cattaraugus, 9; Tuscarora, 3; Saint Regis, 3; total, 16. These offenses were tried by Indian courts on the reservations, except at Saint Regis.

RELIGIONS AND CHURCH STATISTICS FOR 1890.

The total number of churches on the six reservations is 12. Some congregations, however, worship in private houses or halls. The churches cost $25,400. The total number of communicants in an Indian population of 5,133 is 1,074. The cost of the church service was $6,887, of which the Indians contributed $1,262. 18 ministers and missionaries were engaged in the work during the year. Details are given in the tables on the following page and in Part IV of the accompanying report.

The pagans of the Six Nations assemble for their business, ceremonies, and exercises either in the council houses, one of which belongs to each of the nations (except the Tuscaroras), or in groves or private houses.

DENOMINATIONS.

RESERVATIONS.	Total.	Baptist.	Methodist.	Wesleyan.	Episcopal.	Presbyterian.	Catholic.
Total............................	1,074	307	159	21	29	258	a300
Onondaga	68	....	23	21	24	....	....
Tonawanda.....................	94	40	19	....	....	35	....
Allegany	131	21	....	....	....	110	....
Cattaraugus...................	170	35	49	....	....	86	....
Tuscarora.......	238	211	....	....	....	27	....
Saint Regis.....................	373	....	68	....	5	....	300
CHURCHES.							
Number	12	3	4	....	1	4	....
Cost (b)	$25,400	$8,100	$8,200	....	$2,200	$6,900	....
FINANCIAL AID.							
Total........................	$6,887	$1,850	$1,695	....	$570	$2,772	....
Outside aid.....................	5,625	1,300	1,500	....	500	2,325	....
Indian aid	1,262	550	195	....	70	447	....

a Worship at the Catholic church on the Canadian side.
b Estimated total previous cost, with changes and repairs.

NUMBER OF CHURCHES, BY DENOMINATIONS.

RESERVATIONS.	Total.	Baptist.	Methodist.	Episcopal.	Presbyterian.
Total........................	12	3	4	1	4
Onondaga........................	2	....	1	1	....
Tonawanda	3	1	1	....	1
Allegany	1	....	....	....	1
Cattaraugus....................	3	1	1	....	1
Tuscarora	3	1	1	....	1
Saint Regis..............	....	....	....	....	....

STATUS OF THE ENGLISH LANGUAGE.

The total Indian population of the Six Nations of New York on reservations, excluding the Oneidas (106), who are included in the general census of 1890, is 5,133. Of these 2,844 can speak English and 1,985 can not.

STATISTICS OF THE ENGLISH LANGUAGE AMONG THE SIX NATIONS OF NEW YORK IN 1890.

ITEMS.	Total.	RESERVATIONS.					
		Onondaga.	Tonawanda.	Allegany.	Cattaraugus.	Tuscarora.	Saint Regis.
Over 20 years of age who can read English..	1,310	94	125	306	501	201	83
Under 20 who can read English.....................	1,134	57	111	181	509	91	185
Under 20 who can write English.................	765	57	111	165	295	85	52
Persons who can speak English	2,844	186	365	502	983	343	465
Persons who can not speak English	1,985	291	180	275	505	99	635

On the Cornplanter Seneca reservation, Warren county, Pennsylvania, there are 29 persons over 20 years of age who can read English; 19 under 20 years of age who can read English; 19 under 20 years of age who can write English; 57 who can speak English, and 35 who can not. Children not able to speak a language are not noted, and some absentees were omitted from the non-English-speaking enumeration. Some Indians refused the information to the enumerator.

SCHOOLS.

Part IX of the accompanying report gives the practical working of the public schools on the reservations of the Six Nations. Many drawbacks are mentioned, and Mr. Joseph E. Hazzard, the state superintendent of schools on the Cattaraugus and Allegany reservations, writes that he "can not secure competent teachers at the rate authorized". This may have much to do with the causes of complaint of lack of sufficient results from these schools. His letter in full will be found under the head of "Cattaraugus reservation", Part IX.

Mr. T. W. Jackson, enumerator and United States Indian agent, in his report for 1890, in speaking of the schools on the Six Nations reservations, says:

From a careful examination of the reports of the local superintendents of Indian schools made to the superintendent of public instruction of the state of New York, I am led to believe that there is a continued improvement of the schools on the Indian reservations.

Sufficient wages should be paid to secure teachers of brains—teachers who have common sense and who are able to devise means by which not only the scholar can be interested and encouraged to attend the school, but the parents must also be interested in the work.

The pay for teachers on these reservations varies from $250 to $276.50 per year. The total number of teachers is 28; schools, 27; children of school age on the reservations, 1,429; largest daily attendance, 714; average attendance, 306; school accommodations, 1,025. The total cost of these schools to the state of New York for the year is placed approximately at $8,360.69, or an average of $27.32 for each of the 306 in attendance. The Indians' contribution to the expense of these schools is in labor and wood, and is mentioned in Part IX.

Under the heads "Education", "Schools", and "Language" detailed statements show that the record of school attendance for some portion of a year would include attendance even for a day, and that a large number of children were present but a few days during the entire school year. In this connection the attendance for 1 month or more is indicated respecting each school, with notice of exceptional cases of remarkable punctuality, in one case of an attendance with but 1 day's absence, unless sick, for more than 7 years. As the New York school age is from 5 to 21 years, the attendance is indicated of pupils under 6 and over 18 years of age, as well as that usual throughout the country.

STATISTICS OF SCHOOLS AMONG THE SIX NATIONS OF NEW YORK FOR 1890.

RESERVATIONS.	Teachers.	Number of schools.	School age.	Largest attendance any one day.	Under 6 years.	Above 18 years.	Average attendance.	Accommodations provided.	Number of weeks taught. (a)	Cost per annum. (a)
Total............	28	27	1,429	714	46	10	306	1,025	....	$8,360.69
Onondaga...........	2	1	118	53	2	....	20.00	60	40	447.81
Tonawanda........	3	3	125	100	5	1	35.12	105	37	886.51
Allegany	6	6	276	141	17	....	61.67	240	32 ⎫	
Cattaraugus........	10	10	386	219	15	1	115.00	350	32 ⎬	4,874.77
Tuscarora............	2	2	127	71	7	8	27.33	80	36	519.43
Saint Regis.........	5	5	397	130	....	....	47.00	190	40	1,632.17

a These two items, number of weeks taught and cost per annum, are from the official reports of the state of New York.

Adding the number reported as under 6 and over 18 years of age increases the substantial attendance to 770. The data are from reports of superintendents, examination of the registers, and personal visits to the schools. The large percentage of children of school age among the Saint Regis Indians is due to the remarkable size of families on that reservation, there being now, as reported under the head "Saint Regis families", 194 children living out of 254 born in 24 families. 107 children under 16 years of age were also educated at the Thomas Orphan Asylum, viz: From Onondaga, 6; Tonawanda, 6; Tuscarora, 13; Allegany, 20; Cattaraugus, 57, and Saint Regis, 5. Considering the fact that the state of New York has no compulsory school-attendance law, the Six Nations present a fair average attendance of children of school age. The state of New York pays the expense of the Indian schools. The Indians supply fuel and care for the schoolhouses and the state attends to the repairs.

SEWING MACHINES AND PIANOS AND ORGANS ON THE SEVERAL
RESERVATIONS.

RESERVATIONS.	Sewing machines.	Pianos and organs.
Total	283	56
Onondaga..	25	11
Tonawanda............	37	11
Allegany	48	11
Cattaraugus...	120	11
Tuscarora...	20	8
Saint Regis...	27	4
Cornplanter Seneca, Pennsylvania....................	6	....

PROFESSIONS.

The following statistics show that 1,703 of the Six Nations work for a living, of whom 696 males are laborers, and 578 males are farmers. Many minors were enumerated as laborers and farmers. The column of occupations gives details of all callings.

STATISTICS OF OCCUPATIONS.

OCCUPATIONS.	Total.	RESERVATIONS.					
		Onondaga.	Tonawanda.	Allegany.	Cattaraugus.	Tuscarora.	Saint Regis. (a)
Total......................................	1,703	165	174	291	492	182	399
Attorneys..................................	5			4	1		
Basket makers............................	185	7			1		177
Bead workers.............................	14	3				2	9
Bows and arrows, snow shoes, etc............	2	1					1
Canes, whipstocks, etc.....................	1		1				
Carpenters................................	32	1	4	1	19	3	4
Clerks.....................................	2				1		1
Cobblers...................................	1	1					
Doctors....................................	9	1		2		1	5
Domestics.................................	4	1					3
Engineers.................................	1	1					
Farmers...................................	578	37	75	120	186	47	113
Ferrymen..................................	1			1			
Fishing, hunting, and trapping..............	10						10
Gardeners.................................	8		2				6
Guides....................................	3						3
Horse trainers............................	1				1		
Housekeepers (b)	71	10	2	1	24	33	1
Laborers..................................	696	93	84	149	244	78	48
Laundresses...............................	3			1			2
Lumbermen................................	4			2			2
Mechanics.................................	10	2		4	2		2
Merchants.................................	2	1	1				
Missionaries...............................	1					1	
Music and school teachers.................	12	2	3	1	4	1	1
Musicians..................................	14				7	6	1
Preachers..................................	8	2	1	2		2	1
Show people...............................	13	1	1		2		9
Soldiers...................................	2					2	
Stockraisers...............................	1					1	
Storekeepers, grocers, etc	2	1				1	
Surveyors.................................	1				1		
Traveling agents...........................	2				2		
Wood carvers..............................	4					4	

a Among the Saint Regis Indians many children are basket makers. The adults of both sexes engaged in basket making do not number more than 50.
b Housekeepers are generally widows or housekeepers for widowers.

At Cornplanter reservation, Pennsylvania, the occupations are given as follows: Housewives, 3; laborers, 16; farmers, 12; musician, 1; ferryman, 1; lumberman, 1; traveling agent, 1.

THE AREA AND CONDITION OF THE RESERVATIONS.

PROPOSED SIX NATIONS ALLOTMENTS AND LAND IN SEVERALTY—EXISTING LAND TITLES—METHOD OF ACQUIRING AND PERPETUATING TITLE.

The subject of breaking up the Six Nations reservations and investing the Six Nations Indians with citizenship and covering them as other citizens of New York with the general laws of the state is often mentioned. In breaking up Indian reservations, usually recorded or personal land holdings and titles are not found. Allotments and assignments to tracts proceed on the order of the allotting agent. No old and settled occupancy titles are in the way. No allotment can be made of the Six Nations lands, nor can an assignment in severalty of them be had on the basis of a common and general division or absolute removal, as is usual with ordinary reservation Indians. The present occupancy or recorded titles would prevent this, and the courts would undoubtedly protect them.

SIX NATIONS LAND TITLES AND TENURES.

While land tenure among the Six Nations is, as a rule, secure in the families enjoying it, the evidence of title for many years largely depended upon visible possession and improvement, rather than upon the record evidence common to white people. Verbal wills recited at the dead feasts, in the presence of witnesses to the devise, were usually regarded as sacred, and a sale, with delivery of possession, was respected when no written conveyance was executed. Of late years written wills have become common, and among the Senecas, with their peacemakers and surrogate judges, the " proof of a will " conforms very nearly to similar proceedings in the state probate courts. The clerk of the Seneca nation keeps a record of grants made by the council. Generally, the clerk, whether of chiefs, as with the Onondagas and Tuscaroras, or of trustees, as with the Saint Regis, has the custody of the records of official proceedings respecting grants or sales of lands. There is far more carelessness than among white people in securing any record of real estate transfers, the Indians preferring to hold the papers and the records themselves instead of having them moved from place to place, with a change of clerk, there being no regular place or rules for deposit or protection. An applicant for land, after petition, secures a vote of council or of chiefs of a tribe or nation, as the case may be, with the description of the land asked for, and a copy of that vote is the basis of a permanent title to himself, his heirs, and assignees. Indian common law, that of immemorial custom, as with the early English holdings, has generally carried its authority or sanction with effective prohibitive force against imposition or fraud, even when occupation and improvement of public domain have been actual but without formal sanction. No well-ordered system of record for wills, grants, or transfers is in habitual use among the Six Nations, or even among the Senecas. The infrequency of transfer out of a family and the publicity of the act when such a transfer is made have been esteemed sufficiently protective. There is no penalty for failure to make record, and the chain of title is not broken into so many links as to confuse the transmission. During late years farmers having substantial improvements have secured legal advice and perfected their papers in the usual business form common to white people, for deposit or record at county seats in which the lands and reservations are located.

As with white people, there are and will be Six Nations Indians land owners and Six Nations Indians landless.

VALUE OF THE LANDS OF THE SIX NATIONS.

The appraisement of Indian lands is based upon their best local terms of sale, and not upon that of sales by the white people of outside lands; but farms upon some reservations may well be appraised at $50 per acre, when on some other reservations equally good or better lands would range from $25 to $35 per acre. These have a leasehold value, but not the full value of similar adjoining lands, which are unincumbered by their present inalienable Indian title.

The following table gives the number of acres and total value (estimated) for each reservation. The total acreage of the reservations of the Six Nations is 87,327.73, and the value is estimated at $1,810,699.60. The reservation lands, if sold, and the proceeds divided per capita, would give each of the 5,203 Indians and adopted persons $348.01. The acreage to each person on the several reservations is also given, and the names and areas of reservations, tillable and grazing lands, acres cultivated, under fence, fenced during year, leased, new lands broken, pasturage land actually used in 1890, estimated value per acre, and total value of reservations.

ACREAGE, VALUE, ETC., OF THE RESERVATIONS OF THE SIX NATIONS.

RESERVATIONS.	Total number of acres in reservations.	Number of acres tillable. (Estimated.)	Number of acres fit only for grazing. (Estimated.)	Number of acres cultivated during the year by Indians.	Number of acres under fence.	Rods of fencing made during the year.
Onondaga	a6,100.00	4,500	1,100	2,522.25	4,000	(b)
Tonawanda	7,549.73	6,500	500	2,200.00	3,800	60
Allegany	30,469.00	} 11,000	5,000	2,948.00	5,124	100
Oil Spring	640.00					
Cattaraugus	21,680.00	11,000	2,000	4,500.00	5,600	....
Tuscarora	6,249.00	5,800	250	4,200.00	4,635	....
Saint Regis	c14,640.00	9,000	4,500	4,033.50	7,000	3,000
Total in New York	87,327.73	47,800	13,350	20,403.75	30,159	3,160
Cornplanter, Warren county, Pennsylvania	d640.00	599	90	360.00	(e)	....
Total with Cornplanter	87,967.73	48,399	13,440	20,763.75	....	....

a New York commission estimates acreage at 7,300.
b Repairs only.
c With swamp land, estimated at 15,280 acres.

d Actual acreage 679, excess above 640 due to allowance for river bed.
e Nearly all under fence.

ACREAGE, VALUE, ETC., OF THE RESERVATIONS OF THE SIX NATIONS—Continued.

RESERVATIONS.	Number of acres leased to white men.	Number of acres of new lands broken during the year.	Number of acres of pasturage lands used.	Average value per acre. (Estimated.)	Total value of lands. (Estimated.)	Total population, Indian and adopted.	Acres to each person on division or allotment.
Onondaga				$28	$170,800.00	494	12.35
Tonawanda	1,718	50		20	150,994.60	561	13.46
Allegany	}	} 123	2,175	15	457,035.00	} a897	34.68
Oil Spring	640			15	9,600.00		
Cattaraugus				25	542,000.00	1,598	13.57
Tuscarora	1,450			30	187,470.00	483	12.94
Saint Regis		200	1,000	20	292,800.00	1,170	12.51
Total in New York	3,808	373	3,175		1,810,699.60	b5,203	

a 96 white people unlawfully on the Allegany reservation but enumerated in the general census.

b Includes white and colored persons by marriage and adoption, who may or may not have realty rights on allotment under Indian law.

The property valuation of the Indians of the reservations of the Six Nations in New York is $1,284,998, as follows (property valuation includes everything which an Indian owns and can sell to another Indian):

PROPERTY VALUATION.

Onondaga	$118,225
Tonawanda	133,126
Allegany	207,514
Cattaraugus	416,419
Tuscarora	214,222
Saint Regis	195,492
Total	1,284,998

The property valuation of the Cornplanter reservation in Warren county, Pennsylvania, is $24,495.

PROPERTY CLASSIFICATION.

The disparity in acquisition as between society grades is not very different from that in any community of ordinary white people. The large acquisitions are few, and generally are the result of good management and reasonable industry. Inherited estates have been divided and scattered through improvidence, as among the white people. The Indian in New York, as elsewhere, has fewer wants than his white neighbor, and is frequently more indolent or indifferent in the effort to acquire more than his actual necessities require.

PROPERTY CLASSIFICATION AND INDIVIDUAL WEALTH.

RESERVATIONS.	Valuation of $10,000 or over.	$5,000 and less than $10,000.	$4,000 and less than $5,000.	$3,000 and less than $4,000.	$2,000 and less than $3,000.	$2,000 and less than $2,500.	$1,500 and less than $2,000.	$1,000 and less than $2,000.	$1,000 and less than $1,500.	$500 and less than $1,000.	$300 and less than $500.	Less than $300.	$100 and less than $300.	$25 and less than $100.	Under $25.
Total	6	28	13	33	60	1	1	117	9	181	60	147	63	31	13
Onondaga	1	5	1	4	8			12		19		26			
Tonawanda	1	2	3	4	9			25		29		40			
Allegany		3	3	8	17			44		53		49			
Cattaraugus	1	8	3	7	14			20		21		15			
Tuscarora	3	10	3	10	12			16		22		17			
Saint Regis						1	1		9	37	60		63	31	13

The total value of houses on the reservations of the Six Nations in New York is $226,067, and of household effects $63,916.

VALUE OF HOUSES AND HOUSEHOLD EFFECTS.

RESERVATIONS.	Houses.	Household effects.
Total	$226,067	$63,916
Onondaga	20,390	4,882
Tonawanda	25,284	12,670
Allegany	43,735	9,178
Cattaraugus	79,525	22,270
Tuscarora	29,560	7,955
Saint Regis	27,573	6,961

The value of houses on the Cornplanter Seneca reservation is $2,200, and of household effects $1,195.

The Indian population of the Six Nations reservations in New York is 5,133 (2,696 males and 2,437 females). Heads of families, or total families, 1,213. The voters (if they were citizens under the laws of New York, viz, males over 21 years of age) number 1,381. Children under 1 year of age, 163.

The number of houses, frame, log, or plank, on the Six Nations reservations owned by Indians is 1,206.

The house accommodation per person is given under each reservation. The value of the houses is given under the head of "Property valuation". The houses on the Saint Regis reservation are probably the most inferior of all the reservations, but as an illustration of the value of Indian houses, the number and value of those on the Saint Regis reservation are given in full, as follows:

NUMBER AND VALUE OF HOUSES ON THE SAINT REGIS RESERVATION.

$500 and less than $1,000	7
$300 and less than $500	13
$100 and less than $300	66
$25 and less than $100	97
Less than $25	33
Total	216

All Indians on the Six Nations reservations wear citizens' clothes.

STATISTICS OF RESERVATIONS.

RESERVATIONS.	Total Indians.	Indians. (Males.)	Indians. (Females.)	Heads of families.	Children under 1 year.	Males above 21 years.	DWELLINGS. Total number owned by Indians.	Frame.	Log.	Plank.	Average number of persons to each house (a).
Total	5,133	2,696	2,437	1,213	163	1,381	b1,206	1,072	132	2	
Onondaga	494	258	236	117	27	139	105	77	26	2	4.7
Tonawanda	561	296	265	147	22	156	149	c149			3.8
Allegany	880	461	419	250	29	254	242	c242			3.7
Cattaraugus	1,582	850	732	377	56	439	380	303	77		4.2
Tuscarora	459	246	213	110	13	146	114	85	29		4.0
Saint Regis	1,157	585	572	212	16	247	216	c216			5.4

a There are house accommodations provided for the number of persons given for each reservation.

b 89 Indian houses are occupied by Indian renters; the remainder by the owners. The statistics of the Cornplanter reservation, Warren county, Pennsylvania, are: Total number of Indians, 98; males, 57; females, 41; married, 61; single, 37; children under 1 year of age, 4; males above 21 years of age, 18; total number of houses, 27; frame, 18; log, 9; heads of families, 24.

c Frame and log.

AGRICULTURAL STATISTICS.

The following table gives the total agricultural products and values of the Six Nations for the year 1890. The total acreage cultivated, including hay lands, is 20,404; the value of products, $97,887.60. Many of the farmers and farm laborers of the Six Nations hire out during the farming season to their white neighbors, receiving cash for their labor. This, with the products of their small farms, furnishes them a livelihood.

The leading articles of production were: Bushels of wheat raised, 12,366; value, $10,053.60. Bushels of oats raised, 27,774; value, $11,588. Bushels of corn raised, 42,739; value, $17,252. Tons of hay cut, 3,427; value, $27,500. Bushels of potatoes raised, 21,319; value, $17,341. The total value of agricultural products raised by the Six Nations in New York and the Cornplanter Senecas in Pennsylvania for the year 1890 was $97,887.60.

AGRICULTURAL STATISTICS.

RESERVATIONS.	Total value at market rates.	WHEAT. Bushels.	Value.	OATS. Bushels.	Value.	CORN. Bushels.	Value.	BARLEY AND RYE. Bushels.	Value.	BUCKWHEAT. Bushels.	Value.	SWEET CORN, FOR CANNING. Bushels.	Value.
Total	$97,887.60	12,366	$10,053.60	27,774	$11,588	42,739	$17,252	1,971	$1,162	7,011	$5,188	1,145	$595
Onondaga	4,714.60	345	258.60	848	254	1,855	742						
Tonawanda	8,713.00	4,235	3,812.00	2,662	1,025	2,889	1,300	666	499	330	231		
Allegany	16,177.00	330	247.00	2,679	1,072	7,120	3,204	40	30	4,754	3,566		
Cattaraugus	42,904.00	3,525	2,700.00	8,466	3,386	22,604	9,050	100	50	433	325	1,145	595
Tuscarora	14,337.00	3,007	2,256.00	3,853	1,540	2,625	1,050	1,165	583				
Saint Regis	8,411.00	731	607.00	9,049	4,224	5,306	1,753			30	30		
Cornplanter Seneca	2,631.00	193	173.00	217	87	340	153			1,464	1,036		

AGRICULTURAL STATISTICS—Continued.

RESERVATIONS.	HAY.		POTATOES.		TURNIPS.		PEASE, FOR CANNING.		BEANS.		BEETS.	
	Tons.	Value.	Bushels.	Value.	Bushels.	Value.	Bushels.	Value.	Bushels.	Value.	Bushels.	Value.
Total	3,427	$27,500	21,319	$17,341	649	$335	2,020	$1,175	1,758.5	$3,653	240	$130
Onondaga...................	256	2,250	1,169	1,053	19	10	20	20	3.5	7		
Tonawanda..............	89	712							504.0	1,134		
Allegany	349	2,792	4,446	3,556					220.0	440		
Cattaraugus...............	1,536	12,368	14,396	11,558	140	80	1,785	893	757.0	1,514	140	80
Tuscarora	866	7,000	1,143	1,025	490	245	25	25	234.0	468	100	50
Saint Regis...............	210	1,470					190	237	40.0	90		
Cornplanter Seneca.....	121	908	165	149								

RESERVATIONS.	CABBAGE.		APPLES.		STRAWBERRIES.		BLACKBERRIES, WILD.		TOMATOES.		SMALL VEGETABLES, ONIONS, ETC.		BEEHIVES.	
	Heads.	Value.	Barrels.	Value.	Quarts.	Value.	Bushels.	Value.	Bushels.	Value.	Bushels.	Value.	Number.	Value.
Total	1,250	$140	15	$45	300	$30	1,500	$1,250	180	$135	125	$145	34	$170
Onondaga...................	750	90			300	30								
Tonawanda														
Allegany...................							1,500	1,250			25	20		
Cattaraugus...............									180	135			34	170
Tuscarora	500	50	15	45										
Saint Regis.................														
Cornplanter Seneca.....											100	125		

It is estimated that 4,132 cords of wood were cut on the six reservations during the year ended June 30, 1890, mostly for home use.

The Six Nations own live stock valued at $126,860, viz: 967 horses, value $71,710; 4 mules, value $290; 1,222 swine, value $8,219; 9,336 domestic fowls, value $2,255; 1,968 cattle of all grades, value $44,130, and 28 sheep, value $256.

LIVE STOCK.

RESERVATIONS.	Total.	HORSES.		MULES.		SWINE.		DOMESTIC FOWLS.		CATTLE, ALL GRADES.		SHEEP.	
		Number.	Value.	Number.	Value.	Number.	Value.	Number.	Value.	Number.	Value.	Number.	Value.
Total...............	$126,860	967	$71,710	4	$290	1,222	$8,219	9,336	$2,255	1,968	$44,130	28	$256
Onondaga................	3,218	55	495			59	433	200	50	106	2,240		
Tonawanda..............	11,352	113	7,345	2	140	266	1,060	667	167	132	2,640		
Allegany.................	17,074	104	7,250			184	1,288	1,530	306	403	8,060	17	170
Cattaraugus	44,615	308	23,000	2	150	355	2,850	4,267	1,065	682	17,500	5	50
Tuscarora	16,125	121	9,680			220	1,760	1,743	435	173	4,250		
Saint Regis........	34,476	266	23,940			138	828	929	232	472	9,440	6	36
Cornplanter Seneca..	1,260	4	360			24	200	204	40	22	660		

The total value of agricultural implements owned by the Six Nations is $58,702.50.   The value by reservations is as follows:

AGRICULTURAL IMPLEMENTS.

Onondaga..	$2,679.00
Tonawanda...	4,991.00
Allegany	4,691.00
Cattaraugus..	27,751.50
Tuscarora	6,455.00
Saint Regis..	12,135.00
Total..	58,702.50

The value of agricultural implements at the Cornplanter reservation is $4,493.   This includes wagons and other vehicles in ordinary use as well as agricultural implements proper.

UNION SOLDIER AND SAILOR ELEMENT.

The following statement shows the soldier and sailor element in the United States army in the war of the rebellion; also, widows of soldiers or sailors, the data of which were obtained with much difficulty.

On the 23d of July, 1879, an effort was made on the part of ex-soldiers belonging to the Seneca nation to ascertain the names of those who served in the late war, with the result first given below, but without obtaining the dates of enlistment or discharge.

In 1890 the special agent of the census reported that the loss of papers, absence of papers with pension agents, lapse of time since the war, with absolute ignorance for years that any benefits would flow from service, rendered accurate data almost impossible of attainment in many cases, except where some had passed examination for Grand Army posts. Many enlisted under fictitious names. Some failed to pass final examination, but joined recruiting depots for a short time.

The soldiers' widows are also noted by name. The enumeration of 1890 shows that the Onondagas furnished 16 soldiers, the Tonawanda Senecas 13 soldiers and 1 marine, the Allegany Senecas 11 soldiers and 1 sailor, the Cattaraugus Senecas 87 soldiers (in 1879 the total was given as 67), the Tuscaroras 10 soldiers, and the Saint Regis 23 soldiers, making a grand total of 162 soldiers and sailors.

ONONDAGAS:

Charles Lyon, Company F, Second New York Heavy Artillery. Peter Elm, Company F, Second New York Heavy Artillery. Josiah Jacob, Company F, Second New York Heavy Artillery. Jacob Scanandoah, Company F, Second New York Heavy Artillery (musician). Hewett Jacob, Company D, One Hundred and Thirty-second New York Infantry. Samuel G. Isaacs, Company D, One Hundred and Thirty-second New York Infantry. Henry Powlis, Company I, One Hundred and Fourth New York Infantry, enlisted February, 1862; discharged July, 1864 (a pensioner). Wilson Jacob, Company M, First New York Cavalry, enlisted October 16, 1863; discharged July 20, 1865. Joseph Green, Company K, Eighty-seventh New York Infantry. Thomas John, Eighty-sixth New York Infantry; served three months from March, 1863. Martin Powlis enlisted under name of William Martin in the Eighty-sixth New York Infantry; left after two months. Peter Johnson, Company F, Fourteenth Wisconsin (a pensioner). Alexander Sullivan, Company E, Tenth New York Infantry (a pensioner). William Martin, Seventieth New York Infantry.

Soldiers' widows—Mary White, widow of Eli Farmer, who enlisted March 6, 1864; discharged November 6, 1864. Eliza Fish, widow of Moses Jordon.

TONAWANDA SENECAS:

Chauncey Long (Lang) enlisted in the Twenty-third United States Colored Infantry, Company B, May 13, 1864; discharged October 9, 1865. William Bigfire enlisted in the Twenty-third United States Colored Infantry, Company B, July 9, 1864; discharged November 30, 1865. David Moses and Clinton Moses enlisted in the Second New York Heavy Artillery August 1, 1864; discharged October 6, 1864. Erastus Printup enlisted in the Second New York Heavy Artillery March 6, 1862; discharged June 12, 1862. John Peters enlisted in the One Hundred and Thirty-second New York Infantry May 25, 1862; discharged May 25, 1865. Peter Snyder enlisted in the One Hundred and Fifty-first New York Infantry August 25, 1862; discharged June 26, 1865. William Mason, Company D, One Hundred and Thirty-second New York Infantry. Thomas Sky, Company A, One Hundred and Twenty-eighth New York Infantry. John Black, Company A, Second New York Heavy Artillery. Marshall Printup, Company F, Second New York Heavy Artillery. Charles Bigfire, Company B, Second Massachusetts Infantry. Charles Scroggs, William Smith, George Sky, and George Snow, all without data.

Soldiers' widows—Maria Jones, widow of William Jones (marine).

ALLEGANY SENECAS:

Ebenezer Worth, in Twenty-fourth New York Cavalry. Robert Nehew served in Company I, One Hundred and Fourth New York Infantry, under the name of Robert Blacksnake. Amos Snow served on the gunboat Neosha, Captain Samuel Howard, as landsman; enlisted at Buffalo February, 1862. Thomas Scroggs served in the New York Heavy Artillery, Company C. Wooster King served in Company K, Fifty-seventh Pennsylvania Infantry. John Jonathan served in the One Hundred and Forty-first Pennsylvania Infantry; also Abel Jacob. Alfred Halftown served in the Fifty-fourth New York Heavy Artillery. Dennis Titus served in Company B, Thirteenth New York Heavy Artillery. Henry Huff, jr., served in the One Hundred and Second New York Infantry.

Soldiers' widows—Rebecca Blackchief, widow of Samuel Blackchief. Hannah Jones, widow of Belah Jones, One Hundred and Fourth New York Infantry.

CATTARAUGUS SENECAS:

Thirteenth New York Infantry—James Cornplanter, Lewis John, Amos Sundown, Jesse Turkey, William Bluesky, Stephen Gordon, and Stephen Jimerson, Company K; Joseph Warrior, Asher Young, John Jimerson, and George Crow, Company D.

Thirty-first New York Infantry—George Armstrong, Company B.

Fifty-first New York Infantry—Martin Davis, Company H.

Sixty-first New York Infantry—John Jonathan, Company F.

One Hundred and Fourth New York Infantry—Robert Blacksnake, Beeley Jones, James Halftown, Bennett Gordon, Lyman Pierce, James Snow, James Bigfire, and Henry Forest, Company N.

One Hundred and Thirty-first New York Infantry—Henry Sundown, Benjamin Jonas, George Wilson, James Halfwhite, George Snow, and Charles Moore; Jacob Warner and George Jimerson, Company D; Foster Hudson, Company K.

Ninth New York Cavalry—Joseph Halfwhite, Charles Snow, and Cyrus Warrior, Company C.

Twenty-fourth New York Cavalry—George White, jr., and Ira Pierce, Company K; Solon Snow and James Davis, Companies K and M, Joseph Gordon, Horation Jimerson, and Horace Jackson, Company D; John Williams, Samuel Warrior, and Horace Halfwhite, Companies D and M; Lyman Pierce and Ebenezer Thompson, Company M; John Taylor, Company F.

Second New York Mounted Rifles—Moses Turkey, Company A.

Thirteenth New York Heavy Artillery—Young King and Jesse Kenjockerty, Company B.

CATTARAUGUS SENECAS—Continued.

Fourteenth New York Heavy Artillery—Oliver Silverheels, Company C; Jacob Halftown, John Jackson, Lewis Moses, and Sprague Moses; Company D; Lewis Jones, Rawley Jimerson, and James Abram, Companies C and D.

Fifth New Hampshire Infantry—Allen Turkey, Company H.

Twenty-Third Massachusetts Infantry—Cyrus Johnnyjohn, Chicken Bigfire, William Bigfire, and Charles Bigfire, Company B.

Twenty-ninth Connecticut Infantry—Phillip Fatty, Company F.

Eighty-eighth Pennsylvania Infantry—Samuel Logan, Besken Dowdy, and Cornelius Fatty, Company A.

The enumeration of the Cattaraugus Senecas drew out the following additional data :

William Butler, half-blood, enlisted in Seventy-eighth New York Infantry, Company D, 1861; discharged 1865. William Bluesky, Stephen Gordon, Jesse Turkey, and Lewis John, Cayugas, enlisted in the Thirteenth New York Infantry December 23, 1863, all in Company K, and were discharged July 20, 1865. Jacob Halftown, John Jackson, sr., and Oliver Silverheels enlisted in the Fourteenth New York Heavy Artillery, Company D, January 5, 1864. Horace Jackson and George White, jr., enlisted in the Twenty-fourth New York Cavalry, Company D, January 12, 1864, and were discharged August 5, 1865. Cyrus Johnnyjohn enlisted in the Thirteenth New York Infantry January 5, 1864, Company B, and was discharged August 21, 1865. Jesse Kenjockerty and John King served in Company B, Thirteenth New York Heavy Artillery. George Snow, James Halfwhite, George Wilson, and Henry Sundown enlisted in the One Hundred and Thirty-second New York Infantry May 24, 1862, Company D, and were discharged May 25, 1865. Noah Twoguns enlisted in the Sixty-fourth New York Infantry, Company D. Martin Davis, Cayuga, enlisted in the Fifty-first New York Infantry, Company H.

Soldiers' widows—Catherine Jimerson, widow of Jacob T. Jimerson, Company C, Thirteenth New York Heavy Artillery. Elizabeth S. F. Jacobs, widow of Halftown Jacobs.

TUSCARORAS:

Edward Spencer (Anderson), Company A, Thirty-fifth New Jersey Infantry, enlisted March 10, 1865; discharged May 26, 1865. John Bembleton, Company M, Twelfth New York Cavalry, enlisted December 20, 1863; discharged July 3, 1865. Jeremiah Peter, Company D, One Hundred and Thirty-second New York Infantry, enlisted October 28, 1863; discharged July 3, 1865. Ozias Chew, Company M, Twelfth New York Cavalry, enlisted June 26, 1862; discharged June 25, 1865. Cornelius C. Cusick, Company D, One Hundred and Thirty-second New York Infantry, now captain Eleventh United States Infantry.

Soldiers' widows—Charlotte Mountpleasant, widow of Clinton Mountpleasant, who served in the Thirty-first New Jersey Volunteers, Colored Brigade. Sarah Ann Thompson, widow of Nicodemus Thompson, Company M, Twelfth New York Cavalry. Elizabeth Johnson, widow of Elijah Johnson, Battery K, First New York Artillery, who enlisted April 16, 1864, and was discharged November 10, 1865. Eliza Green, widow of Charles Green, of Company K, One Hundred and Twentieth New York Infantry. Sarah Bembleton, widow of Daniel Bembleton, Company M, Twelfth New York Cavalry.

SAINT REGIS:

John Bonaparte and Jacob Williams, Ninety-eighth New York Infantry, enlisted December 25, 1861; discharged July 26, 1862. John Bonaparte also in Company C, One Hundred and Thirty-fourth New York Infantry, from April 30, 1864, to April 20, 1865. John Tarbell, Fifty-sixth Massachusetts, enlisted January 7, 1864; discharged July 17, 1865. John Hoops, Company F, Fifty-sixth New York Infantry, enlisted February, 1864; discharged July 20, 1865. Mitchell Benedict, Company K, New Hampshire Infantry, enlisted December 19, 1863; discharged July 17, 1865. Jacob Pelo, John Billings, Peter Cook, and Peter Gray, Company A, Ninety-eighth New York Infantry. Joseph Bero, Company E, enlisted October, 1861; discharged July 25, 1862. John Tarbell and John White, Company F, Fifty-sixth Massachusetts Infantry, enlisted January 7, 1864; discharged July 17 and 20, respectively, 1865 (Tarbell in Andersonville prison). Jacob Arquette, Company E, New York Infantry, enlisted January 1, 1862; discharged July 25, 1865. Abram Herring (Heron), Company C, Ninth New York Infantry. Frank Papineau. Peter Chubbs served six days and left.

Soldiers' widows—Mary Gorrow (Gareau), widow of Joseph Gorrow. Margaret Gorrow (Gareau), widow of John Gorrow. Hattie C. Torrance (Terans), widow of Frank Currier, Ninety-second New York (pensioner). Sarah David, widow of Loran David. Mary Phillips (absent), widow of John Phillips, who enlisted January 7 and was discharged June 12, 1865, as claimed, but regiment forgotten. Ida Stump, widow of William Stump, Company C, Fifteenth Connecticut; has pension claim; enlistment January 1, 1862; discharged July 5, 1862.

The following were the Six Nations survivors of the United States army of the war of 1812–'14 on June 1, 1890 :

John Adams, Onondaga reservation; age 96. John Joe (Little Joe), Cattaraugus; age uncertain. Henry Phillips, Cattaraugus; age 88. Daniel Twoguns, recently deceased; age 92. Peter Johnson, John Jones, Jack Kenjockerty, and John Jones, very old men, recently deceased, are reported by their surviving families to have served in the same war upon the American side.

THE SIX NATIONS OF NEW YORK.

BY HENRY B. CARRINGTON.

PART I.

HISTORICAL OUTLINE.

The retirement of the Indian westward within the United States has been qualified by two historical factors. The first grew out of the unlimited and conflicting sweep of British land grants, which involved subsequent conflicts of jurisdiction and corresponding compromises. The second was incidental to the passage of the ordinance of July 13, 1787, which organized the northwest territory. The first, especially in the adjustment of the claims of Massachusetts and New York to the same lands, dealt with Indian titles and rights which neither party could wholly ignore. The white men had overlapped and practically surrounded certain internal nations. The United States followed the British precedent, recognizing the independent sovereignty of the Five Nations (a) in New York, and the rival states of Massachusetts and New York made their adjustments upon the same general basis.

Unlike their less fortunate countrymen in the southern states, the Five Nations inherited titles, which they fully maintained in spite of French invasion, compelling Great Britain to honor those titles in her settlement of issues with France. The French claim of discovery was not supplemented by one of conquest. The Iroquois confederacy successfully defended its ancestral homes against both Indian and civilized invaders, even before Plymouth and Yorktown were colonized or Hollanders occupied Manhattan island. At the establishment of the American republic the Five Nations were still too strong to be ruthlessly forced out of their surroundings, and the sentiment of the American people, supported by President Washington, completely suppressed any demonstration in that direction. The campaign of General Sullivan was based upon hostile invasion by the Indians, and its settlement was treated as the end of a necessary war with contiguous states.

The ordinance of July 13, 1787, dealt with the Indian upon the border, whose hunting range had no limit, and whose home jurisdiction had no distinctive definition.

The distinction between the early status of the New York tribes and that of the western tribes is an important one in applying the facts obtained for the Eleventh Census of the United States to the solution of the problem in future dealings with the Six Nations.

The Indians of New York, early recognized as an independent body politic, too strong to be despised and to be conciliated as allies against other enemies, have been comparatively undisturbed by modern progress, but which must inevitably resolve all purely tribal relations into common citizenship. The pressure from without has, in the main, been that of example and ideas rather than that of force. The reduction of their landed possessions and the modification of their governmental forms and social usages have been matters of negotiation, treaty, and friendly adjustment. The grant by King James I of England to the Plymouth colony, afterward known as Massachusetts, from the Indian tribe of that name, and the grant of Charles II to the Duke of York covered in part the same lands, involving questions similar to those which attended Virginia land grants and all others which extended westward to the Pacific ocean at a time when the geographical status of lands " westward " had no clear description.

A brief reference to the substantial settlement of this and other matters affecting the New York tribes is all that is needed in this connection. The numerous national treaties and acts of Congress and other treaties between the state of New York and the Six Nations, which are matters of public record, have been compiled and published by the state of New York in a volume entitled " Report of special committee appointed by the assembly of 1888 to investigate the Indian problem of the state ". The documents occupy 320 pages, octavo size. Additional printed matter of 804 pages embodies the testimony taken by a special commission in prosecuting their inquiries, and an appendix to the volume cites statutes and treaties which have historic relation to the subject-matter.

The state of New York has not been indifferent to the welfare of the Indian nor reluctant to encourage by legislative sanction his efforts to initiate civilized forms of government and modern methods of internal economy in his administration of home affairs, as was shown in the case of the Allegany and Cattaraugus Senecas. 3 of the statutes cited in the volume referred to relate particularly to the Oneidas, 9 to the Tuscaroras, 10 to the Shinnecocks

---

a The Five Nations, or League of the Iroquois, became the Six Nations after 1715 by the admission of the Tuscarora Indians from North Carolina into the Iroquois confederacy.

of Long Island, 13 to the Saint Regis (successors of the Mohawks), 21 to the Onondagas, 14 to the Tonawanda Senecas, and 37 to the Seneca nation, as incorporated by statute, which embraces the Indians of the Allegany and Cattaraugus reservations proper.

These acts, eleemosynary, educational, and general, touch nearly every phase of state supervision and support which does not conflict with the quasi independence of the tribes under original treaties and supplemental agreements in harmony therewith. Their respective bearings upon the census enumeration, as well as the entire testimony procured by the state under its special commission, had careful examination and analysis before the enumeration began, in order to so collect and classify the data that general and state governments might find a remedy for existing evils and save the Indian from any legalized wrong, as well as from the ruinous effects of barbarous rites and customs, which have not been eliminated by a century of contact with the white race. The tendency of attempted legislation and very pronounced utterances from respectable sources have been in the direction of an abrogation of all existing treaties, with or without the consent of the Indians. All such propositions will be confronted by a national judicial negative, and no impatience with slow Indian development can excuse the impairment of his substantial titles and rights or the imposition of terms of conquest. There must be a middle course, just to all. Neither the encroaching white man nor the conservative pagan can resist the wise and safe conclusion that the Indian must come within the pale of civilization and yet lose nothing of intrinsic value to himself or his family.

ANTECEDENTS OF THE SIX NATIONS.

It is impossible to justly apply the tests of to-day without deference to the antecedents of this people and that course of history which has perpetuated their independence while nearly all their contemporary tribes have diminished or disappeared. The advent of the white man in the colonization of the Atlantic coast was at a time when the Iroquois confederacy of the Mohawk, Oneida, Onondaga, Cayuga, and Seneca nations had practically mastered the Algonquin tribes, which in Canada, New England, the middle colonies, and the west had long girdled the New York tribes as a belt of fire. Unlike the Algonquins, whose tribes had nothing to bind them together but certain similar peculiarities of dialect and jealousy of the Five Nations, the Iroquois (the Mohawks, Oneidas, Onondagas, Cayugas, and Senecas) had a constitutional bond of union, described by Lossing as a "barbaric republic, the Iroquois confederacy, existing in the wilderness, simple, pure, and powerful, with its capital 100 miles from the sea, and unknown until Cartier sailed up the Saint Lawrence, until Champlain penetrated its forests, and Hudson discovered the beautiful river that bears his name".

The traditions of the formation of this league are very old, systematic, and carefully preserved. The league was called Ko-ni-shi-o-ni, the "cabin builders" or the "long house", of which the Mohawks held the eastern and the Senecas the western door, with the great council fire or federal capital among the Onondagas. The words attributed to Hiawatha, "the very wise man", mingled with much romantic story, are so descriptive of the family peculiarities of the different nations that they are worthy of notice in the briefest of the two forms preserved among the people. The scene of the conference was on the hill slope north of Onondaga lake, in the state of New York.

THE WORDS OF HIAWATHA.

We have met, members of many nations, many of you a great distance from your homes, to provide for our common safety. To oppose these foes from the north by tribes, and alone, would prove our destruction. We must unite as a common band of brothers, and we shall be safe.

You Mohawks, sitting under the shadow of the great trees, whose roots sink deep into the earth, and whose branches spread over a vast country, shall be the first nation, because you are warlike and mighty.

You Oneidas, a people who recline your bodies against the everlasting stone that can not be moved, shall be the second nation, because you give good counsel.

You Onondagas, who have your habitation at the great mountain and are overshadowed by its crags, shall be the third nation, because you are greatly gifted in speech and are mighty in war.

And you Cayugas, whose habitation is in the dark forest and whose home is everywhere, shall be the fourth nation, because of your superior cunning in hunting.

And you Senecas, a people who live in the open country and possess much wisdom, shall be the fifth nation, because you understand the art of raising corn and beans and making cabins.

You five great and powerful nations must unite and have but one common interest, and no foe shall be able to subdue us. If we unite, the "Great Spirit" will smile upon us. Brothers, these are the words of Hiawatha. Let them sink deep into your hearts.

In 1535, at the site of the future city of Montreal, Cartier made a vocabulary of Indian words, showing that the Iroquois language was then spoken by the Hurons, who were conquered or absorbed by the Iroquois. The confederacy is held to have had its origin about this time. This league, purely aristocratic in spirit, but republican and representative in form, was not political, but chiefly for mutual defense. The carefully preserved wampums of those early times will receive notice in another connection. "Each nation was distinct and independent as to domestic affairs", writes Lossing, "but bound to the others by ties of honor and the general good". Each had its principal sachems or civil magistrates with subordinate officers, in all 200, besides 50 with hereditary rights. These were assigned as follows: To the Mohawks, 9; to the Oneidas, 10; to the Onondagas, 14; to the Cayugas, 10, and to the Senecas, 8. Each nation had subdivisions of tribes or clans, such as Wolf, Bear, Turtle, Snipe, Beaver,

Deer, Hawk, and Heron, 8 in all. The insignia or totem (mark) of each was subsequently placed upon treaties after the European style. These tribes or clans formed one of the closest bonds of union among the confederated nations. In effect, each tribe was divided into 5 parts, and 1 part was located in each nation. The Mohawk Wolf regarded the Seneca Wolf as his brother. Thus if the nations fell into collision it would have turned Bear against Bear, Wolf against Wolf, brother against brother. "The history of the Ho-de-no-sau-nee", says Morgan, "exhibits the wisdom of these organic provisions, for during the whole history of the league they never fell into anarchy nor verged upon dissolution from internal disorders. The whole race was woven into one great family of related households". The 8 tribes were, however, in 2 divisions of 4 each, the Wolf, Bear, Beaver, and Turtle forming one division, and the Deer, Snipe, Heron, and Hawk forming the other. Marriage between members of the same division was nearly as rigidly forbidden as between members of the same tribe.

Other tribes are claimed to have existed besides the 8 principal ones, which are found in many other Indian nations; that of the Eel survives among the Onondagas. The names of birds are confused, according to locality, the "tip-up" (Allegany) evidently being the same as the snipe, and chicken hawk and mud turtle being only a familiar substitute for hawk and turtle. The enumeration follows the Indian's own dictation as a general rule.

It was the sound theory of their wise men that purity of blood could alone perpetuate the empire which their fathers had founded. The initiation of a system of physical decay has been as great a curse to the red men of America as fire water itself.

The league had a president with 6 advisers, and authority to convene representatives of all tribes in cases requiring concert of action. Merit was made the basis and sole reward of office. Oh-to-da-ha, an aged Onondagan, was the first president of the league. The mat upon which he sat is still preserved with care, and the buckskin threads upon which the shell and stone beads were strung are still sound, presenting one of the most beautiful relics of the history of the confederacy.

In the military department chiefs were elected for special causes, nor did they hesitate in extreme cases to depose the civil sachem to give greater force to battle action. The military service was not conscriptive, but voluntary, although every man was subject to military duty, and to shirk it brought disgrace.

Most extraordinary of all, the matrons sat in council with a substantial veto as to peace or war. "With these barbarians", says the historian of New York, "woman was man's coworker in legislation, a thing yet unknown among civilized people". Doctor Colden, in his history of the Five Nations, sagely suggests that "here we may with more certainty see the original forms of government than in the most curious speculations of the learned". Such was their regard for the rights of man that they would not enslave captives; neither did they allow intermarriages among families of the same clan. This has been the prevailing law up to the present time.

At the advent of the Europeans the Iroquois were rapidly spreading their organized power from the lakes to the gulf, and were the dread of other nations both east and west. The Senecas framed cabins, tilled the soil, manufactured stone implements and pottery, made clothing, and showed much skill in military works of defense. When Governor Shirley, of Massachusetts, 100 years later, proposed a campaign against the French he obtained pledges of support from the confederacy, but the British government withheld the promised aid. In 1778 General Lafayette accompanied General Schuyler to a conference with the Six Nations, but while the Oneidas and Tuscaroras remained neutral, the other nations were waiting for the opportunity to avenge their losses in the battle of Oriskany. The subsequent fate of Wyoming and Cherry Valley ended all negotiations, and the campaign of General Sullivan punished the invaders.

As the rival European nations, in founding New France, New Amsterdam, New Holland, and New Spain, had so maintained their murderous rivalry in the new world that the Indians could form no idea of "one religion" governing all white men, the red men, in alliance with the British, who had resisted the French, felt it their right to compensate for their sacrifices by revenge upon the Americans, the enemies of their friends.

In looking back to the landing of the early colonists, the impression prevails that all the Indians of that date were equally and purely savage, and yet Jefferies truthfully says, in his work upon the human race, that "the Five Nations, at the landing of the Pilgrims, constituted a rising power in America. Had not New England been settled by Europeans it is most likely that the Iroquois would have exterminated the inferior tribes of red men". "To this Indian league", writes Morgan, "France must chiefly ascribe the final overthrow of her magnificent schemes of colonization in the northern part of America". Parkham says of the Iroquois: "Among all the barbarous nations of this portion of the continent, these stand most prominent". In 1839 the Hurons occupied 32 villages, with 700 dwellings, and eagerly adopted civilized methods. Schoolcraft mentions Cusick, who not only became a Moravian minister, but wrote a book in the English language upon the aboriginal tribes of America. Doctor Crane, in Crania Americana, says: "These men are unsurpassed by any people. The brain capacity of the skull, 88 inches, is only 2 inches less than the Caucasian". Such men as Joseph and John Brandt, of the Mohawks, are rare, and the American intercourse with every considerable tribe, from the earliest record up to the year 1891, has brought to the front some capable Indians, whose influence, rightly appreciated, educated, and directed, would hasten their people forward in the path of civilized progress. Such men as Cornplanter, the friend of Washington, Governor Blacksnake, and Red

Jacket are noteworthy examples. Photographs of the influential men from each of the Six Nations and from the Saint Regis tribe are not unworthy of companionship with business men among any people.

The briefest outline of the old-time conquests of the Iroquois confederacy challenges as much attention as the triumphs of Cæsar or Alexander. They seized upon firearms as rapidly as they could acquire them, when they learned their use in the hands of Champlain's French followers, and with their new weapons fearlessly extended the range of their triumphs. In 1643 they nearly destroyed the Eries, and extended their successes to northern Ohio. In 1670 they controlled the whole country between Lakes Huron, Erie, and Ontario, and the north bank of the Saint Lawrence to the mouth of the Ottawa river near Montreal. About the year 1670 they became the terror of the New England tribes who had been practically subjugated by the English, so that Colden, writing of that period, says: "I have been told by old men of New England, who remember the Indian wars, that as soon as a Mohawk was discovered in their country the Indians raised a cry from hill to hill 'a Mohawk! a Mohawk!' upon which all fled like sheep before wolves, without attempting the least resistance". In 1680 the Senecas invaded Illinois, even to the Mississippi, at the time that La Salle was preparing to descend that river to the sea. The Cherokees upon the Tennessee and the Catawbas of South Carolina yielded captives to these omnipresent invaders. Michigan and even Lake Superior were visited by them. One well-informed Indian historian uses this language: "No distant solitude, no rugged fastness, was too obscure or difficult to escape their visitation; no enterprise was too perilous, no fatigue too great, for their courage and endurance. The fame of their achievements resounded over the continent". As early as 1607 John Smith met a band of them in canoes upon the upper waters of Chesapeake bay on their way to the territories of the Powhatan confederacy. For a whole century, reaching the pinnacle of their triumphs at last, they became the controlling interior power, with a colossal sway over all other Indian tribes, and only when the protracted wars with the French demanded their constant attention and all their resources did they give up the extension of their growing empire. The Revolutionary war was a trial of their better judgment. The wise protest of the Oneidas divided the league, and the Five Nations did not unite with the British, except as volunteers. The Mohawks took refuge in Canada. The Oneidas and Cayugas after the war gradually sold their lands and departed westward. Their history is a sad one since the dissolution of the confederacy. Even the British government omitted, in its settlement with the United States, to suggest a single paragraph in recognition of their former allies. The broadest and strongest Indian empire north of the Aztec monarchy, fraught with inherent elements of great endurance and substantial strength, succumbed only before advancing civilization, leaving monuments of its wisdom and old-time greatness as suggestive appeals to the generosity, sympathy, and protection of the conquering whites.

THE SAINT REGIS, SUCCESSORS OF THE MOHAWKS: 1890.

Saint Regis river, Saint Regis parish, at the junction of the river with the Saint Lawrence river, Saint Regis island, directly opposite, and Saint Regis reservation, in New York, alike perpetuate the memory of Jean François Regis, a French ecclesiastic of good family, who consecrated his life from early youth to the welfare of the laboring classes. Opposed by his aristocratic neighbors and connections, he sought an appointment as missionary to the Iroquois Indians of Canada. He was unable to leave home, although appointed to the mission, but resumed his previous labors, and died in 1640 at the age of 43, after 26 years of faithful service. He was canonized, upon the joint request of Louis XV of France, Philip V of Spain, and the clergy of France assembled at Paris in 1735, by Clement XII in 1737 in recognition of his disinterested labors (a).

The French jesuits, as early as 1675, established a mission among the Caughnawagas, 9 miles above Montreal, and gathered many of the New York Mohawks under their care. The Oswegatchie settlement had also been established near the present site of Ogdensburg, mainly, according to Abbé Paquet, "to get the Indians away from the corrupting influences of rum and the train of vices to which they were exposed from their vicinity to Montreal".

About the year 1708 an Indian expedition into New England cost many lives, including those of two young men, whose parents permitted them to go only on the condition that if they failed to return their places should be made good by captives. This pledge was redeemed by a secret expedition to Groton, Massachusetts, and the capture of two brothers of the name of Tarbell, who were adopted in the place of the two who fell in the original expedition. They grew to manhood with strongly developed characters and, respectively, married the daughters of Chiefs Sa-kon-en-tsi-ask and At-a-wen-ta. Jealousies arose between them and the Caughnawagas, which the missionaries could not settle, and in 1760 they formed a part of a migrating band in search of a new home and independence. Father Anthony Gordon, their attending spiritual adviser, located them at the mouth of the river Ak-wis-sas-ne, "where the partridge drums" and where peculiar echoes, even at the splash of the paddle by night, still perpetuate the original, suggestive name, although the drumming partridges have almost become extinct. The worthy ambition of Regis to give his life to the welfare of this people was remembered and his name was adopted for the new settlement. Lineal descendants of the Tarbells still survive, and are elsewhere noticed. The well-preserved

_____

a Hough's History of Saint Lawrence and Franklin counties, 716 pages, Albany, 1853, enters fully into the settlement and development of this part of New York.

records of the old parish church and the recollections of the aged grandson of the original Peter Tarbell rescue many floating traditions from vague and conflicting statements.

The Saint Regis Indians have very little in common with the other nations of the old Iroquois confederacy. Only two Oneidas are found among them, and no Onondagas, Cayugas, or Senecas. The Tuscaroras were still in North Carolina when the Mohawks were being gradually drawn into closer relation with the Indians of Canada, and the growth of christianity among them so rapidly severed all associations with the practices and rites of the ancient belief of the founders of the league that even its traditions are little known among their descendants. They had nearly as intimate associations at one time with the Seven Nations of Canada as with the Five Nations of New York, and they still cherish those associations.

PART II.

RESERVATIONS AND LOCATIONS IN NEW YORK: 1721, 1771, AND 1890.

Ho-de-no-sau-nee-ga—"Territory of the people of the long house".

The old map of the province of New York, dated 1723, was copied from the original map now in possession of Mrs. Caroline Mountpleasant, who writes:

This curious map, so quaint in topography, and so generally in harmony with the geographical knowledge of the period of its date, was found among the old papers of the late John Mountpleasant, my husband, one of the most progressive and distinguished of the chiefs of the Tuscaroras. I can give no clew to its early history, except that my brother, General Ely S. Parker, valued it when he assisted Morgan in the preparation of his history of the Six Nations in 1851, 40 years ago.

This map gives the locations of the Six Nations in 1723.

THE GOVERNOR TRYON MAP OF 1771.

The accompanying map was prepared in 1771 under the direction of William Tryon, captain general and governor in chief of the province of New York, and is as nearly suggestive of the then recognized boundary of the Six Nations as any that has had official sanction. In 1851 Lewis H. Morgan, assisted by Ely S. Parker, a Seneca chief, and afterward an efficient staff officer of General Grant, and ex-Commissioner of Indian Affairs, prepared a map for a volume of 475 pages, entitled League of the Iroquois, which aimed to define the villages, trails, and boundaries of the Five Nations as they existed in 1720. Indian names were assigned to all lakes, water courses, and villages, and the various trails from village to village as far as the Ne-ah-ga (Niagara) river. Unfortunately, the plates were not stereotyped, and the book itself is a rare possession. Another map, so ancient as to almost crumble at the touch, represents the territory of Michigan as visited by the Five Nations, and by a footnote relates the visit of 80 Ne-car-ri-a-ges, besides men, women, and children, who came from "Misilmackinac" May 30, 1823, asking to be admitted as a seventh nation into the league, just as the Tuscaroras had been adopted as a sixth. It has some data as to "carrying places" which are not upon the Governor Tryon map. The latter has historic value from its description of "the country of the Six Nations, with part of the adjacent colonies", recognizing at the time the independent relations which they sustained to Great Britain. The vast tract then controlled by the Seneca Indians is clearly defined, and the changes of 120 years appear more impressive when the boundaries and condition of the present representatives of the former Six Nations are brought into close relation to the facts of to-day.

AREAS OF THE SIX NATIONS RESERVATIONS IN NEW YORK AND CORNPLANTER SENECA IN PENNSYLVANIA.

	ACRES.
Onondaga	6,100.00
Tonawanda	7,549.73
Allegany	30,469.00
Oil Spring	640.00
Cattaraugus	21,680.00
Tuscarora	6,249 00
Saint Regis	14,640.00
Cornplanter, in Pennsylvania	640.00
Total	87,967.73

The New York commission estimates the acreage of the Onondaga reservation at 7,300. The Saint Regis, with swamp land, is estimated at 15,280 acres.

RESERVATIONS OF THE SIX NATIONS IN NEW YORK: 1890.

The maps of the existing reservations, as defined in 1890, locate each family, water course, and road, developing, as if by accident, in the clustering of their homes, the differences between those of each nation who "hold to the tradition of the father", and those who welcome the civilization and christianity of the white man.

For a complete and full history of the original treaties and authorities as to the legal status of the Six Nations reservations in New York (beside the report of the New York state commission herein referred to), see the report prepared by Alice C. Fletcher in 1885 and a monograph by Franklin B. Hough, of Lowville, New York, on the Indian tribes of New York, both printed in Executive Document No. 95, Forty-eighth Congress, second session, which are full and most valuable. The various New York reports and especially that of the New York commission, made in 1889, contain much of interest as to the reservations of the Six Nations.

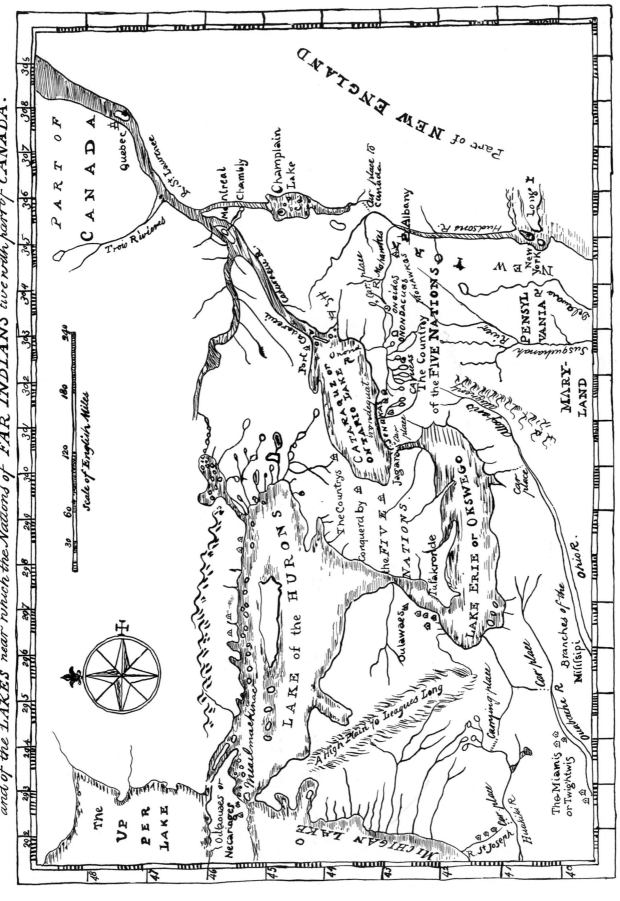

A MAP of the Country of the FIVE NATIONS, belonging to the Province of NEW YORK; and of the LAKES near which the Nations of FAR INDIANS live with part of CANADA.

N.B. The Tuscaroras are now rekoned a sixth Nation & live between the Onondagoes & Oneidas; & the Nearariages of Miedumalinae were recived to be the seventh Nation at Albany, May 30ᵗʰ 1723 at their own desire to many that Nation being present besides women & children.

Reproduction of old map of country occupied by the Five Nations, for report on the Six Nations of New York.

Eleventh Census : 1890

Eleventh Census : 1890.

MAP OF THE PROVINCE OF NEW YORK, 1771, SHOWING THE COUNTRY OF THE SIX NATIONS.

Six Nations of New York.

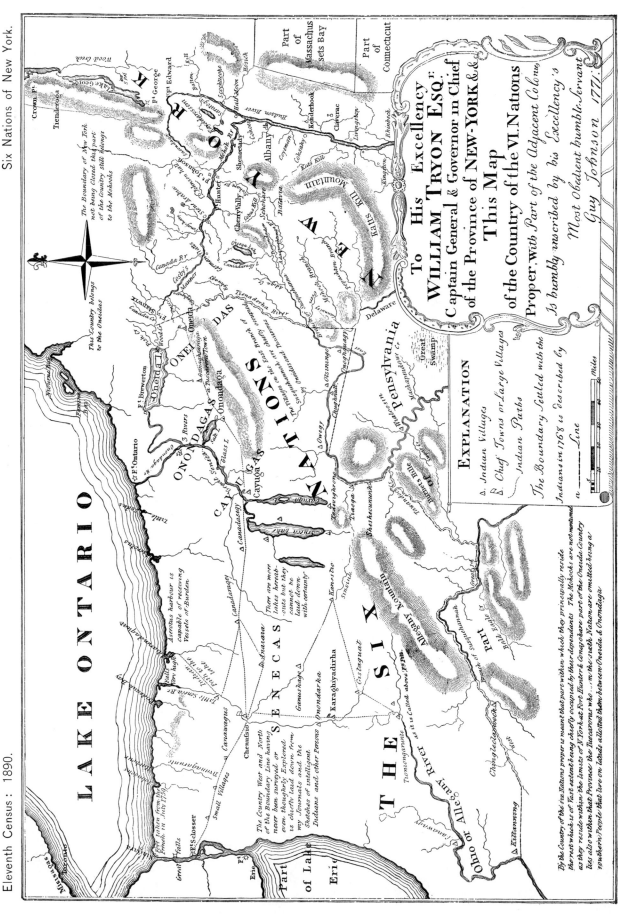

New York Engraving & Printing Co.

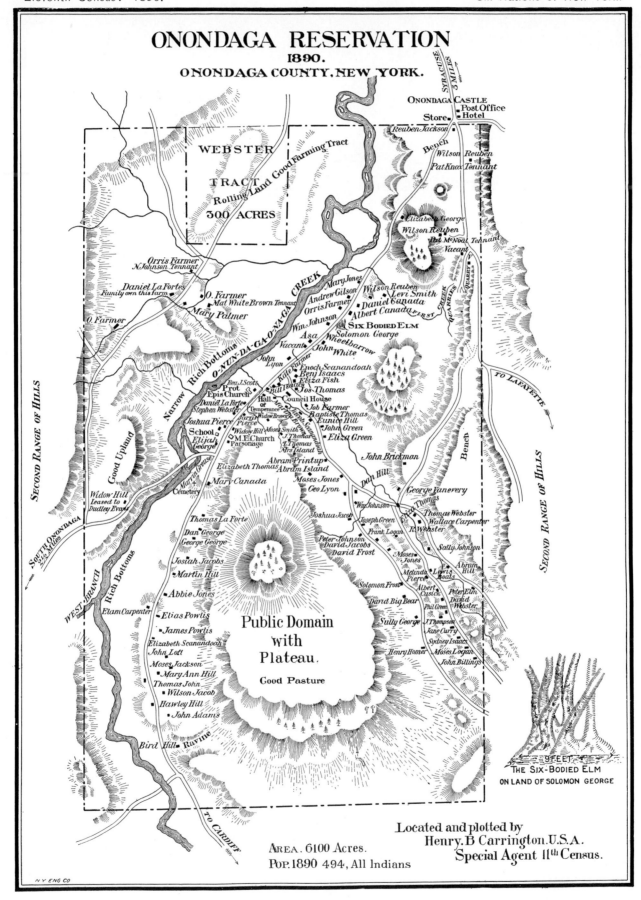

ONONDAGA RESERVATION
1890.
ONONDAGA COUNTY, NEW YORK.

SYRACUSE 3 MILES

ONONDAGA CASTLE
Post Office
Store · Hotel

Reuben Jackson

Bench

Wilson Reuben
Pat Knox Tennant

WEBSTER

TRACT

Rolling Land Good Farming Tract

300 ACRES

Elizabeth George
Wilson Reuben
Pat. McNoal Tennant
Vacant

Orris Farmer
N. Johnson Tennant

Daniel La Fortes
Family own this farm

O. Farmer
Mat White Brown Tennant

Mary Palmer

O. Farmer

Mary Jones
Andrew Gilson
Orris Farmer
Wm. Johnson
Asa
Vacant

Wilson Reuben
Levi Smith
Daniel Canada
Albert Canada
SIX BODIED ELM
Solomon George
Wheelbarrow
John White

John Lyon

Enoch Scanandoah
Ben Isaacs
Eliza Fish
Bill Isaac
Jos. Thomas
Council House

Rev. J. Scott
Prot
Epis. Church
Daniel La Forte
Stephen Webster
Joshua Pierce
School
Elijah George

Hall of Temperance
Harris Pierce
Widow Brown
Widow Hill
Moses Smith
J. Thomas
M.E. Church
Parsonage
Mrs Island

Job Farmer
Baptiste Thomas
Eunice Hill
John Green
Eliza Green

John Brickman

Abram Printup
Elizabeth Thomas
Abram Island
Mary Canada
Moses Jones
Geo Lyon

Dan Hill

George Vanevery
Thomas

Martin Grouse
Cemetery

Widow Hill
Leased to
Dudley Evans

Thomas La Forte

Dan George
George George

Josiah Jacobs
Martin Hill

Abbie Jones

Elam Carpenter

Elias Powlis

James Powlis

Elizabeth Scanandoah
John Lott
Moses Jackson
Mary Ann Hill
Thomas John
Wilson Jacob
Hawley Hill
John Adams

Bird Hill Ravine

Joshua Jacob
Peter Johnson
David Jacobs
David Frost

Solomon Frost

David Big Bear

Sully George

Henry Homer

Wm. Johnson
Joseph Green
Frank Logan
T. Webster

Thomas Webster
Wallace Carpenter

Sally Johnson
Moses Jones
Melinda Pierce
Lewis Roals
Albert Cusick
Phil Green
J. Thompson
Jane Curry
Sydney Isaacs
Moses Logan
John Billings

Abram Hill
Peter Elm
David Webster

Public Domain
with
Plateau.

Good Pasture

SECOND RANGE OF HILLS

SECOND RANGE OF HILLS

TO LAFAYETTE

Narrow
Rich Bottoms
Good Upland

O-NUN-DA-GA-O-NA-GA CREEK

FIRST CREEK
QUARRY

QUARRIES

Bench

WEST BRANCH
Rich Bottoms

SOUTH ONONDAGA 3¾ MILES

TO CARDIFF

9 FEET
THE SIX-BODIED ELM
ON LAND OF SOLOMON GEORGE

AREA. 6100 Acres.
POP. 1890 494, All Indians

Located and plotted by
Henry. B. Carrington. U.S.A.
Special Agent 11th Census.

N Y ENG CO

SOLOMON GEORGE (Wal hah-leigh), "Watchful."
Oneida Chief.

HENRY POWLISS (Was-theel-go), "Throwing up Pins."
Oneida.

JOSHUA JONES (Sa-sun-nah-gan-deeh), "Half name" half blood.
Oneida.

ABRAM HILL (Ga-haeh-da-seah), "Whirlwind."
Oneida.

New York Engraving & Printing Co.

ALEXANDER JOHN (Ska-no-eh), "Fleeting Arrow."
Head chief of the Cayugas.

RUSH S. WILSON (Ha-ja-ah-gwysh`), "He Carries the Fire."
Chief of Cayuga Nation.

EDWIN M. SPRING (Ho-dyah-yoh-gweh), "Spreading Sky."
Cayuga Chief.

HIRAM TALLCHIEF (Dah-eh-Jeh doh), "Burning Hand."
Cayuga Chief.

New York Engraving & Printing Co.

ONEIDA AND CAYUGA RESERVATIONS.

No maps of reservations for these tribes will be found, as they no longer retain their ancestral homes in New York.

Various treaties between the Oneida nation and the state of New York gradually reduced their land area until now (1890) a small remnant of that people retain but about 350 acres, which they hold as citizens and in severalty. The condition of this small remnant is treated of elsewhere. The following data explain the process of their loss of land:

1. By treaty of Fort Herkimer, June 28, 1785, the Oneidas joined the Tuscaroras in selling their lands between the Chenango and Unadilla rivers to the state of New York. Consideration, $11,500 in money and goods.

2. In September, 1788, other lands were sold to the state of New York for cash, clothing, provisions, a mill, and an annuity of $600, excepting certain reservations in Madison and Oneida counties.

3. September 15, 1795, the Oneidas sold to the state of New York another portion for $2,952 in cash and an annuity of the same amount, and another portion for 3 cents per acre, to be paid annually.

4. June 1, 1798, the Oneidas sold additional lands for $300 and an annuity of $700.

5. March 5, 1802, the Oneidas sold to the state of New York certain small parcels of land for $900 and an annuity of $300.

6. In 1805 the conflicting parties among the Oneidas, pagan and christian, settled their otherwise irreconcilable jealousies by a subdivision of their lands in Madison and Oneida counties.

7. In 1846, after 11 successive treaties with the state of New York, the main part of the nation removed to Wisconsin, leaving to the remaining fragment of the band the tract of 350 acres, before referred to.

8. In 1843 the legislature of New York authorized these lands to be held in severalty, as at present.

106 of the Oneidas now (1890) reside on the several reservations of the Six Nations, and 106 in the counties of Madison and Oneida, in the state of New York, in all 212. They have no separate reservation. This is fully shown in the population table.

The Cayugas number 183 and reside on 4 of the reservations of the Six Nations, having no separate reservation.

The Oneidas are scattered, gaining a livelihood by basket making or day's labor, and are less comfortably settled than a majority of reservation Indians. Two groups of small houses, in each of which are 7 families, constitute their representative settlements, viz, Orchard, in Oneida county, about 4 miles south from the city of Oneida, and Windfall, in Madison county. In the former, William and Malinda Johnson own 11 acres, which they rent. William Dockstader occupies 1.75 acre, which he does not till. The school has been abandoned, and the 13 children of these families do not attend any school. Some think the schoolhouse over the hill too far, and Mr. Dockstader claims that the children were not well treated by the white people, but these reasons are not sufficiently supported for serious comment. At Mud Creek, between the 2 villages, are the 2 houses of John Johnnyjohn and Mary Antoine. At Windfall, Mary Webster, widow, is allowed to live out her days in the house of her deceased husband, the mortgage which he gave having cost her the title. Alexander Burning, a chief, lives at Oneida. The total number of all ages, scattered over the original Oneida reservation and the country thereabout, who draw annuities of cloth from the United States, is 106.

These are the facts in 1890, and neither farming nor gardening in either of these villages is to the credit of civilized Indians. They are honest and well behaved, but without sufficient ambition or sympathy to insure much progress. Preaching is attended semimonthly, but all signs conform to their own frank statement, that "before long there won't be any of us left". The few who accept any work they can get and forget that they are Indians assimilate rapidly with their white neighbors, and in another generation will be lost in the mass of the people. Those who remained in New York were too few for combined, mutually-supporting industry, and the experiment of holding land in severalty only hastened their dissolution, without elevating their industry or their condition. Visitors who ride through Windfall, the larger of the 2 villages, should understand that these are no longer Indian villages, and should not confuse any signs of general improvement with ideas of Indian thrift and progress, which do not exist.

ONONDAGA RESERVATION.

An old wampum of 1608, representing the Iroquois confederacy, has for its "center house", to indicate the rank of the Onondagas, a heart. On either side are joined two sister nations, and, although fewer in numbers at present than others, the Onondagas are given the first place in illustration of the Six Nations in 1890.

The Onondaga reservation, lying in Onondaga county, forms a rectangle of a little more than 2.3 miles by 4 miles, commencing about 5 miles southward from the city of Syracuse, and contains about 6,100 acres. The turnpike road to Cardiff enters near the northeast corner of the reservation and leaves it about half a mile east of the southwest corner, cutting a diagonal line nearly 4.75 miles in its course. Onondaga Castle, with hotel, store, post office, and a few houses, is at the "entrance gate". The Lafayette stage road bears southeasterly at this point, from which the reservation road deviates to the right, and at the distance of about three-quarters of a mile sends a branch into the celebrated limestone quarries belonging to the Onondaga nation. This blue limestone is excellent

Of this large area of land, embracing 42 square miles, only 2,948 acres are cultivated by Indians, and 2,175 are used as pasture. This is the land claimed as owned by individuals, and includes the small tracts leased to white people. The narrow belts along the valley are fairly fertile, but the soil is thin and soon wears out. Very few parts are loam or truly rich soil. Frequent floods, bearing sand and gravel over the bottoms and washing out much that has been gained by partial cultivation, have dispirited tenants, so that in the summer of 1890 14 houses were found vacated by the occupants, who took possession with a view to profitable farming. These were all eastward of Salamanca. The tillable land, however, embraces 11,000 acres, of which 7,000 may be properly classed as arable. The hills were stripped of their best timber during the period when rafting logs on the Allegany river and down the Ohio was profitable, bringing quick cash returns without the protracted, patient labor which would have attended clearing the land fully and engaging in agriculture for a livelihood. Hundreds of acres at the foot of the hills, and perfectly level, bear the stump marks of this bygone occupation, and thickly-set brush with small second growth timber show that the ability or disposition to utilize the land for farming purposes is wanting. In fact the soil does not invite farmers to invest largely, even if the Indians had both choice and freedom to sell, for it needs all the fertilization which an energetic farmer can save and use. The cultivated lands have been fairly fenced, but the fences are not kept up with care. Under the head "Farming" the subject will be again noticed. The supply of water from springs and innumerable mountain streams is adequate for all purposes.

OIL SPRING RESERVATION.

Oil Spring reservation, in Cattaraugus county, New York, as indicated on the Allegany reservation map, contains 640 acres in 2 towns and counties. It was by oversight included in the treaty made at Big Tree, in the sale by the Seneca nation of 3,500,000 acres to Robert Morris, and passed with his title to the Holland Land Company. A suit for the recovery of this land was brought in 1856 by D. Sherman, for 13 years the efficient United States Indian agent, and resulted in favor of the Seneca nation. On the trial, Governor Blacksnake, as he was named by Washington when he visited the capital in company with Cornplanter, testified, at the advanced age of 107 years, to being present at the treaty of Big Tree in 1797, and that when the exception was missed upon the public reading of the treaty, Thomas Morris, attorney for Robert Morris, gave to Pleasant Lake, a prominent sachem of the Seneca nation, a separate paper, declaring that the Oil Spring tract was not included in the sale. Governor Blacksnake also produced a copy of the first map of the Holland land purchase, on which this reservation was distinctly marked as belonging to the Seneca Indians. An exhaustive report of Judge Sherman to the Commissioner of Indian Affairs, dated Forestville, New York, October 9, 1877, contains the most succinct, accurate, and just statement of the titles and rights of the Six Nations that has been published. The land is under lease, and, in the language of Judge Sherman, "the Seneca nation own this reservation, unincumbered by any pre-emption right, and it is all the land they do so own".

The place and date of birth of Governor Blacksnake (The Nephew) are unknown. He died at Cold Spring, in South Valley, on the Allegany reservation, December 26, 1859. His Indian name was "Tha-o-wa-nyuths". He was associated with John Halftown and John O'Bail (Cornplanter) in negotiations with Washington, and was greatly esteemed by him. The best estimate of his age is 117, although many have placed it as high as 125 and even 130. The famous trio were Senecas.

The following note, by Charles Aldrich, of Des Moines, Iowa, in the Magazine of American History for July, 1891, on Governor Blacksnake (The Nephew) is of great interest :

When I first began to hear of this notable Indian, and very soon afterward to see him occasionally, I was but 8 years old. This was in 1836. Governor Blacksnake was at that time head chief of the Senecas, living upon their reservation along the Allegany river, just north of the Pennsylvania line, in Cattaraugus county, New York. He may also have had some sort of headship relating to wider intertribal relations. His residence was 1 mile above the little village of Cold Spring, 10 miles or more from the southern boundary of the reservation. That he had been widely distinguished in "the olden time, long ago", was evidenced by the fact that he had received a beautiful silver medal from the hand of Washington. As I remember it, this medal contained from $3 to $4 worth of fine silver and bore upon one side the simple legend "Second Presidency of George Washington". On the obverse was a simple domestic scene, representing a room, as it might be, in a settler's cabin. In the center of the farther side was an open chimney with a blazing fire, a babe lay in a cradle, a spinning-wheel stood in one corner, and two or three women seemed busied with indoor work. The old chieftain was very proud of this medal, generally wearing it suspended from his neck by a cord, for which a hole had been pierced. I often saw him in my boyhood, when he was pleased to hand me his Washington medal for inspection. He understood a little of our language but could not speak it.

The year of Governor Blacksnake's birth was conjectured to be 1736 or close to that time. He died December 26, 1859. If the first date is approximately correct he was not far from 120 years of age. In personal appearance he bore a striking resemblance to one of the portraits of Andrew Jackson in his old age. He was very tall, straight as an arrow, and his abundant hair was both white and long. He sometimes wore a blue overcoat, which came nearly to the ground, and I feel quite sure that it was thickly studded with smooth, old-fashioned brass buttons. His figure was at once striking and venerable. He was always kind and agreeable, genial and pleasant to all who approached him. The people of his tribe, as well as the white people, treated him with marked deference and respect.

Governor Blacksnake, in addition to being a man of authority in his tribe, was an orator to whom his people always listened with profound attention. I shall never forget hearing him, though I did not understand a word of his language. My father's farm adjoined the Indian reservation, half a mile from the river, and one of my Indian playmates "Little Johnny Watts", had died from consumption, and I had frequently gone to the old cabin to see him during his long, wasting illness. One day as I peered into the room where he lay, his poor old mother was indulging in the wildest grief, talking to her poor boy, who was insensible and only gasping at long intervals. Presently the

New York Engraving & Printing Co. GOVERNOR BLACKSNAKE, (Tha-o-na-wyuthe) or ("Tha-o-wa-nyuths,") "The Nephew" (Seneca).

Died at Cold Spring, in South Valley, Allegany Reservation, Dec. 26, 1859, aged 117 or 120 years.

MARSH PIERCE, (Hoh-hoo-e-yoh), "His Good Run,"

Cornplanter Seneca, Warren County, Pa.

gasping ceased, the spirit had fled.   This was the first person I ever saw die.   Meanwhile, not far from the door, stolid and unmoved, sat the father, "Old Johnny Watts", making a bow and arrows of hickory wood for the use of the lad in the "happy hunting grounds".   A day or two later our family attended the funeral in the forest, near the bank of the river, and some 50 Indians (Senecas) and a few white people were present.   The coffin was lowered into the grave, when the father stepped briskly forward and dropped the bow and arrows by its side.

At this moment, with grave and solemn mien, Governor Blacksnake stepped to the top of the mound of earth, and began a half-hour's address to his Indian friends.   He spoke slowly and with great deliberation.   Some one who understood him informed us that he spoke most kindly of the little boy who was gone, depicting the joys of the new existence upon which he was to enter.   He urged his hearers to so order their lives as to be prepared for the better existence in the life to come.   I do not remember, I was but a child myself, that I was ever more impressed by the appearance of an orator, except by Abraham Lincoln at his first inauguration.   Blacksnake's figure was tall and commanding, his delivery slow and distinct, his appearance graceful, earnest, full of dignity, his sympathy for the bereaved family evident and touching. They paid his words the tribute of fast-flowing tears, except the father, who looked on unmoved.

Some time later, about the year 1850, an Indian boy, a relative, I believe, of the old governor, was killed by lightning near his house. A sudden shower of rain was accompanied by lightning and thunder.   The boy fled to a large apple tree to seek protection from the pelting rain, when the deadly bolt came down, killing him instantly.   The Indians at once cut down the tree and rolled it into the pit, where it lay until it was consumed by dry rot.   I was told that some superstition was connected with the cutting of this tree, but it may have been for the simple reason that it was such a sad reminder of the fate of the little boy.

Some notes concerning Governor Blacksnake have appeared in local historical works, but they seem to me to have been more or less fanciful.   It is no doubt true that he fought against our people in the border wars of the Revolution.   He is said to have been at the massacre of Wyoming, and to have been among the Indians of western New York, who were so terribly punished by General Sullivan in 1779.   He must also have made a journey to Washington early in this century.   He retained until his very old age a pass given to him by General Henry Dearborn, the Secretary of War.   It was in the following words :

> To all persons to whom these presents shall come, greeting : It is required of all persons, civil and military, and all others, the good people of these United States, to permit "The Nephew", an Indian chief, with his associates, to proceed from the city of Washington to their places of residence freely and without molestation, and to aid and assist them on their way as friends of the said United States.
>
> Given at the War Office, at the city of Washington, this fourteenth day of February, 1803.
>
> [Seal of the War Department.]   H. DEARBORN.

Governor Blacksnake was the last survivor of the Indian chiefs who had been prominent before their power was broken in the state of New York.   He was a man of much native ability, and he retained his influence with the Senecas to the end of his life.

CORNPLANTER SENECA RESERVATION.

This reservation, in Warren county, Pennsylvania, nominally a tract of 640 acres, owned by Cornplanter's heirs, lies on both sides of the Allegheny river, and is about 2 miles long and half a mile wide, including Liberty and Donation islands, which are formed by the forking of the river.   The land surface, including the river bed and some worthless shoals, contains about 760 acres.   It was a donation to the celebrated chief Gy-ant-wa-hia, "The Cornplanter", March 16, 1796, by the state of Pennsylvania, in consideration, states Judge Sherman, "for his many valuable services to the white people, and especially that most important one, in preventing the Six Nations of New York from joining the confederacy of western Indians in 1790–1791".   The war ended in the victory of General Wayne in 1794.   In 1871, under act of May 16, partition or allotment of these lands was made to the descendants of Cornplanter and recorded in Warren county by the court having jurisdiction, special commissioners having been appointed by the state June 10, 1871, to effect the distribution.   The power to sell the lands thus allotted is limited to the heirs of Cornplanter and other Seneca Indians.   These Indians also have an interest in the Allegany and Cattaraugus lands of the Seneca nation, and draw annuities with them.

A suitable monument rests over Cornplanter's grave in the somewhat neglected burial ground between the Presbyterian church and the house of Marsh Pierce, bearing the following inscriptions upon its four faces :

GY-ANT-WA-HIA,
THE
CORNPLANTER.

JOHN O'BAIL,
ALIAS CORNPLANTER,
DIED
At Cornplanter town, February 18, A. D. 1836,
aged about 100 years.

CHIEF OF THE SENECA TRIBE
AND
A PRINCIPAL CHIEF
OF THE
SIX NATIONS
From the period of the Revolutionary war
to the time of his death.
DISTINGUISHED
For talents, courage, integrity, sobriety,
and love for his tribe and race,
TO WHOSE WELFARE
He devoted his energies and his money
DURING A LONG AND EVENTFUL LIFE.

ERECTED
BY AUTHORITY OF THE LEGISLATURE
OF PENNSYLVANIA,
By act passed May, A. D. 1866.

READING THE WAMPUMS, 1890.

JOSEPH SNOW (Chan-ly-e-ya), "Drifted Snow," Onondaga Chief.

GEORGE H. M. JOHNSON, (Je-yung-heh-kwang), "Double Life," Mohawk Chief and Official Interpreter.

JOHN SMOKE JOHNSON (Sac-a-yung-Kwar-to), "Disappearing Knot," Mohawk Chief.

JOHN BUCK (Skan-a-wa-ti), "Beyond the Swamp," Keeper of the Wampum. Onondaga Chief.

ISASC HILL (Te-yem-tho-hi-sa), "Two Doors Closed," Onondaga Chief.

JOHN SENECA JOHNSON (Ka-nung-he-ri-taws), "Entangled Hair Given," Seneca Chief.

Eleventh Census : 1890.

Six Nations of New York.

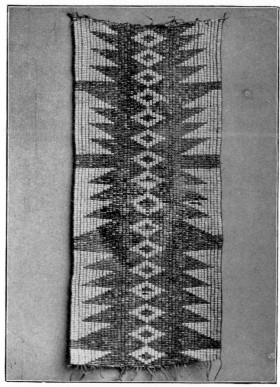

Presidentia of the Iroquois, about 1540.

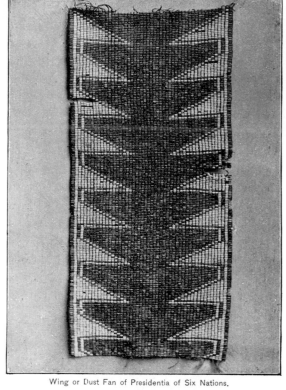

Wing or Dust Fan of Presidentia of Six Nations.

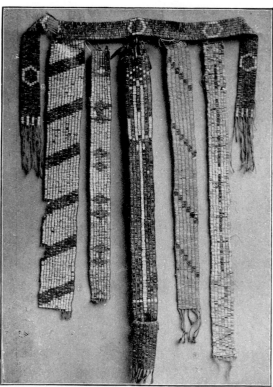

Six Wampums of the Six Nations.

Group of four Wampums and Turtle Rattles, used in Feather Dance.

New York Engraving & Printing Co.

PART III.

ANCIENT AND MODERN GOVERNMENT, PROVISIONS AND INCIDENTS, INCLUDING THE SAINT REGIS INDIANS.

The Iroquois league had its democratic and republican elements, but the separate national governments were essentially oligarchic. The only semblance of written law was the wampum, which was made for special occasions or events and so associated with their leading features as to be afterward suggestive of their lessons and history. It was the duty of the "keeper of the wampums" to store all necessary facts in his memory and associate them with the successive lines and arrangements of the beads so that they could readily be called to mind. At general councils the wampums were produced, solemnly expounded, and made reminders of history and duty.

"Reading the wampums" became therefore a means by which to perpetuate treaties, and the exchange of wampums was an impressive occasion. Both the Canadian and New York divisions of the Six Nations retain as national heirlooms these evidences of the chief facts in their national life.

The Saint Regis Indians, living on both sides of the Saint Lawrence river, have a small collection of wampums, fewer than the Onondagas at Onondaga Castle, near Syracuse. The Onondagas retain the custody of the wampums of the Five Nations, and the "keeper of the wampums", Thomas Webster, of the Snipe tribe, a consistent, thorough pagan, is their interpreter. The "reading of the wampums" to the representatives of the tribes gathered at Saint Regis makes a suggestive picture.

READING THE WAMPUMS.

The following is the group, named from left to right: Joseph Snow (Chan-ly-e-ya, Drifted Snow), Onondaga chief; George H. M. Johnson (Je-yung-heh-kwung, Double Life), Mohawk chief, official interpreter; John Buck (Skan-a-wa-ti, Beyond the Swamp), Onondaga chief, keeper of the wampum; John Smoke Johnson (Sack-a-yung-kwar-to, Disappearing Knot), Mohawk chief, speaker of the council, father of No. 2; Isaac Hill (Te-yem-tho-hi-sa, Two Doors Closed), Onondaga chief, and John Seneca Johnson (Ka-nung-he-ri-taws, Entangled Hair Given), Seneca chief. According to the Narrative of Indian Wars in New England the original wampum of the Iroquois, in which the laws of the league were recorded, "was made of spiral water shells, strung on deerskin strings or sinew, and braided into belts or simply united into strings". Mr. Hubbard describes the wampum as "of two sorts, white and purple". The white is worked out of the inside of the great conch shell into the form of a bead, and perforated, to string on leather. The purple is worked out of the inside of the mussel shell. A single wampum, representing the Onondagas by a heart, in the center of the league, and older than the settlement by the white people, or, as claimed, dating back to Champlain's invasion in 1608, contains over 6,000 white and purple beads made of shell or bone. Another of later date, 6 feet in length and 15 strings wide, and containing 10,000 beads represents the first treaty between the league and the United States. In the center is a building representing the new capitol. On each side is a figure representing Washington and the president of the league, while, hand in hand, the 13 colonies or states, on one side 7 and on the other side 6, in all 15 figures, complete the memorial record. The mat on which the president of the league (to-do-da-ho) is supposed to have sat when the league was instituted, about the middle of the sixteenth century, and the suspended mat to "keep off the dust" are still in good preservation. One wampum represents the conclusion of peace with 7 Canadian tribes who had been visited by the jesuits, having a cross for each tribe, and with a zigzag line below, to indicate that their ways had been crooked but would ever after be as sacred as the cross. Still another memorial of days of craft and treachery while the league was too feeble to take the field against the Algonquin tribes represents a guarded gate, with a long, white path leading to the inner gate, where the Five Nations are grouped, with the Onondagas in the center and a safe council house behind all. There are 11 of these historic wampums, each fraught with traditional story of persons and events.

Daniel La Forte, who has been chairman or president of the league, and also of the Onondagas, and elsewhere referred to, still insists that the wampums, as expounded by Thomas Webster, are "government enough for the nation, and lay down all the rules of duty that are needed".

The fact that the people can have no key to their own "laws", and that the dictum of the wampum reader is binding, just as his memory or interpretation of the emblem shall dictate, seems to weigh little with the pagan party. Notwithstanding the claims made that the wampums can be read as a governing code of law, it is evident that they are simply monumental reminders of preserved traditions, without any literal details whatever. As curious relics they are valuable.

Photographs of all the wampums were obtained to accompany the report of the Six Nations Indians, with the explanation of each as read by the "wampum keeper". The mat of the to-do-da-ho and the wing (mat) used by the headman to shield him from the dust while presiding at the council are well preserved. The first group, from left to right, represents a convention of the Six Nations at the adoption of the Tuscaroras into the league; the second, the Five Nations, upon 7 strands, illustrates a treaty with 7 Canadian tribes before the year 1600; the third signifies the guarded approach of strangers to the councils of the Five Nations; the fourth represents a treaty when but 4 of the Six Nations were represented, and the fifth embodies the pledge of 7 Canadian "christianized" nations to abandon their crooked ways and keep an honest peace. Above this group is another, claiming to bear date about 1608, when Champlain joined the Algonquins against the Iroquois. The second group includes, also in the center, the official memorial of the organization of the Iroquois confederacy, relating back to about the middle of the sixteenth century, and immediately over that of 1608, suspended between the "turtle rattles", which were used at the feather dance at Cattaraugus January 21, 1891, is a ragged wampum of unknown antiquity. Above, and containing the general group, is the wampum memorial of the first treaty made by Washington on behalf of the 13 original states and the president of the Six Nations at the national capital.

GOVERNMENT AND EXISTING CONDITION OF THE RESERVATIONS.

To give a clear view of the government and present condition of the reservations, they will be noticed in the order already adopted.

THE ONONDAGA NATION is governed by 27 chiefs, all but 2 being of the pagan party; 2, however, are sons of christian ministers, and others professed for a time to be christians, but quietly rejoined old associations. Albert Cusick, lay reader in the church of the Good Shepherd, held the office of to-do-da-ho (president) at one time, but was deposed on account of his religion. Those who have thus resumed their former political and social relations are among the most persistent in opposing a change. Daniel La Forte, a genial man in his own house, and once active in church work, is one of this number. It is nevertheless true that many of the most influential, whose property is gaining in value, and whose business gradually increases their dependence upon the white people for a market and like benefits, realize that their own interests would be more secure under some recognized code of law for the government of the nation.

The ruling chiefs, chosen by the females of the families represented, as in very ancient times, are practically in office for life. In case of a vacancy the successor chosen may be under age. In the rules and regulations formulated in 1882 for something like representative government it was provided that minor chiefs should not vote in any matters affecting the finances of the nation. Provision was made for a president or chairman, clerk, treasurer, marshal, 3 peacemakers, or judges, 1 school trustee, 1 pathmaster, and 2 poormasters. A wise provision as to wills, dowers, and the settlement of estates in conformity with the laws of New York, another abolishing the customs and usages of the Onondaga Indians relating to marriage and providing that where parties had cohabited as husband and wife for 5 years the relations should be held to be settled, and another legalizing and authorizing the peacemakers and ministers of the gospel to solemnize marriage found place in the constitution reported on the 3d of May, 1882. A just provision respecting the disposition of lands in severalty was declared to be dependent upon a three-fourths vote of the males and a three-fourths vote of the mothers of the nation. The record states that on the 6th day of May said rules and regulations were adopted at a meeting called for the purpose. A full list of officers was elected, as follows: Daniel La Forte, chairman; Jaris Pierce, clerk; Orris Farmer, treasurer; Cornelius Johnson, marshal; Jimerson L. Johnson, Wilson Johnson, and John White, peacemakers; Simon Scanandoah, pathmaster; Joseph Isaacs, school trustee, and Baptist Thomas and Wilson Reuben, poormasters.

On the 13th of May a resolution was adopted "requesting the president to announce to the people to observe Sunday, to put a stop to Sabbath breaking, such as playing ball and other nuisances, and give it to be understood that the Onondaga Indians as a nation are to become Sunday observers and do all they can to suppress Sabbath breaking". On the 18th of May an appealed land case was decided. On the 30th money was appropriated to send a messenger to the Tonawanda and Cattaraugus families to invite them to come and worship the Great Spirit at Onondaga. On the 13th of June a method for compelling men to work the roads was discussed. On the 28th of September an appropriation was made of $50 to defray the expenses of certain Indians who were desirous of attending pagan ceremonies to be held at Tonawanda for the worship of the Great Spirit. On October 28 the appointment of delegates to meet commissioners appointed by the state of New York to examine into the condition of the Onondaga Indians, and also an appropriation of money for a school site were discussed. On the 16th of November it appeared that charges and complaints had been made by the christian portion of the tribe against the chiefs, and a committee was appointed to canvass every house to see if the people were still in sympathy with the chiefs and favorable to the continuance of tribal relations and the enforcement of the treaty of 1788, made at Fort Stanwix, against the leasing of the lands. On the 1st of December B. E. Cusler addressed the chiefs, claiming that "the deplorable condition of the Oneidas and Cayugas was the condition which awaited the Onondagas if they met the state upon the proposition to divide their lands in severalty". A committee, however, was appointed to wait upon the commissioners and state under oath that they had never seen any immoralities or indecencies at their

THOMAS La FORTE (Sho-heh-do-nah), "Large Feather."
METHODIST MINISTER, Onondaga.

ALBERT CUSICK (Sa-go-neh-guah-deh), "Provoker."
Onondaga.

ORRIS FARMER (Ho-de-gweh), "Absconder."
Onondaga.

New York Engraving & Printing Co.

public places. On the 12th of December a resolution was adopted that " we will not tolerate a change of our laws, nor sign any papers that will tend to our destruction as chiefs or break up our tribal relations ". On the 18th of January, 1883, a delegate was appointed to visit Washington and press the nation's claim to Kansas lands, but an appropriation was voted down. On the 3d of February attention was called to the fact that " chiefs would not attend the meetings ", and a quorum was rarely present. A motion to allow chiefs who would not attend business meetings to resign was carried. A motion to do away with the rules and regulations adopted May 3, 1882, was lost by a vote of 5 in the negative and 3 in the affirmative, 7 being a quorum. On the 13th of February, 1883, an amendment as to quorums (a bare quorum, 7, being present) was proposed, and the rule was so changed that any number present, after due notice of time and place for a proposed meeting, should constitute a quorum, a majority being authorized to appropriate moneys and transact national business. On the 8th of March, after the usual " word of thanks to the Great Spirit " as " opening ceremonies ", the matter of nullifying existing leases was considered. April 3, 4 being present, an appropriation was made to publish a refutation of charges made at Albany against the nation and to defeat the McCarty bill. On April 28 a suggestion was made to give to the christian party a seat among the council chiefs, to prevent the destruction of the tribe as a nation. On the 1st of May occurred the annual election of officers under the constitution of May 3, 1882, and the presentation of the treasurer's report of receipts of rents of farms and quarries ($515) and disbursements ($512). No mention of the chiefs present appears on the record. The record of a meeting held August 3, 1883, and the last meeting until April, 1887, closed with the decision that " through the proper ceremonies of a dead feast " the question of title to land then at issue had been settled.

A MOVEMENT FORWARD.

On the 26th day of April, 1887, a public meeting of the Onondaga people was held at the council house, at which the old rules and regulations were substantially revived, with the following solemn preamble :

DECLARATION of the Onondaga nation of Indians, changing their form of government and adopting a constitutional charter.

We, the people of the Onondaga nation of Indians, by virtue of the right inherent in every people, trusting in the justice and necessity of our undertaking, and humbly invoking the blessing of the God of nations upon our efforts to improve our civil condition and to secure to our nation the administration of equitable and wholesome laws, do hereby abolish, abrogate, and annul our form of government by chiefs, because it has failed to answer the purpose for which all government should be created. It affords no security in the enjoyment of property. It makes no provision for the poor, but leaves the destitute to perish. It leaves the people dependent on foreign aid for means of education. It has no judiciary nor executive department. It is an irresponsible, self-constituted aristocracy. Its powers are absolute and unlimited in assigning away people's rights, but indefinite and not exercised in making municipal regulations for their benefit or protection. We can not enumerate the evils of a system so defective, nor calculate its overwhelming weight on the progress of improvement; but to remedy these defects we claim and establish the following constitution or charter, and implore the governments of the United States and the state of New York to aid in providing us with laws under which progress shall be possible.

Provision was made for a governing body of 12 councilors, two-thirds of which body should constitute a quorum, requiring, however, two-thirds of the entire number to appropriate public money.

On the first Tuesday of May, 1887, the following officers and councilors were elected: For president, Daniel La Forte (a chief), and for clerk, Orris Farmer. The christian element controlled the meeting. The councilors consisted of Joshua Pierce, Baptist Thomas, John Johnson, John White, Jaris Pierce, Wilson Jacobs, Wilson Reuben, Chris. John Smith, Charles Green, Moses Smith, William Johnson, and Thomas Webster. Josiah Jacobs, Jaris Pierce, and Peter George were elected peacemakers.

At a succeeding meeting, on May 10, President La Forte called upon Joshua Pierce to " open the meeting with prayer ".

On the 20th of May a meeting was called to fill vacancies occasioned by the resignations of Daniel La Forte, Orris Farmer, Thomas Webster, John Johnson, and Baptist Thomas. The final meeting of record was held on the 21st of July, 1887, the organization falling to pieces for want of support. A meeting of 10 chiefs was held at the house of Daniel La Forte February 14, 1888, " for the settlement of the Hawley Hill estate ". No other meetings are recorded until one more very decided effort was made to introduce a responsible civilized form of government.

THE STRUGGLE RENEWED.

On the 15th of October, 1889, at a meeting of chiefs, which was held at the council house, when 11 chiefs, viz, George Lyon, Charles Lyon, Baptist Thomas, Thomas Webster, John Hill, William Hill, Andrew Gibson, Peter George, Asa Wheelbarrow, John Thomas, and George Vanevery, were present, the question was discussed of " hiring a chairman, clerk, and treasurer to take charge of meetings and national business ". " As no meetings had been held, nobody took any interest in the affairs of the nation, and something must be done ". Objection was made to such " a traffic of the offices ". With Peter George as chairman and Jaris Pierce as secretary, it was voted 5 to 4 to readopt the constitution of 1882.

"On account of the great importance of the question, so few being present ", a committee of 3, viz, George Vanevery, Jaris Pierce, and John Thomas, was appointed to draft and report a new constitution, and it was also ordered that "notice be given to all of the people of the tribe to be present at the time of the report and election of officers, assigned for the 21st day of October, 1889".

The proceedings of that meeting were as follows:

Chiefs present: Thomas Webster, George Vanevery, Andrew Gibson, Charles Lyon, William Lyon, Hewlett Jacobs, George Lyon, Jacob Bigbear, Peter George, John Thomas, Wilson Reuben, Baptist Thomas, Daniel La Forte, John R. Farmer, and Jacob Scanandoah.

Charles Lyon made the welcome remarks appropriate to the opening services, after which Peter George was chosen chairman of the meeting and Jaris Pierce secretary.

A motion by Baptist Thomas that "we now listen to the committee on constitution" was carried.

Report was then made by Jaris Pierce, by reading the bill as drafted by two of the committee, John Thomas having declined to act.

The constitution reads as follows:

AN ACT for the protection and improvement of the Onondaga tribe of Indians residing on the Onondaga Indian reservation, in the state of New York. Passed October 21, 1889.

SECTION 1. It shall be lawful for the chiefs of the Onondaga tribe of Indians to select annually a president, clerk, and treasurer from among their number, or from the headmen or warriors of the tribe, as president, clerk, and treasurer, whose term of office shall be for one year. The first election under this charter shall be held on the 21st day of October, one thousand eight hundred and eighty-nine, and every year thereafter, to be held annually at their council house for that purpose, at one o'clock in the afternoon of that day. A plurality of all the votes cast at such election shall be sufficient to elect a candidate.

SECTION 2. There shall be a book provided, to be called "The register of election", and a certificate of the election of any officer under this act shall be entered in such register and be signed by the presiding officer and clerk of such meeting, and shall be evidence of such election.

SECTION 3. The chiefs of said Onondaga tribe of Indians, their names, shall be enrolled in the book of records kept by the clerk. Fourteen of their number shall constitute a quorum, and shall be competent for the transaction of national business. Two-thirds of their number voting for any resolution shall be deemed carried, but to all bills for the appropriation of any moneys the assent of twelve of the chiefs in council shall be necessary.

SECTION 4. It shall be the duty of the president to call a meeting of the chiefs from time to time and to preside at all of the meetings of chiefs, etc.

SECTION 5. It shall be the duty of the clerk to keep the records and minutes of the proceedings of the council, and issue warrants on the treasurer for moneys appropriated by the chiefs in council, and he shall be their secretary.

SECTION 6. The treasurer-elect shall, within five days after his election, issue bond or security to the nation to the amount of $1,000, to the satisfaction of the president and clerk of the nation, for the faithful performance of the duties of his office as a treasurer of the nation. The treasurer-elect, after giving security aforesaid, may receive all moneys belonging to the nation. He shall not pay out any of said moneys except upon the warrant of the president and clerk of the nation. At the expiration of his office he shall deliver up his books, papers, and vouchers to his successor, or to the chiefs in council assembled. His books shall always be opened for the inspection of the nation.

Baptist Thomas moved that the constitution be adopted. Voted and carried.

The election for officers was then proceeded with.

The election of the president and clerk was by acclamation, viz, Daniel La Forte, president; Jaris Pierce, clerk.

After which Frank Logan was elected treasurer by ballot.

Meeting then adjourned.

JARIS PIERCE, Secretary.

It would be almost impossible for any community of white persons, whether of a high or low social grade, whether educated or ignorant, to live in peace under the loose restraints which the Six Nations call their governmental system, and yet there are very few disorders, few crimes, and petty offenses against person or property are very infrequent. Pride in the old systems of the confederacy and in the traditions and memories of early times have much to do with the involuntary respect paid to the chiefs, sachems, or councilors, who are officially recognized as their government by the respective nations; but natural indolence or indifference to the future, provided the immediate present be tolerable, has its effect, and suspicion that the white people urge citizenship upon them for the purpose of a more ready control of their lands prevents decided action toward citizenship.

At all the reservations in New York, except the Tuscarora, the executive control is in the hands of the pagan party, and a majority of the population thus ruled is also pagan. This element is more largely political than religious, although the old men and women are, by long habit and abject ignorance, firmly set against a change. Just at present any hearty accord with the rapidly maturing wishes of the progressive party would be regarded as treason to the nation, but even this objection to any change is largely controlled by the settled conviction that the offices could not in that event be controlled, as at present. The fact is that the governing officials will not account to the people for the management of public affairs, and there is no concentrated effort thus far to compel such accounting.

At a meeting held December 2, 1889, Chiefs Charles Lyon, George Vanevery, William Lyon, George Lyon, Baptist Thomas, James Thomas, Abbott Jones, William Hill, John Hill, Wilson Reuben, Peter George, John R. Farmer, Asa Wheelbarrow, Hewlett Jacobs, Jacob Bigbear, Enoch Scanandoah, and Jacob Scanandoah were present. The president and treasurer elected on the adoption of the constitution having declined to act, Baptist Thomas was elected president and Wilson Reuben treasurer. The constitution was also signed by all of the above named except William and George Lyon. It was also signed by William Isaacs, John White, Thomas R. Farmer, William Johnson, Daniel Hill, Benjamin Isaacs, and Frank Johnson, "headmen and warriors". The quorum basis was changed so that a majority present at a called meeting could transact business, but the assent of 12 chiefs was required to appropriate moneys. "A committee was appointed to examine into existing leases and report at a future meeting".

On the 9th of December real business was transacted, and a clear business report was made of individual leases, rentals of land as well as of quarries, propositions for cutting timber, etc. At an adjourned meeting, held December 16, only 10 were present at the opening exercises. Mr. T. D. Green, state agent, who was present, understanding that there was a difference of opinion as to the new rules and regulations, thought it best to take a vote. Meanwhile other chiefs were called in, so that all but George Crow, James Thomas, and Hewlett Jacobs were present. The

JOHN GRIFFIN (Wer-dyah-seha), "Cheap."

WILLIAM COOPER (Her-nohn-gwe-sers), "Seek a Wife."

DAVID MOSES (Jo-Weese), "Chipping Bird."

CHAUNCEY H. ABRAM (Nis-hea-nyah-nant), "Falling Day."

New York Engraving & Printing Co.

vote in favor of sustaining the new constitution was 10, against 12, William Lyon neutral. The analysis of the vote does credit to Indian imitation of the white man's methods. Jacob Scanandoah, who has a small hall opposite the green for public use, and Asa Wheelbarrow and George Vanevery changed their votes, and Jacobs and Thomas, friends of the constitution, were absent. The vote on the 21st of October had 16 in favor of the adoption, as already noticed. At a called meeting for December 17, 6 chiefs being present, a protest was entered against the action of the previous day, and the clerk, Jaris Pierce, was appointed a committee to draft a bill and prepare a petition to go before the legislature for relief.

The nation is near the point where well-considered advice and support would be of saving value.

The names of the present chiefs are as follows, those marked with a * being unable to read or write:

*Thomas Webster (Snipe), age 64 ; *John Green (Wolf), 74 ; *Asa Wheelbarrow (Eel), 64 ; Charles Green, 30 ; *William Hill, 52 ; *John Hill, 56 ; *Peter George (Eel), 38 ; John R. Farmer, 28 ; *James Thomas, 42 ; George Vanevery (Snipe), 36 ; *Frank Logan (Wolf), 35 ; William Lyon (Turtle), 50 ; *Billings Webster, 31 ; Daniel La Forte (Wolf), 58 ; *George Crow (Wolf), 34 ; *Baptist Thomas (Turtle), 64 ; *Abbott Jones, 76 ; *Charles Lyon, 57 ; *Andrew Gibson (Beaver), 29 ; *Wilson Reuben (Beaver), 50 ; Jacob Scanandoah (Beaver), 70 ; *George Lyon (Eel), 42 ; *Levi Webster, 35 ; Hewlett Jacobs (Eel), 48 ; Jacob Bigbear (Turtle), 56 ; John Thomas (Turtle), 30 ; Enoch Scanandoah, 24.

Abbott Jones and Enoch Scanandoah are not pagans, the former attending the Wesleyan church.

THE TONAWANDA SENECAS are governed by 34 chiefs, elected by the women of families entitled to fill a vacancy, the chiefs already in office having the power to remand the selection back for reconsideration if there be well-founded objection to the first nominee. This does not impair the right of the families of a clan or tribe to recognition. The people vote for executive officers, and at the annual election for president, clerk, and peacemakers in 1890 such was the doubt as to the fairness of the vote that the state courts were called upon to declare and decide the question upon trial of the issue raised by the christian party.

David Billy (Wolf), an illiterate pagan, was elected president, and a majority of the chiefs, of which the president must be one, is also pagan. The most influential of the party is Chauncey A. Abram (Snipe), while the progressive or christian party is well represented by Edward M. Poodry (Turtle), David Moses (Hawk), and Jacob Doctor (Hawk). Here, as on all the reservations, the changing political interests or ambitions involve changes from one party to another without regard to religious views. No ward politician, seeking small offices, a little patronage, and the control of public funds, can more shrewdly manipulate the voters or pledge small favors for votes than the ambitious Indian chief. In proportion as the granting of leases brings in good rentals, so does the struggle to control the funds become earnest. This is more conspicuous where, as on the Allegany reservation, the rents amount to thousands of dollars per annum. This tendency at Tonawanda is modified by the small amount of public money that accrues to the nation from outside sources.

The contest becomes more closely drawn between the old and progressive divisions of the people. Poodry and others of his education, business independence, and force of character are inclined to stand aloof, mind their own business, and abide developments. Two of the chiefs, Nickerson Parker (Hawk), living at Cattaraugus, and his brother, Ely S. Parker, living in New York, married white wives, and take no active part in the national councils, although Tonawanda was their birthplace and the old homestead still stands, as indicated on the map. To a very marked extent the do-nothing party (the old party, the party of the sixteenth century) depresses nearly all national enterprises.

There is, however, a maturing sentiment among many of the pagan chiefs here, as on every reservation, that affairs are drawing to a crisis in their national history, and that customs which inspire idle gatherings, whether religious, social, political, or sportive, are becoming obsolete. There was an inquisitive inquiry respecting the purpose of the exhaustive interrogatories attending the enumeration, and perfectly plain words of warning and encouragement were received respectfully by pagan as well as christian.

The most impressive representation of folly on the part of the governing chiefs is the vacant manual school building. A state act of 1869 initiated the enterprise. The Tonawanda trust-fund income supplied $1,600 and the state expended $5,500 more. A farm of 80 acres, well located and of the best quality, was provided; buildings, furniture, teams, and implements were also purchased, but in 1877 all was abandoned, and the buildings are rapidly falling into decay. The state committee, in its report, very justly says: "It is well located and perfectly adapted for the work it was designed to accomplish. It stands there to-day a monument to mismanagement or neglect on the part of the state or its representatives, as well as to manifest indifference on the part of the Indians". The report adds: "The committee believes that it might have been of great value to the Indian youth if it had been carried out as originally intended". It was poor economy, or indifference, or want of an appreciation of the existing opportunity to stimulate the Indians to co-operation by liberal support that fastened upon the reservation such an unnecessary warning that the Indians, poor as they are, must look out for themselves. Pagan chiefs say that "if it could be even now turned into a high or mechanical school for teaching trades they would do something for it". At present the governing body is by a decided majority unwilling even to keep the roads in repair.

The year has been one of general good order, and the action of the peacemaker court has rarely been appealed to 6 chiefs, as authorized by law, in cases unsatisfactorily decided.

The following is a list of the chiefs, those marked with a * being unable to read or write:

*David Billy (Wolf), age 51; Chauncey Lone (Bear), 53; Chauncey A. Abram (Snipe), 52; *Samuel Bluesky (Turtle), 59; Isaac Doctor (Beaver), 77; Jacob Doctor (Hawk), 45; Nickerson Parker (Hawk), —; Addison Charles (Heron), 61; *Henry Spring (Snipe), 40; Solomon Spring (Hawk), 31; Edward M. Poodry (Turtle), 56; Jesse Spring (Beaver), 75; John David (Snipe), 40; *Lewis Hotbread (Bear), 69; Milton Abram (Snipe), 52; Robert Sky (Snipe), 31; David Moses (Wolf), 51; Charlie Doctor (Hawk), 57; Isaac Sundown (Deer), 36; Daniel Fish (Bear), 60; *Charles Clute (Beaver), 60; Erastus Printup (Beaver), 55; Wallace Jimerson (Hawk), 34; *Charles Hotbread (Hawk), 35; Andrew Blackchief (Wolf), 68; Howard Hatch (Wolf), 57; Clinton Moses (Wolf), 61; *Elan Skye (Snipe), 73; Fox Poodry (Hawk), —; *Eli Johnson (Hawk), 56; *Peter Doctor (Wolf), 29; *George Mitten (Bear), 33; *William Strong (Hawk), 49; Ely S. Parker (Hawk), —.

The ALLEGANY and CATTARAUGUS reservations are organized and incorporated under the laws of New York as " The Seneca nation", with a constitutional system giving them large independent powers. This constitution, as amended October 22, 1868, provides for a council of 16 members, of whom 8 shall be elected annually for each reservation on the first Tuesday of May every year. A quorum consists of 10, and the affirmative vote of 10 shall be necessary to appropriate public moneys. Expenditures of more than $500 require the sanction of a majority vote at a popular election, duly ordered. The president, also elected annually, is the executive officer of the nation, has a casting vote upon a tie in the council, fills vacancies until the next election thereafter, decides cases of impeachment, and is authorized to initiate by his recommendation any measures he may deem for the good of the nation not inconsistent with the true spirit and intent of the laws of the state of New York. A peacemaker court on each reservation for 3 years, one-third of the peacemakers being elected annually, has jurisdiction in all matters relating to wills, estates, real estate, and divorces, with forms of process and proceedings similar to those of justices of the peace in New York. An appeal lies to the national council, to which the evidence taken below is certified, and a quorum of the council is competent to decide the case upon arguments submitted, or, upon due application of either true party in interest, to submit the facts to a jury. A treaty, however, must be ratified by three-fourths of the legal voters, viz, " males above 21 years of age who have not been convicted of felony", and also by the consent of three-fourths of the mothers of the nation. A clerk, treasurer, and 2 marshals, 1 from each reservation, are provided for. The salaries of these officers are determined by the council, and are not to be enlarged or diminished during their term of office. Provision is made for amendment of the constitution and for the enactment of any laws not inconsistent with the constitution of the nation or the constitutions of the United States and the state of New York.

Section 13 of the constitution of the nation contains the following provision:

The laws heretofore enacted by the legislature of the state of New York for the protection and improvement of the Seneca nation of Indians, also all laws and regulations heretofore adopted by the council of the nation, shall continue in full force and effect, as heretofore, until the statutes of the state of New York shall be repealed or amended by the councilors, to the extent, and in the manner, as the attorney of the nation shall deem lawful and proper.

No provision is made whereby the nation may exercise its choice of an attorney, the plain purpose being that they are to have the disinterested advice of competent legal counsel, at the expense of the state, in matters in which they would lack discretion without legal advice. The contingency of having an attorney whose engagements might conflict with those of the nation, or whose habits and character would militate against its highest moral progress, was never considered in the preparation of the above section. The importance of having an attorney, if not a religious man, who would support and foster and not offend the christian agencies at work among the people is of the highest concern in their development. All other officials are chosen by them. In this they have no choice or suggestion of a choice. No people are more approachable if their confidence be won. However slow to change old customs and dull to forecast the future, they are suspicious of outside advice, if it be not entirely free from any possible antagonism to their own business and social relations.

The present council consists of the following members, those marked with a * being unable to read or write:

FROM ALLEGANY.—Sackett Redeye (Plover), age 49; Dwight Jimerson, 32; *George Gordon (Deer), 47; *Stephen Ray (Hawk), 50; Alfred Logan (Bear), 50; Abram Huff (Turtle), 40; Cyrus Crouse (Bear), 59; Marsh Pierce (Beaver), 69.

FROM CATTARAUGUS.—*David Stevens, age 73; *Chauncey Green, 45; *John Lay, jr. (Heron), 45; *Howard Jimerson (Wolf), 30; Elijah Turkey (Hawk), 34; Lester Bishop (Wolf), 41; *Robert Halftown (Snipe), 45; Thomas Patterson (Turtle), 36.

Andrew John, jr. (Gar-stea-o-de, Standing Rock), elected president in May, 1889, as elsewhere noticed, is a strict pagan, a shrewd politician, and an expert in applying the white man's methods of improving the opportunities of office. He presides over the council with self-possession, and is attentive to evidence upon questions of impeachment which come before him. A somewhat perplexing case was fairly adjudicated in September. Frequent journeys to Washington and abundant reticence in political matters have given him a large but varying influence with both parties. He is a steadfast upholder of his nation, while never making unnecessary sacrifice of his personal interests for anybody. This is his third but not consecutive term of office.

WILLIAM C. HOAG, Treasurer Seneca Nation, Allegany Seneca.

HARRISON HALFTOWN (Dar-gus-swent-gar-aut), "Drop Gun Stock,"   ALFRED JIMERSON, Allegany Seneca.
Allegany Seneca.

New York Engraving & Printing Co.

SOLOMON O. BAIL (Ho-noh-no-oh), "Not to be Persuaded or Convinced,"
Great grandson of Cornplanter.　Cattaraugus Seneca.

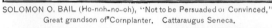

THEODORE F. JIMERSON (De-hah-teh), "Enlightened,"
Great-grandson of Mary Jimerson, the captive white woman.
Cattaraugus Seneca.

CHESTER C. LAY (Ho-do eh-ji-ah), "Bearing the Earth."
Official interpreter and ex-president of the Seneca Nation.
Cattaraugus Seneca.

THOMAS WILLIAMS (Ta-ker-yer-ter),
President of the Tuscarora Nation, 1890—Beaver Clan.

DANIEL PRINTUP (Da-quar-ter-anh),
Sachem of the Wolf Tribe and Treasurer of the Tuscarora Nation.

LUTHER W. JACK (Ta-wer-da-quoit), "Two boots standing together,"
Sachem Chief of Wolf Tribe and Clerk of Tuscarora Nation.

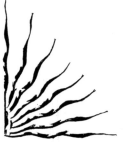

ELIAS JOHNSON (To-wer-na-kee),
Historian of the Tuscaroras—Wolf Tribe.

ENOS JOHNSON (Ka-re-wah-da-wer), "Warming-toned Voice."
Bear Tribe.

GRANT MOUNTPLEASANT (Ne-no-kar-wa),
Warrior Chief—Turtle Tribe.

New York Engraving & Printing Co.

Chester C. Lay (Ho-do-eh-ji-ah, Bearing the Earth), his predecessor, a man of good manners, education, and large experience (a proficient, as well as an instructor in instrumental music), stands among the foremost of the progressive men of his people. Thomas Kennedy and Theodore Jimerson are strong progressive men. Two professional attorneys, A. Sims Logan and Noah Twoguns, have great capacity to advance the interests of their people as soon as the consideration of fees shall allow opportunities in that direction. Harrison Halftown, the deputy clerk, and for nearly his whole life identified with the public concerns of the nation, has good judgment as well as experience, and will slowly but firmly follow that course which makes for the prosperity and peace of his people.

At present very grave matters agitate the Seneca nation. The present council is considered by many as being incompetent to manage public affairs. Wholesome laws are not enforced. Necessary legislation is neglected. The purchase of a "road machine", too late for autumn use, was a spasmodic attempt to do some work upon the mail route between Versailles and Lawton. Suspicion of federal and state legislation and reluctance to admit any wedge of reform that may endanger old-time rites and customs prevent all consistent legislation to meet the most essential conditions to real prosperity and development. The late winter session of the council witnessed such crude and fickle action respecting encroachments by the Rochester and Salamanca railroad authorities upon their lands near Red House station that they threw away, through penny-wise pride, an occasion for replenishing their exhausted treasury and conciliating their neighbors without injury to themselves. A strong undercurrent is in motion to elect a council in the spring of 1891 which shall be invulnerable to bribery, have a sufficient knowledge of the English language to read and understand the legislation of the federal and state governments, and so adjust their relations to the leasehold estates at Salamanca and other corporations in Allegany as to neither do nor suffer wrong.

THE TUSCARORA INDIANS were admitted to the Iroquois league on the ground of a common generic origin, retaining their own hereditary chiefs, but without enlarging the original framework of the confederacy. They had authority to be represented and enjoy a nominal equality in the councils. They are styled "sons", and in turn use the term "fathers" in their official relations with the league. No authority exists by which they can be disturbed by the league in the management of their own affairs. The prevalent opinion to the contrary is an error. In the Revolutionary war and in the war of 1812 they were faithful to the white people, and in the war of the rebellion furnished a reasonable contingent of volunteers to the union cause.

Vacancies among the chiefs are filled by the women of the clans entitled to the appointment. Here, as among the Onondaga and Tonawanda bands, the ruling chiefs arrogate and occasionally exercise the power of displacing chiefs by formal deposition, or make the place so uncomfortable as to force a resignation. It is a stretch of prerogative to exercise this power except for a cause that would require a substantial impeachment, but there is no method of redress, and the Indian dislike to bother about local legislation, even in their own behalf, represses organized effort to find a remedy.

The laws are few; the income is small; the people as a rule are orderly, peaceable, and accommodating; so that society moves along evenly but sluggishly, with rare infringement upon personal rights or disturbance of the public peace. The crossroads are poor, because the nation is poor, and, though not destitute, public funds are inadequate to pay for their repair. There is not sufficient constraining or sanctioning power in the governing body to enforce "working the roads". Fences, however, are well maintained under regulations well enforced by the governing chiefs. The distinction of sachem chiefs is retained by the governing chiefs as a title, but no practical difference in authority is recognized.

The government during the census year was constituted as follows, those marked with a * being unable to read or write:

Thomas Williams (Beaver), president, sachem, age 36 ; Luther W. Jack (Wolf), clerk, sachem, 31 ; Daniel Printup (Beaver), treasurer, warrior, 50 ; Phillip T. Johnson (Sand Turtle), warrior chief, 30 ; Simon A. Thompson (Wolf), warrior chief, 55 ; William J. Johnson (Turtle), sachem, 32 ; Grant Mountpleasant (Turtle), warrior chief, 22 ; Marcus Peter (Beaver), sachem, 42 ; Nicholas Cusick (Beaver), warrior chief, 30 ; Isaac Patterson (Sand Piper), Snipe, sachem, 54 ; George Williams (Sand Piper), Snipe, warrior chief, 24 ; *James Bembleton (Bear), warrior chief, 60 ; Jefferson Chew (Beaver), warrior chief, 22 ; *James Bembleton, sr. (Eel), warrior chief, 62.

THE SAINT REGIS INDIANS formed part of the Seven Nations of Canada. In 1852 their numbers were 1,100, or nearly the present number of the American Saint Regis Indians. By a provision of the first constitution of New York, adopted April 26, 1777, no purchases or contracts for the sale of lands by the Indians since the 14th day of October, 1775, were to be valid unless made with the consent of the legislature. Among the documents in the possession of the nation at the present time none are more prized than the treaty made May 4, 1797, exemplified, signed, and sealed by John Jay, governor, February 28, 1800. Three of the most noted parties to that treaty, viz, Te-har-ag-wan-e-gen (Thomas Williams), A-tia-to-ha-ron-gwam (Colonel Louis Cook), and William Gray, who was made captive in his boyhood and adopted by the Indians, are still represented among the families enumerated upon the schedules. Thomas Williams was third in descent from Rev. Thomas Williams, of Deerfield, Massachusetts. Louis Cook was captured with his parents, his father being a colored man, at Saratoga, in 1775. He raised and commanded a regiment on the colonial side, and on August 1, 1775, was entertained by Washington at Cambridge, Massachusetts. On the following day he was received by the general court of the commonwealth, and John

Winthrop, chairman of a special committee to confer with this Caughnawaga, or Saint Regis chief, made a report as to the successful terms of friendship then established. Sparks' Life of Washington and the American State Papers are generous in their recognition of the services of Cook and the Saint Regis Indians at that period, and the history of the war of 1812 is equally creditable to their loyalty to the United States. No student or observer of their gradual advance in civilization should overlook or slight their antecedent history in a patient development of their future.

By an act of the legislature passed March 26, 1802, William Gray, Louis Cook, and Loren Tarbell, chiefs, were also appointed trustees on behalf of the Saint Regis Indians to lease the ferry over the Saint Regis river, with authority to apply the rents and profits for the support of a school and such other purposes as such trustees should judge most conducive to the interests of said tribe. The same act provided for future annual elections of similar trustees by a majority of adults of the age of 21 years, at a town meeting, on the first Tuesday of each May thereafter. This system is still in force.

The powers, functions, and responsibilities of these trustees are hardly more than nominal in practical effect. The peculiar credit which the Six Nations attach to all preserved treaties, however old or superseded, developed during the census year a new departure in the Saint Regis plan of self-government. The old or pagan element among the Onondagas, supported by Chief Daniel La Forte, Thomas Williams, keeper of the wampum, and others, maintained that their rights to lands in Kansas and similar rights rested upon treaties made between the Six Nations (exactly six) and the United States, and at a general council, held in 1888, the Saint Regis Indians were formally recognized as the successors of the Mohawks, thus restoring the original five, while, with the Tuscaroras, maintaining six. The theory was that an apparent lapse from the six in number would in some way work to their prejudice. The same element at once proposed the revival of the old government by chiefs, which had become obsolete among the Saint Regis Indians. A meeting was held, even among the Cattaraugus Senecas, with the deliberate purpose to ignore or abandon their civilized, legal organization as the Seneca nation and return to former systems. The impracticability of such a retrograde movement did not silence the advocates of chiefship for the Saint Regis Indians. The election through families, after the old method, of 9 chiefs and 9 alternate or vice chiefs was held, and these were duly installed in office by a general council, representing all the other nations. Practically and legally they have no power whatever. Two of them, Joseph Wood and Joseph Bero (Biron), are still trustees under the law of 1802.

By tacit understanding the Indians avail themselves of the New York courts in issues of law or fact so far as applicable, and submit their conduct to ordinary legal process and civil supervision, so that they have, in fact, no organic institution that antagonizes civilized methods. The distinctions by tribe or clan have almost disappeared, those of the Wolf, Turtle, Bear, and Plover only remaining. Thomas Ransom, the third trustee, retains in his possession the old treaties and other national archives, while the people, ignorant of the reasons for any change, vibrate between the support of the two systems, neither of which has much real value. The small rentals of land are of little importance in the administration of affairs, and the more intelligent of the prosperous Indians distinctly understand that the elected chiefs have no special authority until recognized by the state of New York as legal successors of the trustees. Either system is that of a consulting, supervising, representative committee of the Saint Regis Indians, and little more.

The following is a list of the chiefs, those marked with a * being unable to read or write:

*Peter Tarbell (Ta-ra-ke-te, Hat-rim, or Neck-protection), great grandson of Peter Tarbell, the eldest of the Groton captives; Joseph Wood (So-se-sa-ro-ne-sa-re-ken, Snow Crust), Heron clan; *Peter Herring (Te-ra-non-ra-no-ron-sau, Deerhouse), Turtle clan; *Alexander Solomon (A-rek-sis-o-ri-hon-ni, He is to Blame), Turtle clan; Angus White, chief and clerk (En-ni-as-ni-ka-un-ta-a, Small Sticks of Wood), Snipe clan; Charles White (Sa-ro-tha-ne-wa-ne-ken, Two Hide Together), Wolf clan; also, Joseph Bero, John White, and Frank Terance. Alternate or vice chiefs are Joseph Cook, *Matthew Benedict, *Paul Swamp, *John B. Tarbell, *Philip Wood, and *Alexander Jacob (two vacancies).

Angus White is an intelligent business man of excellent character and gracious address, thoroughly competent for his position.

There is a pending question among the Saint Regis Indians, which may require settlement by both the state and federal governments, respecting their intercourse with their Canadian brethren. Even the census enumeration is affected by its issues. The early treaties, which disregarded the artificial line of separation of these Indians and allowed them free transit over the line with their effects, are confronted by a modern customs regulation, which often works hardship and needless expense. The contingency of their purchasing horses beyond the line and introducing them for personal use, while really intending to sell them at a profit greater than the duty, is not to be ignored; but such cases must be rare, and the peculiarly located families near the line, who worship together, farm together, and live as people do in the adjoining wards of a city, is a question which seems to call for a special adjustment to the actual facts.

Meanwhile the development of the basket industry and the ready market at Hogansburg, where a single resident firm bought during the year, as their books show, in excess of $20,000, have attracted the Canadian Saint

PHILIP TARBELL, Chief (Ta-ra-ke-te), "Hat-rim Protects the Neck."
Wolf Clan of St. Regis Indians.

PETER HERRING, Chief (Tier-a-nen-sa-no-ken), "Deer House,"
Turtle Clan of St. Regis Indians.

ANGUS WHITE, Chief and Clerk (En-neas-ne-ka-unta-a),
"Small Stick of Wood,"   Snipe Clan of St. Regis Indians.

ALEXANDER SOLOMON, Chief (Arch-sis-o-ri-henn), "He is to Blame,"
Son of old Chief Solomon of the Six Nations.

JOSEPH WOOD, Chief, (So-se-sais-ne-sa-ke-ken), "Snow Crust,".
Heron Clan of St. Regis Indians.

CHARLES WHITE, Chief, (Saro-tha-ne-wa-na), "Two Hide Together,"
Wolf Clan of St. Regis Indians.

New York Engraving & Printing Co.

Regis Indians across the line, so that the schedules indicate the term of residence of quite a number as less than a year upon the American side. Their right to buy land of the American Saint Regis Indians and erect buildings has been discussed, and the question as to trustees or chiefs as their advisory ruling authority has had this political element as one of the factors. Clerk Angus White furnishes a list of those on the American side whom he declares to be Canadians proper, drawing Canadian annuities, and on the American side of the line only to have the benefit of its market for profitable basket work. The two parties made their statements, and on one occasion the Canadian chiefs, Alexander Thompson, Mitchell Jacobs, and Richard Francis, with their clerk, Roland Pike, sought an interview to explain that no encroachment upon the rights of others was the object of their people. The loose holdings or tenures of land among the Saint Regis Indians makes them jealous of extending privileges beyond their immediate circles; at the same time indispensable daily intimacies prevent the establishment of any arbitrary law of action in the premises. Petitions have been sent to the New York legislature demanding that the Canadians be forcibly put across the line. There is no occasion for such summary legislation. A wise commission could adjust the matter equitably without injustice to any or bad feeling between the adjoining families of the same people. The list of Clerk White is made part of this report, specifying which of those enumerated and resident are deemed Canadian Saint Regis Indians. The list is not to be accepted without qualification, for some who are denounced by one party as Canadians have reared children on the American side of the line and call it their home. John McDonnell is one of the most prosperous farmers on the American reservation. Jealousy of his prosperity is at the foundation of a purpose to do him injury, although Angus White does not fully understand the spirit which prompts the outside antagonism to McDonnell, who is rightfully where he is. The trustees or chiefs, or both, are continually at work to have stricken from the New York annuity list all whose mixture of white blood on the female side is decided. The only just rule is to give to both parents equal rights. The reputed list of Canadian Indians on American soil is as follows:

Mitchell Stovepipe, Joseph Martin, Joseph Sam, John Paul, George Peter, Peter Papineau, Mary White, Mitchell Hemlock, Joseph Simoe, Peter McDonnell, John Phillips, Peter La France, Roran Stovepipe, Mitchell Papineau, Jacob Day, Hannah Brass, John McDonnell, John Papineau, Louis David, Christie Bonaparte, Louis Benedict, John Hoops, Mitchell Leaf, Peter Oak, Thomas Jacks, Andrew David, John Peter, Kate McDonnell, Sarah Mitchell, Mitchell Johnson, Paul David, Mitchell Monroe, John Benedict, Thomas Hoops, Mitchell Oak, John Oak.

All such questions as those involved in this controversy can only find permanent solution through some ultimate appeal to state or federal authority for distinct and binding settlement.

As a general rule, the state agent is able to adjust the distribution of the state annuity without friction, but he should reside at Hogansburg, with powers to adjust local difficulties. This would largely bridge the chasm over which the Saint Regis Indians slowly but certainly advance toward a matured citizenship.

7

PART IV.

RELIGION AMONG THE SIX NATIONS, INCLUDING SAINT REGIS INDIANS.

With the exception of the Tuscaroras, each of the Six Nations has one or more council houses, in which the people assemble for business or purely Indian ceremonies, religious or social. There is also a council house or town hall on the Mount Hope road of the Tuscarora reservation, but the pagan party has no footing among this people. The council houses, formerly built of logs, are practically in disuse, and frame buildings, about 40 by 80 feet, with fireplace or simple chimney at each end, which allows separate sittings for the sexes, have taken their place. A new building of this kind on the Tonawanda reservation, and 1 at Carrollton, on the Allegany reservation, are indicated on the maps of these reservations. The sites of 3 ancient council houses at Cattaraugus and of 2 at Tonawanda are also indicated. The religious differences of the Indians actually characterize grouped settlements on each reservation. Thus, the majority of the christian Indians live upon the central road in Onondaga; upon and east of the main road of Tonawanda; between Salamanca and Red House, in Allegany, and upon the main route from Versailles to Irving, in Cattaraugus. As a general rule, both internal and external comforts, conveniences, and indications of thrift are alike in contrast. The pagans chiefly occupy the western and southeastern parts of Tonawanda, the Carrollton district, and the country below the Red House, in Allegany, and almost exclusively people the Newtown and Gowanda roads, in Cattaraugus. There are exceptions, as in the case of Andrew John, sr., one of the most successful farmers of Cattaraugus, but the groupings are everywhere maintained.

ONONDAGA RESERVATION.

At Onondaga the council house is central upon what is known as " the public green ", thus retaining for this open space the name common throughout New England even up to a recent date. In this building the pagan rites are annually performed.

The Protestant Episcopal church, a handsome and well-equipped structure, having Rev. John Scott as rector and 24 communicants, is also near the " public green ". The responses are devoutly rendered, the singing is rich, full, and expressive, and an hour's " talk " to the Indians, interpreted by Jaris Pierce, an advanced man in English education and civilized manners, was eagerly listened to and received a rising vote of thanks. The occasion was improved to impress their minds with the value of school training and a sacred regard for the marriage and family relations as essential to their true prosperity and development. The venerable Abram Hill (Oneida, of the Snipe tribe), Albert Cusick (Onondaga, of the Eel tribe), the latter preparing for examination to take deacon's orders, and Marvin Crouse (Seneca, of the Wolf tribe) are among the most active members. The singing was under the direction of the rector's wife, Mrs. Scott, who presided at the organ. Mr. Scott's compensation, including morning charge of the state school, amounts to $500 per annum, and the people contribute current expenses.

The Methodist Episcopal church, also a handsome building, with stained glass windows, is situated opposite the schoolhouse, 180 rods south of the Episcopal church. Rev. Abram Fancher is the minister, with a salary of $500 per year and use of parsonage. There are 23 communicants, and nearly 60 persons were present at the afternoon class meeting. The audience was addressed without an interpreter, and there were expressions of cordial satisfaction from the people. Josiah Jacobs (Onondaga, of the Wolf tribe) and Abram Printup (Eel tribe) are among the most efficient workers. A third christian organization, the Wesleyan Methodist, is worshiping at private houses under the spiritual care of Rev. Thomas La Forte, a brother of the influential and most prominent chief of the present Onondagas, Daniel La Forte (Onondaga, of the Wolf tribe). This minister was for 13 years among the Saint Regis Indians, and has a fair English education. His brother, Chief La Forte, was at one time a member of the christian party, and took an active part in the erection of the church edifice.

A singular sequel attaches to the building of this church, growing out of alleged aid in its erection. Rev. Thomas La Forte claimed that his society helped build it. Among the few records preserved, the following ex parte statement, taken literatim from their pages, indicates the attitude of the pagan party respecting the question referred to :

The undersigned, chiefs of the Onondaga nation of Indians, hereby certify that our nation heretofore has given permission to the Wesleyan Methodist people & Church to build a church and passage [parsonage] on our reservation. We further certify that we have never given to any other church or society the right to hold or occupy the building enter [entered] no more occupied [no more either to be occupied] that church by the Protestant Episcopal church, thereby the Wesleyans church people as [has] the lands on which the building stands.

We believe that the said wesleyans church and people to be lawful owner & holder of the church and other buildings ented [entered] on our reservation by them, & hereby willingly consent to their taking & holding possession of the same.

Done at Onondaga Castle this 24th day of September, 1886.

Name for chiefs :

his George x Lyon. mark.	his Thomas x Webster. mark.	his Baptist x Thomas. mark.	his Jacob x Big Bear. mark.	his Charles x Green. mark.
his John x Johnson. mark.	his William x Lyons. mark.	his Wilson x Reuben. mark.	his John x Hill. mark.	his Joseph x Isaac. mark.
his Abbott x Jones. mark.	his William x Hill. mark.	his William x Joe. mark.	his Andrew x Gibson. mark.	

(Signed) BAPTIST THOMAS, Chairman for Nation.
DANIEL LA FORTE, Clerk for Nation.

Some of the above chiefs can write, but the record reads as above given.

Here, as in many frontier settlements, the number of churches is disproportionate to the population. The stimulus to competitive, earnest work, which often follows the existence of more than one religious body, does not wholly prevent church jealousies or impress upon pagan minds the highest idea of christian spirit, or that christianity is the object sought and denominational connections are matters of judgment and choice. The property episode is therefore given, not to expose the crudeness of the record, but as indicative of local christian differences, which hinder rapid progress.

TONAWANDA RESERVATION.

At Tonawanda there are 3 church buildings, each well adapted to its purpose. The Presbyterian church is languishing through internal discords. The Baptist church, built of brick, and having a good organ and 40 members, cost nearly $3,600. The annual contributions to its support are a little more than $200. Mr. John Griffin (Seneca, of the Bear tribe) has lay charge of the meetings, the pulpit being vacant. He is a prosperous farmer, and, with his wife Margaret and daughter Nellie (Senecas, of the Wolf tribe), struggles hard to restore the church to its former pre-eminence on the reservation. The wealthiest member of the church and of the nation, and prominent among the entire Six Nations for business experience and practical wisdom, is Edward M. Poodry, a Seneca of the Turtle tribe, but through difference of opinion as to church management has recently attended the Presbyterian church and acted as interpreter. Mr. Poodry, who is an independent thinker, perfectly alive to the demands of the times, and successful in bringing his sons into profitable employment upon his large farm, acted as interpreter on the occasion of one " talk " to this congregation, and earnestly seconded the request that fresh effort be made to arouse the people to throw off the weight of " old-time " superstition and hasten into full accord with the progress of the times. This partial withdrawal of Mr. Poodry from the Baptist meetings has chilled attendance and crippled their usefulness.

The Presbyterian church, costing $2,500, is another good structure that would do credit to any country town. Rev. John McMasters, of Akron, preaches on alternate Sabbaths, and Rev. M. F. Trippe preaches once a month. Three excellent elders, Warren Sky (Seneca, of the Wolf tribe), a prosperous farmer; William Cooper (Seneca, of the Hawk tribe), an enterprising young man, who commands the full confidence of sensible white people, and William H. Moses (Seneca, of the Wolf tribe), have charge of the active work of the church, and prove efficient laborers. The number of communicants is 35, and the annual contribution by the church is $30.

The Methodist church, with a small but neatly furnished place of worship, has nominally 19 members, Mr. Stephen Sky (Seneca, of the Hawk tribe), one of the 5 non-backsliding male members, being earnest in his endeavor to secure regular preaching services as soon as possible. Their contributions for church work are $30 per annum.

ALLEGANY RESERVATION.

There is but 1 church edifice on the Allegany reservation (Presbyterian), costing $1,500, of which the Indians contributed $750. There are 110 communicants, according to the church records. The pastor, Rev. M. F. Trippe, thoroughly enthusiastic in his work, in addition to the occasional aid of Rev. William Hall, who has spent more than a third of a century in this field, has had strong support by members and elders of his church. Two members of this church died during the enumeration under circumstances which evinced the power of the christian's faith in the dying hour, and the statement of their experience is worth more than columns of figures in establishing a strong bond of sympathy between the christian people of America and the people of the Six Nations. Joseph Turkey (Cayuga) had been preacher, exhorter, and colporteur, laboring with indefatigable zeal for the conversion of the people. Elder William W. Jimerson (Seneca, of the " Eagle " tribe, probably Hawk), while dying of consumption, expressed his greatest " regret that his work for Jesus had not been better done ". Three days before his death he " wished he could have been at their prayer meeting the previous evening ". David Gordon (Seneca, of the Wolf tribe), Elder Alfred T. Jimerson (Seneca, of the "Plover", properly Snipe tribe), an efficient aid during the enumeration, as well as a church elder, and Willit B. Jimerson (Seneca, of the Wolf tribe), who has a piano instead of an organ or melodeon in his parlor, are among the efficient workers to rescue the Allegany Senecas from the controlling influence of the pagan party.

The Baptists have a nominal membership of 21, and meet at the old school building at Red House, having lost their small church by a storm. Their minister, Rev. Harvey Blinkey (Seneca, of the Wolf tribe), and his wife Letitia (Seneca, of the "Flamingo", really Heron tribe), clerk of the church, are taking measures to revive their organization and recall "professional backsliders" to duty, but the church is at low-water mark.

CORNPLANTER RESERVATION.

Closely associated with Allegany, under the same pastoral care, and allied by community of blood and annuity interests, are the few families of Cornplanter's descendants across the line in Warren county, Pennsylvania, on the Cornplanter reservation. A well-built Presbyterian church, with 39 communicants, a good organ and Sabbath school, testify to progressive work. Marsh Pierce (Seneca, of the "Tip-up", properly Snipe tribe) is the active representative of the church and a real force in the elevation of his nation. He owns property to the value of $10,000, is an industrious, careful farmer, and one of the progressive members of the "national Seneca council".

CATTARAUGUS RESERVATION.

Cattaraugus reservation has 3 churches, all on the road from the courthouse to the town of Irving. The Methodist church, on Courthouse square, is a building costing nearly $2,000, and $300 has recently been appropriated by the missionary society of the Methodist Episcopal church for improvements. Rev. A. A. Crow, of Gowanda, preaches every Sabbath afternoon, followed by a class meeting. A divorce suit pending before the peacemaker court and challenging much attention and sympathy brought out on one occasion such prayerful expressions of sympathy as might be evoked under corresponding circumstances among the most earnest christians. The membership is 39. The ladies' sewing circle realized $100 during the census year for church purposes. As in all churches throughout the Six Nations, "familiar talks" upon personal duty at this critical period of the Indian history elicited appreciative responses and an avowed purpose to struggle for a higher plane of living.

The Presbyterian church, near the parting of the Brant road, cost $2,500, and will accommodate from 400 to 500 people. It has a reliable membership of 86, some having been dropped from the rolls. 10 additions were made upon profession of faith after the enumeration was formally taken, and nearly 30 others had consulted the pastor with a view to admission. Rev. George Runciman succeeded Rev. M. F. Trippe 2 years ago, and this church has been especially blessed in an awakening of the people to the value of christianity as the only thoroughly effective civilizing force.

The Sabbath school numbers nearly 100, including the pupils of the Thomas Orphan Asylum, who worship at this church with Mr. and Mrs. Van Volkenburg, who have charge of that institution. Instead of a choir, as in many of the Indian churches, the asylum pupils, nearly 70 in number, lead the singing with great effect. During the census year the sum of $272 was contributed by the congregation for church purposes. Mr. Lester Bishop (Seneca, of the Wolf Tribe) is superintendent of the Sunday school, and in its management, exposition of the International lessons, and general church work exhibits rare tact, spirituality, and judgment. He is also one of the most respected and efficient members of the national Seneca council.

The Baptist church, cost about $1,500, is a convenient building, with good horse sheds near by. It has 35 communicants, but is without a minister, and is in a languishing condition. The sum of $60 was contributed during the census year for a temporary supply, and about $70 for other church purposes.

TUSCARORA RESERVATION.

At Tuscarora there are 2 substantial church buildings, the Presbyterian, on the mountain road, visited monthly by Rev. M. F. Trippe, of Salamanca, who formerly preached at Cattaraugus, but now has general supervision of the Indian Presbyterian churches of Allegany, Tonawanda, and Tuscarora, as well as at Cornplanter, in Pennsylvania. The number of communicants is 27, with a good Sunday school, good singing, and an intelligent, but small attendance, except under favoring conditions of the weather, when this congregation, as in most Indian churches, is large, the Indians, equally with the white people, regarding clear weather and clear roads as passports of attendance. The American board assists this church $175 per annum. The contributions for sexton and other expenses reach $75 per annum.

The Baptist church, under the care of Rev. Frank Mountpleasant (Seneca, of the Turtle tribe), is a large edifice, and has capacious horse sheds, after the old New England style, and a nominal membership of 211. The Sabbath school numbers 85, and the active support of Mrs. Caroline Mountpleasant, sister of General Ely S. Parker, a woman of refinement, education, and culture, greatly adds to the efficiency of the church work over which her nephew presides. A choir of 20 persons renders excellent music, in which the congregation often joins with spirit.

The minister's salary is but $50 from the Baptist convention, but the congregation, which contributes $220 per annum toward church expenses, and the proceeds from a profitable farm make up a sufficient sum for his support. A ladies' home missionary or sewing society in behalf of the church inspires additional interest among the people. The comparatively large number of communicants, embracing many very young people, is far above the real number of working members. A new roof upon the church by voluntary labor indicates the enterprise of the congregation.

RELIGION AMONG THE SAINT REGIS INDIANS.

Three-fourths of the American Saint Regis Indians belong to the Roman Catholic church and worship with their Canadian brethren at the parish church of Saint Regis, immediately over the Canada line. The church building, which was once partially destroyed by fire, has been restored, made cheerful, and is both well lighted and suitably heated. It accommodates about 600 persons, and at one morning service it was crowded with well-dressed, reverential people, whose general decorum and prompt responses indicated a sincere regard for the service and the proprieties of the day and place.

Few churches on American soil are associated with more of curious tradition. One of Mrs. Sigourney's most exquisite poems, "The Bell of Saint Regis", commemorates the tradition of the transfer of the bell stolen from Deerfield, Massachusetts, February 29, 1774, to the Saint Regis tower. The bell went to the church of the Sault Saint Louis, at the Caughnawaga village, near Montreal. The three bells at Saint Regis, including the largest, which was cracked and recast, came from the Meneelay bell shops of Troy within the last 25 years.

The old church records are well preserved, and since the first marriage was solemnized there, February 2, 1762, both marriages and christenings have been recorded with scrupulous care.

The Canadian government withholds from annuities a small sum to maintain the choir and organist by consent of the Canadian Indians, but no organized support flows from the American Indians as their proper share. Although the American Indians are welcomed to the church service, there is a church need which can not be fully supplied by the present arrangement.

The Methodist Episcopal church is located just on the margin of the reservation, north from the village of Hogansburg and within the town limits, in order to secure a good title. It is a substantial building, commenced in 1843 and finished in 1845, at a cost of $2,000. The bell was presented by Bishop Janes. The church has 68 communicants, representing one-fourth of the inhabitants of the reservation, and is in a growing, prosperous condition. It is in charge of Rev. A. A. Wells, an earnest preacher, and a whole-souled, sympathetic, visiting pastor. The music, the deportment, even of the boys, and the entire conduct of the service, with the loud swelling of nearly 200 voices in the doxology at the close, as well as the occasional spontaneous "amens" and the hand-shaking before dispersion, left no occasion for doubt that a thorough regenerative work had begun right at the true foundation for all other elevation, whether educational or social. Weekly prayer meetings at private houses present another fact that emphasizes the value of the work in progress. Mr. Wells' assistant, who is both exhorter and interpreter, and as enthusiastic as his principal, is John Wesley Woodman, an Oneida, and son of a pious Indian woman, Mary Benedict Woodman, one of the founders of the society. The annual contribution for church expenses is $25. The Methodist Episcopal Missionary Society pays the minister's salary of $500.

RELIGIOUS CONTRASTS.

The mere statement of the value of church buildings and the number of church members of each organization does not afford an entirely sound basis for testing their real influence and progress. To a greater extent than usual among the white people other motives than those of spiritual, soul religion enter into the mind of the Indian in making the change. The minister of the gospel who seeks to make of the church a training school, and accepts members upon a short test of the applicant's real experience of a change of moral motive, must find that early "backsliding", as the Indians term it, is almost as certain as a soundly progressive development. Leading Indians who have returned to their pagan associations admit that they did not gain what they expected in the way of influence or position when they "joined the christians". Both terms have a political meaning among the Six Nations. Members of the christian party are not of necessity christian at heart, neither are members of the pagan party necessarily of pagan faith.

Examinations of all church records, visits to all christian churches during service, as well as conferences with pastors, church officers, and laymen, show that every church roll needs some purging, and that the social and political relations are so commingled that the real number of converted Indians is but vaguely determined; at the same time truth requires the statement that, according to the reports of ministers in charge of churches for the white people adjoining the reservations, the derelict membership is very little greater among the membership of Indian churches than those of their neighbors. This startling fact induced a more careful inquiry among the Indians themselves, without entire dependence upon the church records. The result was to find in every Indian church some members, and in several of them many, whose faith, life, and example would do honor to any christian professor. In every case the reservations have white neighbors who are as destitute of religious principle as any Indian can be, and who have no other idea of the Indian than that he has land, which the white man does not have, and as an Indian is incapable of honor or right motive, he is to be dispossessed and gotten rid of as soon and as summarily as possible. Hence came a more minute inquiry into the real religious motive, if such could be found, of those Indians who were not merely pagan in a party sense, to conserve old customs, but pagan in actual belief.

THE PAGAN FAITH.

The statement of Andrew John, jr., that "knowledge of the pagan faith would show it to be more beautiful and moral than the christian", was a step in the inquiry. He was interpreter for the Quaker minister, Rebecca K. Masters, at Carrollton council house when George S. Scattergood and party from Philadelphia made a visit in the fall of 1890. The contrast of the interpreted words with pagan ideas led to fuller inquiry as to the ceremonies among the pagans which they call "religious" and subsequent attendance at all of them, from the autumn green-corn dance and worship to the closing "feather dance", which closes the celebration of the Indian New Year. Friend George S. Scattergood, following the example of his father, had also fallen upon the same line of inquiry, and formed the opinion that many of the old people in the ceremonies of their belief actually render unto God the sincere homage of prayerful and thankful hearts. The simplest form of inquiries, slowly interpreted, left the same conclusion upon the mind of the enumerator of this people. At the same time it was equally apparent that the younger portion, almost without exception, treated days of pagan ceremony much as they would a corn husking, full of fun, but without religion.

THE NEW RELIGION.

The " new religion ", as the teachings of Handsome Lake have been called, did not displace the old ceremonies of earlier times. He was a Seneca sachem of the Turtle tribe, a half-brother of Cornplanter, was born near Avon about the year 1735, and died in 1815 at Onondaga while there upon a pastoral or missionary visit. About the year 1800, after a dissipated life and a very dangerous illness, he claimed to have had dreams or visions, through which he was commissioned by the Great Spirit to come to the rescue of his people. His first efforts were to eradicate intemperance. He mingled with his teachings the fancies of his dreams or convictions, claiming that he had been permitted to see the branching paths which departed spirits were accustomed to take on leaving the earth. His grandson, Sase-ha-wa, nephew of Red Jacket and his delegated successor, long resident of Tonawanda, amplified his views in many forcible addresses, which are full of wild poetic conceptions, yet ever teaching the value of marriage, respect for parents and the aged, and many lessons from the old Hebrew Bible, which, besides the Ten Commandments, had been incorporated into the " new religion " of Handsome Lake. Of the future state, he taught that " one branch road, at death, led straight forward to the house of the Great Spirit, and the other turned aside to the house of torment. At the place where the roads separated were stationed 2 keepers, 1 representing the good and the other the evil spirit. When a wicked person reached the fork he turned instinctively, by a motion of the evil spirit, upon the road which led to the abode of the evil-minded, but if virtuous and good the other keeper directed him upon the straight road. The latter was not much traveled, while the other was so often trodden that no grass could grow in the pathway ". " To a drunkard was given a red-hot liquid to drink, as if he loved it, and as a stream of blaze poured from his mouth he was commanded to sing as when on earth after drinking fire water ". " Husbands and wives who had been quarrelsome on earth were required to rage at each other until their eyes and tongues ran out so far that they could neither see nor speak ". " A wife beater was led up to a red-hot statue, which he was to strike as he struck his wife when on earth, and sparks flew out and burned his arm to the bone ". " A lazy woman was compelled to till a cornfield full of weeds, which grew again as fast as she pulled them ". " A woman who sold fire water was nothing but bones, for the flesh had been eaten from her hands and arms ". " To those who sold the lands of their people it was assigned to move a never diminishing mound of sand ". By such terrific and pertinent imagery Handsome Lake and his successor wrought a deep place in the confidence of the old pagan party throughout their field of labor.

RELIGIOUS DANCES.

With all this, the more ancient rites do not yield their place, and the perpetuated songs of remote ancestors still echo to the beat of the kettledrum and the turtle rattle at every recurring celebration of the days observed several hundred years ago. Only now and then is found a man who can carry the whole text of the refrain through the protracted measures of the leading dances, but there are a few such, and the heart throbs with strange emotions, never lost, even after hearing several recitals of their stirring appeals. They embody all the true spirit there is in the Iroquois religion.

The war dance, still preserved, has the striking feature of allowing witty speeches, cutting repartee, personal hits, and every conceivable utterance that will stimulate either laughter or action. The great feather dance, the religious dance, consecrated to the worship of the Great Spirit, is given in part as an illustration of the religious sentiment which pervades their old music, rising far above the ancient ceremonies of Greece or Rome, and so contrasted by Elias Johnson, a genial and companionable Tuscarora, in his interesting book upon the history of his people.

At the New Year's festivities at Newtown council house, in the pagan section of Cattaraugus, January, 1891, this dance followed the thanksgiving dance and rounded out the ceremonies of the closing year.

At a great fireplace at one end of the council house large caldrons were fiercely boiling, stirred with long poles by the shawl-wrapped women, who were preparing the feast of boiled corn and beans, while 2 other kettles, equally large, suspended by chains over a fire behind the building, provided a relay of repast if the first should fall short. Astride a bench placed lengthwise in the middle of the hall sat vis-a-vis the leader and the prompter of dance and song, surrounded by 2 raised benches filled with men, women, and children of all ages. 8 representatives of the Iroquois tribes, in divisions of 4, had been selected to lead off the dance. At the appointed hour there gathered from the cabins that surrounded the large open space where the council house is located nearly 80 men and boys, who were costumed appropriate for the occasion. The headdresses were of varied patterns, from the single eagle feather to the long, double trailing feather ornament which the Sioux wear in battle, and which, streaming out behind as he dashes about in action, more completely represent him as some uncouth beast than a real man. The men wore ornamental aprons before and behind, while every muscle stood forth round and compact through the closely fitting knit garment that covered the upper part of the body, and rarely has there been such a display of athletic forms. Silver bracelets, armlets, necklaces, and brooches, the inheritance of generations, were parts of their adornment. Strings of bells were fastened around the knees, and the costumes varied from the rich variety of Ed. Cornplanter's equipment down to that of an old man who had pinned 2 faded United States flags to the skirt of his coat through want of anything older or richer. Unlike the parties to the green-corn dance at Cold Spring in September, only 1 used paint upon the cheeks. The women wore their good clothes, as if on a social visit.

All was ready! The slight touch of the turtle rattles gradually increased in rapidity as party after party fell into line and caught step and cadence, which constantly developed in volume, until the leader sounded the opening chant for the dance to begin. The whole song, lasting nearly an hour, consisted of a series of measured verses, each of 2 minutes duration. It is difficult to describe the step. The heel is raised but 2 or 3 inches and brought down by muscular strength to keep time with the drum and make a resounding noise by the concussion and at the same time shake the knee rattles. Every figure is erect, while the arms assume every possible graceful position to bring the muscles into full play. Although 80 men and 40 women engaged in the dance and slowly promenaded during the necessary rests from the violent exercise of such swift motion, all was orderly, decent, and without vulgarity or rudeness. The recitative portions were varied by addresses of gratitude to the Great Spirit, acknowledging every good gift to man. A few passages of the refrain are given as translated many years ago by Ely S. Parker and sung by his grandfather. They have been handed down from generation to generation.

Hail! Hail! Hail! Listen now, with an open ear, to the words of Thy people as they ascend to Thy dwelling! Give to the keepers of Thy faith wisdom to execute properly Thy commands! Give to our warriors and our mothers strength to perform the sacred ceremonies of Thy institution! We thank Thee that Thou hast preserved them pure to this day.

Continue to listen. We thank Thee that the lives of so many of Thy children have been spared to participate in the exercises of this occasion.

Then follow thanks for the earth's increase and a prayer for a prosperous year to come, then for the rivers and streams, for the sun and moon, for the winds that banish disease, for the herbs and plants that benefit the sick, and for all things that minister to good and happiness.

The closing passage is given as the rapidly increased step and tread almost die out in a subdued cadence.

Lastly, we return thanks to Thee, our Creator and Ruler! In Thee are embodied all things! We believe Thou canst do no evil; that Thou doest all things for our good and happiness. Should Thy people disobey Thy commands, deal not harshly with them; but be kind to us, as Thou hast been to our fathers in times long gone by. Hearken to our words as they have ascended, and may they be pleasing to Thee, our Creator, the preserver of all things visible and invisible. Na ho!

Thus strangely do the elements of revealed and natural religion come into contrasting and yet sympathetic relation. The Six Nations Indian is never an atheist. The pagans point to their quiet homes, however lowly, rarely protected by locks, to the infrequency of crimes, and even of minor offenses, unless when fired by the white man's whisky or hard cider, and challenge proof of greater security or contentment. During 7 months of enumeration of this people neither vulgarity nor profanity was noticed, while it was repeatedly forced upon the attention when resuming contact with the white man's world outside. Neither does the deportment of the old people at these dances belie the claim that they sincerely worship. The women move in an inside circle, with faces bowed and turned toward the turtle rattles or the kettledrum, with all the solemnity of real convictions that in some way they are recognizing and invoking divine aid.

THE INDIAN BELIEF.

The cardinal difference between the pagan Indians of the Six Nations and the ancient philosophers of Greece and Rome lies in the Indian recognition of one great spirit, to whom all other spirits are subject. They do not worship nature or the works of nature, but the God of nature, and all physical objects which minister to their comfort and happiness are His gifts to His children. It is this "unknown god" whom Paul unfolded to the superstitious Athenians in the heaven-arched court space of the Areopagus on Mars' Hill that the Indians in vague forms of heathen faith seek to worship. It is through this avenue of approach that these Indians must be approached. John Eliot's success was in deliberate but simple effort to explain that the white men had in their hands the revealed record of the attributes and providential dealings of the same Great Spirit whom they ignorantly worshiped. It will be by a renewed, earnest, consistent, and fraternal work, discouraged by no failures and without sectarian jealousy or sectarian dogmas, that the red men can be reached; and now is just the time for the religious denominations which operate in this field to redouble their efforts in the spirit of the Master. The crisis has come upon the Six Nations. They know it. They have strong and willing men ready for their emancipation from pagan control, and if the struggle be to save them on their lands, and not merely to possess their lands, their future will be safe.

A RELIGIOUS RELIC.

The embodiment by Handsome Lake of so many Hebraic ideas, gathered from Old Testament history, was not a new departure. Theories that the red men hold peculiar relations to the lost tribes of Israel are not peculiarly modern. The sacrifice called the "burned dog", no longer made, was, according to their faith, "sending back to the Great Spirit, as a pledge of their unwavering allegiance, the most faithful friend of the Indian on earth". It was killed without torture, taking away its earthly breath that it might have breathed into it a new life, and in the happy grounds of the blessed testify of the loyalty to the Great Spirit of its former master, who remained on earth.

In the autumn of the census year John Bembleton, an old soldier of the Grand Army, while looking over the plowed sides of one of the Tuscarora mounds (indicated on the map), discovered what the searchers from the Smithsonian Institution failed to find, a curious group of statuette figures cut from stone, much marked by age, and yet sufficiently suggestive of Abraham, Isaac, and the sheep to recall the theories of the red men's remote antecedents. Cushing, so long with the Zuñis, relates its history as far back as about 3,000 years. The Indians recognize it as in harmony with some of their traditions. The suggestion that it was of early Jesuit origin is not borne out by the marks, which indicate a patriarchal beard, and are equally inconsistent with its being of recent manufacture. The illustration is from a photograph taken while the mold still filled the crevices.

A SENECA MONUMENT TO WASHINGTON IN HEAVEN.

According to Indian tradition no white man enters the Indian heaven. As the Hebrews regarded Jehovah as exclusively their God, so the Indian regards the Great Spirit. After General Sullivan's invasion of the Iroquois country the Indians gave to Washington the name "Ha-no-da-ga-ne-ars", the "Town Destroyer". The Indians, as before intimated, were practically abandoned by the British when peace was made in 1783. The subsequent enlightened and humane treatment of this people by Washington was never forgotten. Their traditions respecting his state of being after death is thus stated by Morgan:

Just by the entrance of heaven is a walled inclosure, the ample grounds within which are laid out with avenues and shaded walks. Within is a spacious mansion, constructed in the fashion of a fort. Every object in nature which could please a cultivated taste had been gathered into this blooming eden to render it a delightful place for the immortal Washington. The faithful Indian, as he enters heaven, passes the inclosure. He sees and recognizes the illustrious inmate as he walks to and fro in quiet meditation. But no word ever passes his lips. Dressed in his uniform, and in a state of perfect felicity, he is destined to remain throughout eternity in the solitary enjoyment of the celestial residence prepared for him by the Great Spirit.

Handsome Lake, in his ecstatic relation of being visited by messengers from Washington, used to close his address thus:

Friends and relatives, it was by the influence of this great man that we are spared as a people and yet live. Had he not granted us his protection, where would we have been? Perished, all perished.

A RELIGIOUS RELIC—Ancient Tuscarora.

Dug up by JOHN BEMBLETON, 1890.

PART V·

INDUSTRIES OF THE SIX NATIONS INDIANS.

FARMING.

Farming is the chief employment of the Six Nations Indians, and the products are typical of the varying soils of the different reservations. While more land is under cultivation than heretofore, the barns are mainly old and in bad condition. This is largely true of similar buildings upon the adjoining farms of the white people, as farming has not of late netted an amount sufficient for repairs. The Indians, with no cash capital, as a rule, have been compelled to lease their lands to the white people for cash rent or work them on shares. The death of influential men, such as John Mountpleasant and Asa Thompson, of Tuscarora, left large estates under pecuniary burdens without ready money to develop the land. The general failure to maintain fencing has been partly due to crop failures and scant returns, but in a large degree to the improvidence of the farmers themselves. Such men as Daniel Printup and Isaac John, of Tuscarora; Moses Stevenson, Theodore Jimerson, Thomas Kennedy, and Andrew John, in his prime, of Cattaraugus; Edward M. Poodry and Warren Sky, of Tonawanda; William C. Hoag, of Allegany; Marsh Pierce, of Cornplanter, and Josiah Jacobs, of Onondaga, who work their lands and seldom rent them, and who maintain buildings and fences and take fair care of their implements, keep steadily on the advance. In nearly all directions valuable agricultural implements are exposed to the weather, and no economy attends farm work generally.

With the exception of Tuscarora, old orchards are on the decline, and more than one-half of the 4,823 apple trees of Cattaraugus are not in condition, through age and neglect, to bear large crops. A few new orchards have been started, but there is neither Indian labor attainable nor sufficient money realized from crops to hire other labor; neither is there any method by which tillable and arable land can be turned into money. With few exceptions, farming is done under wearing conditions, and many young men prefer to seek other employment.

The business of farming, except by a few of the Saint Regis Indians, is carried on only to the extent of barely securing crops for home use. A larger proportion of the Saint Regis than of any other Indians own at least 1 horse, and a cow is regarded as a necessity; hence, small crops of corn and oats are found quite general among those of small means; but this sort of farming does not improve the soil. Neglect of the few implements used and the wretched condition of the fences testify to a lack of ambition in agricultural labor.

For many years each reservation had its agricultural fair grounds with annual exhibitions, which stimulated both stock raising and farming, and handsome profits were realized. Premiums were awarded, and the state of New York contributed its part. Horse races, foot races, and games attracted large attendance, but their management fell into speculative hands, and, being distrusted, the best farmers ceased to compete for premiums and withdrew their support. All the grounds, except those of the Iroquois Agricultural Society, on the Cattaraugus reservation, have been converted to other uses. The annual fair held at Cattaraugus in 1890 was widely published, and the programme included not only games, races, and premiums, but a Grand Army reunion, at which several posts were to be present, and the attractions of dress parade, review, and sham battle were to mark two days of the entertainment. Colonel T. G. Parker, of Gowanda, a veteran of sterling merit, consented to preside over the military department, and actually pitched tents sufficient for a small battalion, but he left at the close of the first day. The attendance was small, even from the immediate neighborhood, the exhibition hardly more than several good farms could have furnished singly, and the receipts, a little more than $100, were insufficient to pay the incidental expenses of the enterprise. The result was that at the annual meeting for election of officers the old life members rallied their strength and made a clean sweep of the incumbents, electing as a new board the most efficient men on the reservation, with the declared purpose of governing the society, independent of speculators and local pools. The ability, responsibility, and influence of the new board, consisting of Moses Stevenson, Walleck Scott, Sylvester Lay, sr., Thomas Kennedy, William Kennedy, Chester C. Lay, Samuel Jimerson, Job King, T. F. Jimerson, Nathaniel Kennedy, John Lay, and N. H. Parker, will command the confidence of the people and of their white neighbors. The recognized decline of interest in county fairs elsewhere had its effect upon these reservation fairs; but they had become occasions for questionable games and ceased to command respect and support.

The value of farm implements and the crop statement afford a fair idea of the real farming done on the respective reservations. Steam thrashers, self-binding reapers, and the best adjuncts to hand labor have accumulated, but the tendency of late to lease lands has caused a suspension of the purchase of these implements. Specific details of the implements owned are found upon the special schedules. Much that is called farming is simply living off the small patches of land adjoining houses or cabins—a listless existence, with little ambition or means to do better. At the same time they erect their own buildings and do good work. The house of Jaris Pierce, at Onondaga, was built entirely by himself, and exhibits tasteful inside finish, furnishing, paper, and paint.

STOCK RAISING.

The contrast between this enumeration and those enumerations heretofore reported by Indian agents, by the Society of Friends, and by the New York state officials is especially noticeable in the matter of stock. Only 22 sheep are carried upon the schedules. Formerly many were raised in Tuscarora, Cattaraugus, and Allegany, and some on the other reservations. Each reservation having open boundaries on all sides, except where the better farmers build to the line, and pasture land being almost invariably unfenced, with the added fact that the public lands, as a rule, are open to an entire nation, there is such danger from dogs that the industry has been abandoned. Now and then one man, like Job King (Beaver), of Cattaraugus, a professional horse-jockey, keeps good stock for propagation as a business. He also raises "game" or "fighting cocks", but in this respect he stands alone, professionally. There are in all 11 stallions and 9 bulls upon the reservations, belonging to farmers who desire to raise their own stock for draught or other home purposes. E. M. Poodry, of Tonawanda, makes a specialty of "Chester white" swine, but mainly for his own use. With the exception of the fancy stock of Job King, the ordinary domestic fowls fall into every farm list as barnyard fowls for home use. This diversion of Indian farmers from stock raising accounts for the fact that very little butter is made for the general market, especially at Cattaraugus, in the vicinity of cheese factories. The large amount of green peas and sweet corn noticed on several schedules is accounted for by the existence of large "canning establishments" on the eastern border of the reservation.

BASKET MAKING.

Basket making is a success, and many of the old people are proficients in this work. The summer resorts of Niagara and Saratoga, as well as the state and county fairs of New York, afford a ready market for their wares. Besides the ash and hickory splint, corn husks are also used for baskets, salt bottles, and sieves. Among the old-fashioned people, partly from habit as well as for economy, the domestic industries of their ancestors are still practiced.

Basket making has recently risen to the most important place among the activities of the Saint Regis Indians. It occupies the time of one or more of nearly every family, and the schedules show that nearly one-sixth of the entire population have suddenly concentrated their energies upon this occupation. It guarantees a good support, with prompt pay, and the beauty, variety, and artistic combinations of the new designs prove the enterprise a success. The sales made during the census year by the Saint Regis Indians netted a little more than $55,000, or an average of $250 to each family, and nearly ten times as much as was realized from the sale of crops by the few farmers who made farming their regular business.

Already enterprising firms have seized upon this expanded basket industry, so that a single house at Auburn has extended its agencies throughout the United States. To the Indian a new field is opened, and this work becomes a legitimate, standard occupation, on as sound a basis as any other hand manufacture, and is stimulative of systematic industry. The introduction of the Diamond dyes and the obligation to follow patterns, instead of indifference as to similarity in the stock of any single invoice, develop the Indian where he is most deficient. It also cuts off his roaming, peddling habits, and secures for him not only home work but a home market. The subdivision of the labor, as witnessed in many families, also has its good effect.

The Tuscaroras near Niagara are especially skillful in bead work, but every reservation has its experts as well as its novices at this calling. Among the Saint Regis Indians 10 or 12 still engage in bead work, but the demand is very small and confined mainly to summer watering places. 27 sewing machines were in use. Berry picking and nutting employ many, especially women. Mr. William C. Hoag, of Allegany, gave employment during the census year to as many as 50 persons, who earned from $2 to $4 per day, realizing 1,000 bushels of blackberries alone during the season.

Sugar making, which formerly figured largely upon the annual reports of Indian agents, has disappeared with the maple trees, which were sold for wood. A small but young maple grove at Tonawanda, owned by Chauncey Abram, also one of 200 trees at Cattaraugus, owned by John Jimerson, several groves of small trees at Saint Regis, and a few hundred scattering trees are the only hints of this once profitable industry.

Rooting or herb gathering has almost disappeared. Dr. David Hewett (Kar-ner-to-nah-ner), of the Turtle tribe, at Tuscarora, and now 75 years of age, has had prolonged success as an Indian doctor, and Dwight Jimerson, of Allegany, devotes much time to collecting and drying the black cohosh and stone root for Buffalo druggists; but the days of the old "medicine man" have passed away. Young men from each of the reservations, including Chief Phillip T. Johnson, of Tuscarora, are "traveling men" for so-called Indian medicines, and make themselves welcome and successful through the prestige of their Indian character and good address.

Other young men, like Ed. Cornplanter, of Cattaraugus, have joined traveling shows as acrobats or minstrels, and others have played the part of musicians in theatrical orchestras or bands. These classes of industry, with their contact with the world and fair wages, draw enterprising men from home and largely reduce the percentage of intelligent labor.

TRAPPING, HUNTING, AND FISHING.

Trapping and hunting are almost unknown. A few Saint Regis Indians, as indicated upon the special schedules, act as professional guides to tourists, who make the vicinity of Saint Regis the base of visitation to the streams and forests of Canada.

Fishing still occupies a few families of the Saint Regis, at the mouth of the Raquette river. The only suits at law brought against these Indians were such as grew out of their resistance to the execution of the New York game laws. The Indians claim that their fishing rights under formal treaties can not be set aside by state statutes. As a matter of fact, the sawmills so fill the channel with sawdust that the number of game fish that can reach the vicinity of white settlers is absolutely insignificant. The few families that do fish catch suckers and mullets for the most part, and just about enough to supply the market demand of the reservation each spring; so that the imposition and execution of the law have neither necessity nor equity for their support.

The following, copied from the special schedule of John Jimerson's family, illustrates what one thorough farmer exhibited as his standing during the census year:

UNDER CULTIVATION.—A peach orchard of 90 acres, an apple orchard of 200 trees, 200 maple trees, and 1 acre of raspberries.

CROPS.—Oats, 300 bushels; wheat, 100 bushels; buckwheat, 20 bushels; beans, 40 bushels; corn, 100 bushels; turnips, 20 bushels; potatoes, 150 bushels; onions, 20 bushels; 250 cabbages, and 15 tons of hay.

STOCK.—3 horses and 1 colt, 8 cows, 4 heifers, 3 calves, 5 sheep, 29 swine, 2 hives of bees, and 150 domestic fowls.

IMPLEMENTS.—Self-binding reaper, mower, fanning mill, harrows, 2 large and 13 small cultivators, plows, horse hoe and corn sheller, hoes and hand potato diggers, lumber wagon, spring wagon, buggy, sled, sleigh, and cutter.

MECHANICAL TRADES, ETC.

Mechanical trades are followed by few and apprenticeships are rare. The Indians are unable to buy tools, and carpentry, smithing, and house painting are only engaged in sufficiently for local demand 2 carpenters, 1 blacksmith, 1 stonemason, and 3 "job workers" constituting the force of professional mechanics, and 2 doctors, 1 nurse, 1 teacher, and nearly 20 traveling showmen complete the occupations of the Saint Regis Indians.

Among the Six Nations Indians, while many are poor, there are but a few absolute paupers. 1 old man on the Tonawanda reservation, mentioned in the special schedules, is a wanderer from house to house, and 2 upon the Cattaraugus reservation, alike aged, depend upon transient charity. During the year 1890 the state agent at the Onondaga reservation furnished relief to several needy families upon the order of the chiefs from funds in his possession, collected for the nation as the rent of quarries placed in his custody. Overseers of the poor appointed by the Indians have general oversight of needy cases, and the general hospitality among these people rarely fails to meet every case with prompt relief. There are a few chronic loafers on each reservation, who hang around and live upon their neighbors at random, but the proportion of such cases is not greater than among white people. Sympathetic aid to the really needy is proverbial and exemplary.

PART VI.

SOCIAL LIFE, GAMES, AND AMUSEMENTS.

There is as much variety in the social life and manners of the Six Nations Indians as between the white people of different states or sections. Among the pagans the regular stated dances afford the chief occasions for "parties and suppers". The "maple dance", when the sap first flows in the spring, has lost much of its zest, as the sugar maple has almost disappeared. The "berry festival" (ha-nun-da-yo) celebrates the advent of the strawberry, "the first ripening fruit", and the berries, prepared in large bark trays and sweetened with maple sugar, attract old and young to the delicious repast and the general merrymaking at its close. When the whortleberry comes, "the first fruit of trees", a similarly jolly occasion is experienced. The green-corn festival (ah-oake-wa-o) honors the first standard product of tilling the soil. A previous "planting festival", where Indians had "spells" of helping each other, as they still do in chopping wood and raising houses and barns, brought many together, but "good things to eat" formed the chief attraction. There are 13 annual festivals; all of them, aside from exercises that are strictly "religious", abound in stories, wit, repartee, and badinage, characteristic of the Indian, who has a keen sense of humor, is ready with practical jokes, and quick to see the grotesque or ridiculous. Double meanings are quickly caught and played upon, and loud peals of laughter mingle with ceremony, feast, or sport. Even at annuity distributions and trials before the peacemakers a keen sense of humor involuntarily manifests itself. At the adjournment of an exciting divorce case at the Cattaraugus courthouse, when the Iroquois Agricultural Society was holding its fair in 1890, an invitation was sent to the court and attendants to "take dinner on the fair grounds at the expense of the society", which action was promptly denounced by Noah Twoguns, a quick-witted attorney, in the most solemn manner, while the whole arraignment of the society was but the introduction to an equally solemn motion, that the invitation be accepted on condition that it be changed to read "to take dinner on a table on the fair grounds". The incident is one of hundreds to show how watchful they are for fun. This comes partly from good nature and partly because it is not hard work, significant of the Indian's habit of making things easy and living for the present, whatever may betide the morrow.

The same spirit prevails among the christians, but as their religious observances follow different methods their social reunions are usually "surprise parties", although every year has its picnic, in which everybody joins. On one occasion nearly 100 persons, old and young, gathered, without warning to the host, well supplied with choice cake, cold meats, and accompaniments that would have been acceptable anywhere. Instrumental and vocal music, jokes, and merrymaking ran on until 4 o'clock in the morning without an incident to mar the occasion. At an Onondaga reception in Jacob Scanandoah's hall a brass band furnished music, and a bountiful modern supper followed. Christmas has its usual civilized observances, of which the Christmas tree is a grand spectacle. In 1890 the Presbyterian church at Cattaraugus had three large trees as high as the ceiling, loaded with presents, including photograph albums, books, sleds, handkerchiefs, shawls, neckties, and other useful articles, as well as bags of candy for each of the 300 or more who were present. Not the least suggestive series of articles successively "called off" were an immense pumpkin, a large squash, a turkey, a chicken, a bag of flour, and some smaller tokens for Mr. Renciman, their minister. During the whole distribution, introduced by spirited music, the witty comments of Porter Kennedy upon the articles taken from the trees and upon the characteristics or names of the recipients kept old and young alike in constant good humor. The victims of these witticisms laughed with the rest, and the whole occasion was suggestive of a way of approach to this people.

The nations differ in manifestations of this common social peculiarity. A large party at Thomas Kennedy's had both music and ordinary dancing, and with the musical training of the Thomas Orphan Asylum and the two brass and string bands on the reservation the social gatherings are more largely musical. At Tuscarora the large society connected with the Baptist church and the limited number of large parties mutually shape social life into a mere industrial form; but an annual picnic is observed by everybody, and public grounds, as represented on the map, are assigned for that purpose. Tonawanda, Allegany, and Onondaga have less of the social spirit, outside of the pagan dances, but the growth of sensible, social reunions is apparent. The accusation that these Indians indulge in vulgar stories is refuted by careful observation and the judgment of trustworthy writers upon Indian life and character. Indian vocabularies are especially deficient in the means of profaning the Great Spirit. Their manner of living has been degraded and at times beastly, but no worse than among the debased white people in well-known sections of the United States. No customs, practices, or "orgies" attributed to the pagan dances of the Six Nations are as low, sensual, and demoralizing as those which have from time to time been the accompaniment of some licensed entertainments in American cities.

THE NATIONAL GAME.

The favorite " national game " is " ball " (o-ta-da-jish-qua-age), of great antiquity, and the origin of the modern game of " lacrosse ". Pontiac's stratagem, by which his disguised warriors sent their ball inside the fort at Detroit to excuse an entrance, has given it memorial interest. Representatives of the four brother tribes or clans, the Wolf, Bear, Beaver, and Turtle, are matched against their cousins, the corresponding brothers, the Deer, Snipe, Heron, and Hawk. Victory falls to the credit of the nation represented instead of to the players. Two poles are set into each end of the grounds, at a distance of from 1 to 3 rods, and the contest is for competing parties of 5 or 7 to carry the ball through its own gate a designated number of times. 5 or 7 counts make a game, and 9 games are allowed if, after playing 8, the game be tied. The play begins in the center, and neither party is allowed to touch the ball with hand or foot. Managers are pledged to honorable umpire duty. Betting was systematically regulated formerly, and the friends of players were kept on opposite sides of the field to avoid possible collision during the wild shouts and demonstrations which followed victory. Suitable diet and training were then more systematically required, as in preparation for a foot race.

The game of javelin (gi-geh-da-ga-na-ga-o) is played by throwing a javelin of hickory or maple at a ring, either stationary or in motion, and is still a favorite spring and autumn game. Snow-snake (ga-wa-sa) is still popular, and consists in sending a long shaft of hickory, with a round head slightly turned up and pointed with lead, swiftly over the snow in an undulating course to the distance of 300 yards, and even a quarter of a mile. Archery continues in favor, and the " deer button " or " peach stone " is a fireside game for winter evening sport. It is a game of chance, with a pool to draw from, each person receiving 5 at first and playing until he loses. The shaking of the buttons, stones, or beans, which are marked and have different values, is on the principle of throwing dice, and hours are often taken to decide a game. Blindman's buff is another house game in high favor.

These qualifying social elements are a maturing counterpoise to the fading influence of the pagan dance, which is already taking on the shape of an innocent masquerade, stripped of immoral and offensive associations. At Newtown, the pagan settlement near the eastern line of Cattaraugus, where no white man's games were permitted, George Wilson has introduced a billiard table. He is a Grand Army man and sufficiently popular to secure its introduction, notwithstanding the prejudice against admitting any amusements not having the sanction of their fathers. All games are now public, without any attempt at secrecy or mystery, and decently conducted. With the Saint Regis Indians games are few, that of lacrosse being most prominent. Occasionally shows or public performances take place, and even attempts at stage performances have their turn ; but while this, which savors more of French than Indian precedent, is enjoyed, the people are deficient in the musical taste which distinguishes members of the other nations of the league, especially the Senecas.

PART VII.

MARRIAGE AND THE INDIAN HOME.

Statistics very inadequately convey exact ideas respecting marriage customs and family relations among the Indians of the Six Nations. Relating to Indian or pagan marriage, using the term "pagan" in the Indian sense, the Indian divorce, separation, or "putting away" has been a matter of choice, not necessarily mutual, but at the will of the dissatisfied party. The chiefs have sanctioned it and practiced it, as well as the people, and to a considerable extent still uphold the custom. The laws of New York forbid its exercise, but the extension to the peacemaker courts of the power to legalize separation and divorce is but feebly and often wrongly exercised. The discussion before the New York general assembly and the visitation and report by the legislative committee have already done much to consolidate the convictions of the educated men of the Six Nations that the election of able men as peacemakers has become vital to their prosperity, if not the only barrier to a sweeping interference by the white people with all internal Indian affairs. The tendency of congressional legislation to abolish all tribal relations, regardless of treaties as old as the republic, has added its influence to strengthen the progressive party among the Indians of New York.

The standing method of report by Indian agents has been to accept the Indian heads of Indian families as husband and wife and enumerate them as "married", and many western tribes have formal ceremonies of instituting this relation; but among the Six Nations of New York marriage, separation, and divorce have no ascertainable ceremony except as performed by ministers of the gospel or the Indian judges or peacemakers. The pagan party expressly regard marriage by a minister as treason to their system and absolutely wicked. Some of them do not hesitate to say that they "put away their wives" even as Moses directed a Hebrew separation. The schedules of enumeration of the New York Indians have so generally followed the Indians' own declaration, in the absence of any other detailed proof, that the tables must necessarily be qualified. Thus, at Onondaga, a list was furnished of more than 60 persons who sustained the relation of husband and wife without any ceremony whatever, and most of these had held the same relation to several parties without other law than choice for the change.

At Tonawanda the most careful inquiry of responsible Indians, who knew every family upon the reservation, revealed only, as a certainty, 26 legal marriages. At Allegany and Cattaraugus the question, " How many wives have you "? or " How many wives have you had "? was met with laughter or evasion, rendering an accurate record impossible. Divorces, unless a struggle for property be involved, are rare in the peacemaker courts. The records of the peacemaker courts were examined, and in one case a transcript was taken. Its process, the service, return, and trial compared very favorably with that of a country justice of the peace. One trial, where all the proceedings, including the part taken by the Indian counsel in the conduct of the case, was without legal error. At Tuscarora there is no pagan organization and only one family called pagan, and yet there were those of whom no evidence of legal divorce before entering upon a second marriage relation could be secured. That there are pagans who are thoroughly loyal to home ties is certain, but they will neither expose nor prosecute their derelict neighbors. The statutes of New York in this respect are practically inoperative, and those who openly deprecate the fact only make enemies.

As a matter of history, while a change of wife was permissible among the Iroquois, polygamy was forbidden. In case of family discord, it was the duty of the mothers of the couple, if possible, to secure peace. Marriage itself was a matter of arrangement and not of choice, and at an early period a simple ceremony, like the interchange of presents, consummated the agreement made between the parents. " Except at the season of councils or of religious festivals ", writes Morgan, " the sexes rarely met, and sociality in such cases was limited ". As the children always follow the tribe of the mother the nationality of offspring was never lost; hence it is, that on every reservation there are families wholly different in nationality from the family head. The children of an Indian woman having a white husband have rights, but the children of a white woman having an Indian husband have no rights. Either husband or wife controls his or her property at present, each independent of the other. The custody of the children is absolutely that of the mother, and upon her falls the burden of their support when deserted by the father. Neither the civilized nor canon law controls the degrees of consanguinity among the Iroquois, so that the Indians in giving their lists often reported nephews and nieces as sons and daughters. As the purpose of the Iroquois system was to merge the collateral in the lineal line through a strictly female course the sisters of the maternal grandmother were equally grandmothers, the mother and her sisters were equally mothers, and the children of a mother's sister were equally brothers and sisters. Thus, while under the civil law the degrees of relationship became lost through collaterals, the principle of the Iroquois system was to multiply the nearer family ties, and this shaped the basis both of their civil and political systems.

54

The establishment of christian churches among the Indians involved a christian marriage ceremony, but this had restraining force with the Indian only as he became a christian at heart and conscientiously canceled every obligation and margin of license that marked the old system. A backsliding or relapsing Indian at once threw off at will his marriage obligation as a void act; hence, Rev. Mr. Fancher, at Onondaga, kept no record of the marriages of Indians, reducing, unconsciously on his part, the marriage ceremony to a seeming farce. During the recent religious interest on the Cattaraugus reservation, the most difficult question to solve, when application was made for admission to the church, was how to dispose of successive family relations previously sustained to several parties still living. There is at present no peacemaker court among the Onondagas, and the chiefs practically recognize the pagan custom to be in force. This confused condition of affairs even led Bishop Huntington to marry two Indians who had long cohabited as husband and wife, but who had otherwise deported themselves correctly, without a rigid test of their previous relations to others; and now the eldest daughter of the male who had been once married by a clergyman to a wife still living is neighbor to the former husband of her father's present wife. The bishop was at a loss how to act in this case. The effect of this state of things is to paralyze christian effort and harden the Indian against every dawning sentiment that might win him to a purer and better life, and to instill into the minds of Indian youth the conviction that they are independent of all moral restraint and moral duty. It also exposes those who would modestly and honestly prefer the proprieties of civilized society to contamination by vampire white people, who hover about the borders of reservations to ruin a dependent people, in defiance of those sentiments of honor which the Iroquois, in the days of their proudest military achievements, rarely ignored, even when dealing with captives of their spear and bow.

The enumeration under the Eleventh Census and the enjoined inquiry into every phase of Indian life brings to the front the fact that, "to save the Indian, he must be saved from himself as well as saved from the aggressions of the white people".

THE INDIAN HOME.

Among the Indians the home has as many varied phases as among the white people. Comfort and want, cleanliness and dirt, good order and confusion, neatness and slovenliness furnish like contrasts. Neither extremes are more common than among white communities where a corresponding number of people are unable to read and write. On the maps which accompany this report every house, cabin, hovel, or shanty is noted, and the family schedules give the value of each dwelling and its household effects, ranging from totals of $25 to $2,500 and upward. The property tables in this report show a basis for comparing those of varied valuations with those of civilized society generally, showing that even the single-room cabin, with scant blanket screens or those not divided at all, are more common among immigrants at the extreme west than among these Indians.

A grouping of the special schedules of Cattaraugus presents the following suggestive exhibit, independent of the value of lands, crops, and implements:

Houses of value of $25 and less	26
Houses of value more than $25 and less than $100	130
Houses of value more than $100 and less than $300	110
Houses of value more than $300 and less than $500	47
Houses of value more than $500 and less than $1,000	41
Houses of value more than $1,000 and less than $2,000	11
Houses of value more than $2,000	4
Total	369

Household effects present a still more significant idea as to modes and styles of living:

Household effects in value $25 or less	59
Household effects in value more than $25 and less than $100	217
Household effects in value more than $100 and less than $300	80
Household effects in value more than $300 and less than $500	9
Household effects in value more than $500	4
Total	369

This ratio applies to the other reservations, with perhaps a better class of household effects at Tuscarora. The usual furnishing of the home consists of a second-hand stove, plain bedsteads, tables, utensils, crockery, home-made quilts, muslin curtains, a few cheap chairs or benches, and other absolute essentials. The comfort and appearance of the homes depend naturally upon the pecuniary resources, taste, education, and religious associations of the occupants, and a comparison of an equal number of homes of the same grade at Tuscarora with those of any other reservation would show to the credit of the former. It is no reflection upon the equally kind entertainers among the pagan party to say that, with rare exceptions, the home reflects the political (Indian or christian) character of its inmates. The rule already applied to neighborhoods and roads is as conclusive here; but the refined home of Mrs. Caroline Mountpleasant at Tuscarora affords no better example of home comfort than the

1-story 3-roomed house of Mary Bempleton, who attends as faithfully to her 150 chickens in the barnyard as she does to her household duties. In the smallest, poorest shanty of Tuscarora, with bed, stove, bench, some shelves for dishes, and suspended strings of corn all around, lives Eliza Green, caring for her grandson and the household needs. Here the broom, which the humble Indian housewife stands outside the door as a signal "not at home" for want of lock, is not wanting. On a small donation, the cheerful "thank you; I'll get nails with that to patch my roof", savored of domestic cheer to be remembered and honored.

This report exacts definite ideas of the Indian condition in all its phases, and the data of special schedules can only be illustrated by reference to some homes of all grades, the better class as well as the most repulsive. The houses of Thomas Kennedy and Chester Lay, of Cattaraugus, with modern comforts and the best of good home living, contrast with the quaint slab shanty of old Mary Jack, who is innocent of anything better; yet the two little windows let in light and the cabin is not absolutely filthy. In one cabin, somewhat larger than the one occupied by Mary Jack, on the bluff overlooking Cherry Hollow, and said to be the "poorest affair on all the reservation", a bedstead, stove, crockery, shelves, and a bench, which answered for seats or table, comprised the furniture. The bed was occupied by visitors, but on the bench, kicking their feet and playing together, were 5 Indian children, whose good shoes, neat clothing, and clean faces showed that somebody had carefully prepared them for this neighborly visit. The house of Bill Hill, in a ravine near the foot of Onondaga reservation, is one of the poorest; but it can, on the frontier at least, be called decent. The log house of genial, accommodating, witty Bill Isaacs, who lives in one room with his aged mother, and who was confirmed by Bishop Huntington on a recent Sabbath, furnished an interior view of very forbidding features, and yet it, in its wilderness of articles of clothing, corn, potatoes, flour sacks, and old traps of half a century's accumulation, is the abode of an affectionate son and a noble soul. Indian like, he takes things easy. He "agreed to light the schoolhouse fire for 3 cents a day, but didn't get it, and guessed he could stand it". Clapping his hands, with a merry twinke of his eye, he added: "I don't care much; I'll get paid some time" (pointing upward). He has a curious coat of many pieces and all conceivable colors, such as the "first Isaac's wife made for Joseph once". He is known as "Buffalo Bill", and "runs chores" for everybody, and the rector of the church of the Good Shepherd says: "I trust my house with Billy every time". Politically he "wants everybody to own his own land, to have the children made to go to school, to have chiefs account for public money, to stop their spending it on pagan dances and heathen 'tomfoolery', and for everybody to pick up and get citizenship as soon as they know enough; don't care how soon it comes—next week, if a good chance comes". Buffalo Bill, who is thus philosophical, and so good natured as to offend no one, has the courage of his convictions, knows the wants of his people, and daily sows good seed in a soil ready for immediate development.

Names are freely given in this report for the purpose of opening to any inquirer the same avenues of information which prompt its statements. Access to nearly a thousand homes, meeting with never-failing politeness, however inquisitive or intrusive the interrogation might seem, among those speaking several different languages, and surprised in every phase of home or farm life, with only now and then a warning of the visit, furnished evidence that the good-natured and simple welcome came from real kindness of heart. No apologies were made, as a general rule, for want of neatness or order, and, with the exception of one pig and occasionally a dog, no beast or fowl shared the home with the family. Old Eliza Parker, of Tonawanda, surrounded with a family of 9, including grandchildren, threatened a rough reception. The house was a type of aggravated disorder. Old shoes of many shapes and sizes, onions, potatoes, corn, and an indescribable collection of worthless things lay in the corners and under the tumbled beds. The old woman suspected there was a plot to get hold of her land, and she put a stake in the stove to make a firebrand for defense of her rights; but her face relaxed its fierceness at last, and her loud declamations, as well as wild gestures, subsided. With all the resultant disorder from want of closets, and with strings along the walls, instead of nails, to suspend everything that can be hung up, it is a very rare thing to find a place that can be called really filthy. There are such places, but continental life, as well as frontier life, has similar exhibitions to disgust a visitor. In such cases deferred washing of bedding, clothing, floors, and dishes is too suggestive for description to do justice to the abomination.

CLOTHING.

All the Six Nations Indians wear the same kind of clothing as the white people and "fix up" for church, festivals, picnics, and holidays, indulging especially in good boots and shoes. At the "green-corn dance", at Cold Spring, Allegany reservation, the majority of young men wore congress ties or gaiters. The head shawl is still common, but at more than 30 assemblies "store bonnets" or home-made imitations appeared. Sewing machines are much used.

The old women among the pagans still wear the beaded leggings, as the "pantalet" was worn by the white women and girls in New England some 50 years ago. Old Martha Hemlock and her husband Joseph, of Cattaraugus, are about 80 years of age, and are representatives of the oldest pagan type. The woman, notwithstanding her age, quickly finished a beautiful basket, hammered loose a sample bark from a soaked black-ash limb for another lot of splints, put up her corn-husk sieve, and afterward appeared in "full regalia", as if about to act a chief part in a "thanksgiving dance". A cape over her bright, clean, and stiffly starched calico dress bore closely uniting rows of silver brooches, 12 deep on the back. From the throat to the bottom hem in front similar silver brooches, mostly of eagles' heads, in pairs, widened out, until the bottom cross-row numbered 16. Each brooch, well hammered out and punched through in somewhat artistic openings, had been made long years ago from quarter and half dollar pieces and Canadian shillings, and was the representative of so much money, the cape being valued, with a front lapel, at $75. At Mary Wilson's, on the Tonawanda reservation, old Jo-geh-ho, a Canadian Cayuga woman, 83 years old, who "had danced her last green-corn dance", reluctantly, and as if with some misgivings as to duty, parted with a pair of leggings which she had used on solemn occasions "for nearly 60 years". The white beads, yellow from age, arranged in bands and loops, were still in good order, and the cloth, although threadbare from age and use, was neither ragged nor torn.

Sick were found in many households, but they seemed to take for granted that they could not be expected to have "things nice" about them, and the patient sufferers from consumption, wherever found, left no heart for criticism; nor are the sympathies of the Six Nations Indians often withheld or coldly manifested toward those in sorrow. During 8 months of daily contact with families and individuals, never forbidden access to house or council hall, church or school, not an occasion was found for considering dress as immodestly worn or too scantily provided. Poor and often ragged and soiled clothing is the consequence of their "bunched" family living, their small quarters, and their infrequent use of water; but their attitude, deportment, dress, surroundings, and internal accommodations, or want of accommodations, do not reflect the conditions which belong to the "hotbed of filth and vice", as some have imagined. This conviction is not impressed upon the mind by enthusiastic missionaries, who, in their sympathy, see the signs of a swift regeneration of the ignorant Indian, but by comparison with Indians of other tribes, with the lower orders of society in other countries, and by contact with white people in America.

THE PARLOR.

More than one-third of the small houses have but one room. And yet a log or "block house", as many are called, is not of necessity a mere cabin, nor rude within. Some are two stories, and some have frame additions or framed upper story. Daniel Printup, of Tuscarora, and Philip Fatty, of Allegany (a veteran of the Nineteenth Connecticut regiment, and sometimes an attorney for his people), have enlarged their log accommodations by framed additions, and in 30 two-storied houses, already erected or in progress, a special regard has been had for a company room, or parlor, which is often furnished with a carpet and sometimes with a musical instrument.

Among the Onondaga homes 10 organs and 1 piano were found, at Allegany the same number, and at Cattaraugus 10 organs and 1 melodeon; in all, 30 organs, 2 pianos, and 1 melodeon distributed among these Indian families. Elias Johnson, of Tuscarora, author of "Legends, traditions and laws of the Iroquois, or Six Nations, and history of the Tuscarora Indians", and several other heads of families have small but well-selected libraries, and many a parlor has its pictures and table albums. The Indian parlor is not a "spare room", rarely used, but more often borrows heat from the kitchen stove, and is a true parlor or place for talking when work is over.

THE KITCHEN.

The Indian is not an early riser nor an epicure. The antecedents of the hunting period, which involved one substantial meal each day and long absences from home, with only dried meat or parched corn for lunch, still hold their place with those of the poorer class. Scarcity of fuel largely restricts its use to the kitchen stove, as was the case not many years ago in New England, when meals were eaten where cooked, and the only other room having a fire was the familiar "family keeping room". With the poorer Indian families, and especially among the older pagans, cracked corn, skinned-corn hominy, corn bread, dried corn, succotash, beans, and squash are in common use. Old-time tea of wild spice or the sassafras root is now supplanted by the common tea and coffee. Pork is the principal meat, but chickens and eggs are plentiful. The old mortar, with its double-headed pounder, is still in use. The corn is first hulled by boiling in ashes and water, then pounded to a powder, strained through basket sieves, and boiled or baked with dried currants to give it flavor, and is both palatable and nutritious. Three kinds of corn are raised by the Senecas, the red, the white, and the white flint, ripening progressively, so that their graded growing corn has the appearance of careless instead of systematic planting. The red corn is esteemed most highly for hominy, the white for charring or roasting, and the white flint for flour. When stripped from the stalk the husks are braided and strung by twenties, and hung up for future use. "Strings of corn" are measured for about as many half bushels of shelled corn. Besides these primitive kinds of food, one finds choice varieties of cake, as well as simple gingerbread, in many households for festive occasions, though, for the pagan dance, boiled hominy and beans, sometimes with pork, supply the meal. A few shelves often take the place of a pantry, where the plates are stood on edge, as in earlier times among the white people. The kitchen is in many cases all there is of the house, often uninviting enough, but always more than half civilized in its appointments, and generally with a sufficiency of food; but, whether well or poorly supplied, hospitality is gracious and hearty.

The Saint Regis people are certainly poor, but there is little destitution or suffering. The aged are treated with respect, and national pride in their ancestry and history finds expression whenever interested inquiry is made in that direction. Tenacity of old treaty rights, however unsuited to their present relations with the surrounding white people, is characteristic of nearly everybody, as if neither time nor conditions had changed.

The French element binds the Saint Regis Indians closely to the observance of the christian forms and ceremonies, so that legal marriage, baptism of children, and burial of the dead are well recognized modes of procedure. The social life is informal, and the home life is quite regular, with an air of contented simplicity. All family obligations are well maintained, and the humble homes, the co-operative industry of the children, the rarity of separations, and the number of large households are in harmony.

Among the Saint Regis Indians a curious marriage custom exists, that of having 3 successive suppers or entertainments after the ceremony. The first is at the house of the bride, the second at the house of the bridegroom, and the third at the residence of some convenient friend of both. A procession, bearing utensils, provisions, and all the accessories of a social party, is one of the features. Another custom observed among the Saint Regis Indians bears resemblance to the " dead feast " among the pagans of the other nations, viz, that of night entertainments at the house of a deceased person until after the funeral, much like the " wake " which is almost universal among the white people in the vicinity of Hogansburg, and combines watching the dead body with both social entertainment and religious service.

The predominant thought during the enumeration of this people was that of one immense family, as, indeed, they consider themselves. This sentiment is strengthened by the fact that the invisible boundary which both separates and unites 1,170 American and 1,180 Canadian Saint Regis Indians is practically a bond of sympathy, multiplying the social amenities or visits, and cheering their otherwise lonely and isolated lives. The river Indians also contribute their share in these interchanges of visits.

The large diffusion of French blood and the equally universal relationship of most of the representative men and families to the Tarbells, Cooks, Gareaus, Torrances, Grays, and Birons (Beros) blend the families more closely than upon any other reservation, not excepting even that of Cornplanter, where all directly inherit from one family head.

ANDREW JOHN, Jr. (Gar-stea-ode), "Standing Rock."
Seneca.

Rev. HENRY SILVERHEELS AND WIFE,
Ex-Chief and Ex-President of the Seneca Nation.

AUNT DINAH, 107 years old.
Onondaga.

PART VIII.

TEMPERANCE AND MORALS.

TEMPERANCE.

A temperance society has been in active operation for 60 years, and its annual meeting was held on the Onondaga reservation during 1890. A special car brought the Seneca delegates from Cattaraugus at reduced rates, accompanied by one of the Indian bands, but the attendance from the other reservations was unusually small. Speeches, music, and the usual incidents on such occasions had place in the exercises.

The Tuscaroras and Onondagas have comfortable audience rooms, that of the latter, at Onondaga Castle, being known as "Temperance Hall", and is occupied by Ko-ni-shi-o-ni lodge No. 77, I. O. G. T.; motto, "Our world".

No stranger on a casual visit to the Six Nations could avoid the conviction that the white men and women who skirt the reservations, wherever a convenient crossroad will assure the easy temptation for the Indian to drink himself drunk, are more deadly enemies of the red man than are all the pagan rites and dances on their most ancient calendar. Old Allen Mohawk, who has suffered himself in earlier times, but now, with agony and tears, pleads in behalf of his sons for some rescue from the power of these cold-blooded destroyers of Indian homes, is only one of hundreds who cry for help. No poverty, untidiness, or want of civilized comforts was so piteous as the silent appeals of this people for deliverance, and there is an actual, persistent claim that only through outside legislation can saving relief come.

During the census year 3 fatal accidents on the railroad track near Tuscarora, 1 at Tonawanda, and 1 on the Allegany reservation were the result of this remorseless traffic of the white people. The village of Carrollton, on the last-named reservation, is a "drunkard-manufacturing center", with but little to illustrate civilization in the other lines of business. Nearly 50 saloons or their equivalents at Salamanca make it almost a "banner town" for its ratio of saloon facilities to each hundred inhabitants. Almost daily interviews for nearly 2 months with the 2 policemen failed to elicit any definite information as to the parties who sold strong drink to the Indians. Verbal requests and written inquiries equally failed to elicit from Hudson Ansley, the official state attorney of the Seneca nation, any reply as to "offenses committed by or against Indians, or the number of whisky sellers prosecuted", or any facts whatever. The otherwise business aspect of this important railroad center is conspicuously marred by the prevalence of this traffic. A combination in 1890 levied even upon druggists a tax to limit the sale of whisky within the corporation bounds, but the druggists might have added dignity to their calling and character to the town by obligating themselves, under penalty of exposure and punishment, not to sell to Indians at all. The suggestion was favored by some but not by the majority, although suspension of such sales to Indians would not have materially affected the receipts of these places.

The sweeping denunciation of the Allegany Indians as a nation of drunkards is slanderous. In proportion to numbers the visible signs are not greatly to their discredit.

There are intelligent Indians who know the habits and tendencies of every other Indian on the reservation, Mrs. Blinkey, clerk of the Indian Baptist church, explained the backsliding of 5 church members to flow from the drinking habit, and others equally interested to give honest testimony, specifically went over the entire list of Indian names and defined the peculiarities of each in this respect. As compared with white people who daily exhibit this habit before the public the Indians, who habitually drink to excess when they visit the town, are not many in number. One argument in favor of giving citizenship to the Indian was repeatedly and seriously urged, that then "he could come boldly to the counter and get his drink under legal sanction". The Indian rarely betrays his entertainer. Ingenious ruses, in form of package or hiding place for exchanging money for a bottle of spirits, often obscure the transaction. Public sentiment is pained by the presence of drunken Indians, but public sentiment, aroused at last, has not fully concluded that the religious, educational, and social atmosphere is polluted by the large liberty which the liquor traffic now enjoys. The corporation of Salamanca can stop this wrong to its Indian landlord if it wishes to do so. It is cruel, degrading, and inexcusable not to do so. There is law enough as well as occasion, when the people are ready. The best property owners and business men, who know that a great development is within their immediate reach, have commenced the work for the sake of both Indians and white people alike; but the apple-growing counties in apple years will brook no legislation against the cider traffic, neither will they permit the product of their mills to occupy its natural level with the product of the still.

On every reservation the demand is made, "Give us some protecting law"! Even the hiring of Indian labor is coupled with a partial equivalent in cider pay. Mr. Poodry, of Tonawanda, thus illustrates his own experience: "We have hard work to hire sometimes, unless we give them liquor. One year plenty of men passed my house, but wouldn't hire. I got mad. Next year I put 6 barrels of hard cider in my house cellar, putting in enough strong whisky to keep it on edge, and when some men came along I got them. One day 2 lay drunk the whole afternoon. That did not pay. Then the children got hold of it. I couldn't stand that, and have bought none since".

Irregular habits and employment on the farm or other labor expose the Indian to easy temptation, and the border dealers, who wholly depend upon Indian patronage for their own support, not only quickly absorb the pittance annuities, but as promptly secure written orders, practical liens, upon the amounts due a year in advance.

The United States Indian agents have for 25 years made annual reports upon this destructive use of hard cider, but these statements of the agents seem to be taken as innocently as if they only said "the Indian is addicted to basket making", and no action follows by the authorities. Not the least evil that results from the inability of state legislation to reach this wrong is the reaction against active temperance movements which had matured, greatly to the credit of the Indian, and were full of hope for the future.

On February 19, 1830, a temperance society was formed at Tuscarora, and had as its chief founders the late William and John Mountpleasant, men of wisdom, piety, patriotism, and progress. On March 1, 1832, a general temperance society was formed at Cattaraugus. On the 27th of January, 1833, the Tuscarora society was reorganized. Almost immediately afterward the National or United Temperance Society added the following article to its constitution, viz: "In the temperance assemblies the following subjects are to be lectured upon: temperance, industry, education, and moral reform". A temperance cornet band was organized, and at a grand reunion on the 19th of October, 1876, 4 consolidated bands, with 50 instruments, rendered music, and the entire assembly sang, in the Indian language, "O, for a thousand tongues to sing my dear Redeemer's praise". The society also took on a new name, "The Six Nations Temperance Society of the United States and Canada", which it still retains. Waves of blessing swept over the people of the Six Nations as this organization developed. Some of those who figured actively then have fallen back to paganism and some have renewed old habits, but the organization still survives.

Oppressed by assaults from without, and in the family relation and religious experience divided and confused as to duty, there abides among this people a passive sense of helpless isolation and a longing for guidance and support, with a distrustfulness of the white people, while impotent to protect themselves.

MORALS.

The statistics which only concern vice and immorality in a sensual sense are not conclusive tests of Indian life and character; neither can public opinion be accepted as a rule if the morals of the people of the Six Nations are to be solely judged by the difference between their marriage custom and that of the surrounding white people. The first official census of the Six Nations can not be shaped by previously conceived notions as to their morals, but must develop its own facts as gathered directly from Indian homes, thus supplying an independent basis of judgment.

The history of the Six Nations is not that of a licentious people, for while the natural pursuits of war and the chase produced strong and athletic men, who looked with contempt upon the labor of tilling the soil, it is not true that the idle intervals spent in their villages or homes were given up to sensual pleasure. This has been the testimony of the most reliable writers upon the life of the native American from the days of the first narrative of Captain John Smith to the present time. Even the young people of neighboring cabins in those days were not social in a society sense. Morgan has already been cited to show that even at their public dances the ceremonies, which were formal, were not immoral. Two historic facts have direct bearing upon the question: first that no race on the earth was more jealous of outside infringement upon the rights of the family circle than some tribes of the red man. His exercise of authority at home might be harsh and the exacted service might be severe, but violators of that home could expect no mercy; second, that the hard physical service of the women, coupled with a hereditary recognized responsibility for the transmission of the pure blood of their mothers to future generations, left neither time nor inclination for dalliance with impure surroundings. As a result of these two related facts, it can be truthfully asserted that until the advent of the white man and his appliances of spirits and money, a prostitute woman, in the modern sense of that term, was as greatly abhorred by the Seneca Indians as a cowardly man; even more so, for the coward was turned over to the women to share their drudgery, but an erring woman was held to have sacrificed the glory of her maternity and dishonored her people.

These facts had their bearing upon the development of the Six Nations when they began their companionship with the white people. The machinery of their social and political systems, as heretofore developed, had special regard for the purity of their line of descent and the limitation of all alliances which could deteriorate the stock or impair the legitimate succession. Coupled with these fundamental laws of their social and political life is another fact, that while a conquering band might adopt prisoners, the laws of the Iroquois were opposed to personal slavery, and even the penalty of defeat in resisting an invading force was not the surrender of the female prisoners to the victor's lust. The more thoroughly the history of such alleged practices is examined the more vague becomes the evidence of their use.

It is as impossible to reach the Indian with a view to his deliverance from the immoral tendencies of his present mode of living, without regard to his antecedents before admixture with the white people, as to approach him religiously, while treating him as wholly without reverence or conscience. Through every phase of his life, as already illustrated, he is shown to possess qualities which have sterling social value and strong bearing upward instead of downward in the social scale; hence, in increasing numbers, in longevity, and in gradual acquisition of property he is holding his own with his neighbors in proportion to his advantages.

Something more than statistics should be noticed. In the light of existing surroundings, compelled to associate with white people, and under obligations to advance with them in harmony with the governing laws, moral, social, and political, the Indian has neither right nor power to hold back. His ancestral codes no longer apply to his present condition. A tribe or race has ceased to be the unit of value. That unit is the individual man, the individual woman, the individual child. Wampum associations must be exchanged for written law, and irresponsible chiefs must be held to strict account under intelligent codes, voluntarily adopted, under the sanction of the state, or by the interposition of the state in behalf of the people, who have no power to protect themselves.

Lingering pagan customs, which, no longer having a specific reason for their existence, repress aspiration, confuse all social relations, demoralize youth, antagonize the spirit of the age, outrage the public sentiment of those who would be their friends, do not stand as rights on the level with the right of soil, to be exercised in the face of the evils they engender. The perpetual guarantee by the United States and the state of New York of their titles to the land they rightfully own never can be held to be a guarantee that the social and political customs of the sixteenth century shall be assured at the close of the nineteenth century.

Inquiry was diligently made respecting the number of recognized immoral characters living on the respective reservations. These inquiries were made with the population list in mind, and always of different persons. There was almost an invariable concurrence of testimony, specifying how many and who openly violated the laws of chastity. The largest estimate for any reservation was less than 20; at some reservations not even 6 could be named. The latest divorce suit tried before the peacemaker court at Cattaraugus witnessed a bold and earnest assertion of the plaintiff's rights, warmly supported by the people, which rang out as if new life and courage had possessed the friends of reform. The inferior and sometimes corrupt men who have almost invariably held judicial positions long kept in the background many who desired justice. 9 marriages at Cattaraugus and 6 at Tonawanda during the census year, with additions to the churches only after rigid examination into the antecedents of the parties, have done much to quicken the progressive party and evoke an outspoken challenge of the pagan party to a final contest for deliverance from the existing evil. The moral tone is low, but residence in the small cabin, or even in the single-room cabin, elsewhere sufficiently described, is not the prime source of the evil. It is when different families come into improper associations, as in crowded tenement houses, that all natural restraint is lost; and the people of the Six Nations, with all their unhappy surroundings and poverty in this matter, have suffered opprobrium beyond their true desert in the judgment of christian America.

At the Onondaga reservation, where there is no semblance of a court and no regular method of approach to any organized and certain source of relief, the moral plane is below that of the other reservations. The condition is deplorable; jealousies, local antagonisms, and the rapidly ripening struggle for an advance, even here, lead both parties into much injustice, and the statements of neither were accepted as fully reliable; but the sweeping charges so often promulgated have neither truth nor christian grace to qualify the wrong they do.

The New York Indians are not, as are many western Indians, a decided gambling people, nor more given to betting on games than the white people. Debased by early associations with white people, without the restraints of education or religion, they are an example of a demoralization from without rather than from natural causes within. A day among them and their immediate surroundings, a Sabbath day in August, 1890, presented facts bearing upon this statement. The Indian Presbyterian church at Tonawanda, adjoining Akron, had a morning service and Sabbath school, the exercises in all respects befitting the day and occasion; while nearly a mile westward, at the new council house, 65 young men of the pagan party were playing the javelin game and getting ready for an evening pagan ceremony. Near the house of George Moses, southward, about 20 pagan women were boiling supper for the coming entertainment. Still farther south, in view from the front steps of 2 christian churches, about 130 white men and boys were racing horses on a regular track, or looking on, and the barrooms of the village were open, but the Indians were present at neither. These pagan sports were taking place between the Indian's and the white man's center of christian effort. The object lesson is a statistical fact bearing upon the condition of the Six Nations during the census year.

TEMPERANCE AND MORALS AMONG THE SAINT REGIS INDIANS.

With the Saint Regis Indians quarrels are rare. When once disarmed of suspicion their hospitality is generous for their means, and rudeness or discourtesy has no natural place in their intercourse with visitors and strangers.

Ignorance is the key to much of their passivity, and the safeguards which religious forms have placed about their homes lack intelligent application to their outside relations through the unfortunate failure to combine with religious teachings and observances instruction in any other language than their own. This will be noticed elsewhere. Their social life and their homes must have intelligent communication with the outside world before they can aspire to a higher life.

The temptation to use spirits, which easily masters the unoccupied classes of any community, has had its effect here as on the other reservations, and, aside from the church influence, there is little formal effort at temperance work. Intemperance is not general, but, as at Cattaraugus, it is often found among the men who have the greatest capacity for good, and these intemperate leaders stand in the way of the immediate start of their people toward a strong life.

Immorality among the Saint Regis Indians, other than intemperance, is also rare. The statistics of the family relation show that constitutional diseases have not destroyed their vigor, nor have they become debased through immoral practices. However humble the home, it commends its home loyalty and home increase to the respectful consideration of the native-born white citizens of the United States. The Saint Regis people, like the other Iroquois people, have noble blood in their veins and are better qualified for useful citizenship than several of the white races which seek America for a change of living. There are men upon each reservation who honor and illustrate the virtues and capacities of true manhood, and women who are conspicuous for their domestic life, purity of character, and christian grace.

PART IX.

EDUCATION, SCHOOLS, AND LANGUAGE.

EDUCATION.

The pagan element, as a general rule, is opposed to education, because only through ignorance can the force of old traditions and tribal independence be retained. Exceptions are sometimes found to this opposition, as in the case of an old man at Allegany, who said: "They wouldn't let me go to school when a boy. Now I see how I missed it". Jackson Gordon (Snipe) also said: "There is no school near us, but 20 pupils could be had for a school when we want it". Another, at Tonawanda, who had to employ an interpreter to sell his hay, said: "They used to tell us that the devil would roast us in a red-hot kettle if we went to school. Now, every time I am bothered to do business with white folks I wish the devil had roasted them".

Families with small means, unwilling to make any effort to change their condition, claim that they need their children for home work. Even when they enter them at the beginning of the term they do not enforce their attendance. The children themselves, to a large extent, inherit careless, sluggish, indolent natures, and a lazy spirit, which forms a decided element in Indian life. Punctuality is confessedly "not Indian". There is no remedy for the existing apathy and opposition but the compulsion of law through some methods not yet realized. Indian children do not lack capacity or reasonable industry when they are held by systematic constraint to their work.

In some respects their capacities are above the average standard of the white people. They are more uniformly good penmen, good musicians, and excel in drawing; but the statements of the Indians themselves as to reading, writing, and speaking the English language magnify the facts. Their reading, as a general rule, goes little beyond the slow mechanical utterances of fixed lessons. Letters are merely objects easily memorized and related to each other in their fixed order, but the thought involved is rarely recognized. There are bright exceptions in all the schools, as well as among adults; but the ability to read ordinary books and papers is an aftergrowth. Writing, to many, is even more difficult than reading, but their mechanical copying, for which they have a natural faculty, will compare favorably with that of the best schools of the same grade in any state, girls and women doing better in this respect than boys and men. In several families the educated women have the care of their husbands' books and correspondence, and their social temperaments lead to letter writing, as among the white people. Thus, Mrs. Abbie Parker, of Cattaraugus, conducts a successful school at Cornplanter, across the Pennsylvania line, which is attended by 9 white boys and 3 white girls, and her letters are examples of good composition, and their tone is that of a faithful, earnest, christian worker. She has a good normal-school training, to which at least 20 of the Seneca girls now aspire. Mrs. Hattie Spring (Heron), wife of Hanover Spring (Wolf), also a normal-school graduate, speaks and writes with purity of diction and expression, has refined manners, grace and dignity, and a personal carriage which would not discredit the best society. Mrs. Hattie E. Poodry, a retired teacher, who also taught freedmen in the south, Mrs. Spring, and Elizabeth Scanandoah, the afternoon teacher at the Onondaga state school, all had the benefit of normal-school training at Albany. Discrimination against advanced education for the reservation or elsewhere is poor economy and wholly unsound in principle.

In contrast with these cases is the fact that very few of the men who can conduct ordinary conversation in fair English can clothe the same ideas with correctly written forms. Their court records, books, and correspondence, with the exception of those portions of the records of the Seneca nation kept by Sylvester Crouse, the clerk, are generally full of errors. A fairly written constitution, elsewhere cited, was revised by a citizen lawyer. " I do it if you want me do it" illustrates one form of a common statement, and the simplest connection of subject and predicate is the most common. This is partly because their own language is limited, and only careful training can secure good results. Edward M. Poodry thus illustrates this idea: " The Seneca language can not carry what the English can ". Taking from his parlor table the Buffalo Courier, he read the following sentence: " The diplomatic correspondence concerning the Bering strait embroglio does not seem to relieve the situation from embarrassment", adding, "You can not translate that into Seneca. There is no mental preparation or material out of which to explain the matter ".

The Indian mind, which is quick to catch practical relations and natural correspondences or associations, lacks the mental discipline and the mental qualities which grasp pure logic. Their language seems to lack the stock from which to frame a compact and harmonious postulate. This accounts for the unusual backwardness of their children in pure mathematics. Mr. Poodry also has a suggestion upon this matter. He says: " Our people, especially our old men, have no conception of numbers any farther than hundreds. When you get to thousands it is always a box or so many boxes, because in old times the annuities were paid in gold, the amount, $1,000, being so marked on the box ".

The deportment of Indian children in the schoolroom is exemplary. Those who attend are well dressed and well behaved. At fully 20 schools visited there was no whispering or side play when the teacher's attention was diverted. Obedience is willing and prompt; but tardiness and irregular attendance, as elsewhere intimated, seem to be instinctive, as punctuality at church or other definite appointments proves to be a missing factor in their life. The success of the Friends' school, of the Thomas Orphan Asylum, and of normal-school training in the education of the Indian lies in the enforced system and routine of duty which exact punctuality and accept no compromise; hence, the restriction of the school to rudimental grades has a radical defect, and ends almost at the threshold of real education. They return home after mere primary training and at the very point where the more intelligent can catch glimpses beyond their reach of opportunities for teaching or some other profitable calling in life through educational development. Once at home they drop into the old ruts, utterly unable to put their primary training to practical use. For this and related reasons the failure to convert the unfortunate manual labor and farming school into a mechanical or high school form was a double disaster. Even now the revival of the enterprise, so well initiated and with property and buildings susceptible of immediate use, would send a current of vitalizing force throughout the Six Nations and arouse anew those aspirations for education which have fallen off during late years because of poverty and want of systematized hearty support from the state of New York or the Congress of the United States.

SPECIFIC SCHOOLS.

The New York schools upon the 5 reservations are as follows, viz: 1 at Onondaga, employing a male teacher in the morning and an Indian female teacher in the afternoon; 3 at Tonawanda, employing 1 male and 2 female teachers; 6 at Allegany (a seventh building being abandoned), employing 2 male and 4 female teachers; 10 at Cattaraugus, although numbered to 11 (the Thomas Orphan Asylum school practically counted as number 4), with 2 male and 8 female teachers, and 2 at Tuscarora, one being taught by Miss Emily M. Chew, a native Tuscarora woman of good education, winning address, and admirable tact both for teaching and government.

With the single exception of the dilapidated, unattractive, unwholesome "mission boarding-school building" at Tuscarora, long ago unfit for school use, all the state buildings are well lighted, ventilated, and attractive. In this building, against all adverse conditions, Miss Chew makes the best of her discouraging surroundings, and holds her pupils fairly well by her magnetic force. Prevalence of the measles kept an unusual number at home the past year, and the interest of educated and christian parents seems to be lessened by the failure of the state to build a new schoolhouse. The Tuscarora nation has repeatedly declared a readiness to share in the expense of such an enterprise.

The old dormitory of the former boarding school is partly woodhouse and partly barn. In one wing Miss Abigail Peck, the veteran former teacher and missionary, resides, and at the age of 80 retains a fresh memory of her earnest work, which began in 1853. The original school was organized as early as 1808 as a mission school, in charge of Rev. Mr. Holmes, the first missionary to the Tuscaroras. In 1858 the American board of foreign missions transferred the school to the state of New York.

The second school at Tuscarora is taught by Miss Alla Sage, daughter of Mr. William Sage, who devoted many years to teaching and promoting the welfare of this people, and he and his family have been among the most patriotic and self-sacrificing pioneers of Niagara county. This teacher, as well as Miss Chew, is compelled to endure another discrimination against the teachers of Indian schools in receiving only $7 instead of $8 per week. There are special difficulties in teaching Indian youths. The conditions require patience, tact, and endurance beyond that required for pupils who can at least understand the spoken English language and promptly associate the words with familiar objects or thoughts.

SCHOOL DETAILS.

The Onondaga school, first in order, is taken as an illustration of the difficulties and embarrassments attending the teacher's work. The building, erected by the state of New York at a cost of $500, is especially attractive and well located. A glance at the map will show that a great majority of the families live within a mile's distance. Rev. John Scott teaches in the morning and Miss Elizabeth Scanandoah, an Indian, teaches in the afternoon. At the fall term, 1889, the school opened with 12 scholars. The daily attendance during the 5 days of the first week was, respectively, 12, 19, 28, 21, 19, a total of 99. The totals for the succeeding 8 weeks were, respectively, 145, 132, 127, 159, 129, 81, 172, 177, the last being during the week before Christmas. Average daily attendance for first week was 19.8; for the succeeding 8 weeks as follows, viz: 29, 26.4, 25.4, 31.8, 25.8, 16.2, 34.5, 35.4. The total number entered on the register during that period was 64. At the winter term only 45 pupils were registered, the attendance being, by weeks, 61, 84, 68, 75, 91, 112, 89, 113, 80, 130. At the spring term 50 registered, the attendance being, by the week, 89, 130, 123, 103, 62, 88, 123, 90, 108. The highest attendance on any one day during the year was 32, on the 10th of April, 1890. Only 12 attended every day, even during the Christmas week, and one of these worthy of mention was Julia Hill, aged 13, daughter of Daniel Hill, who missed but one day in the term. 9 other pupils attended 40 or more days, and 26 were quite regular, securing more than a month of fairly conservative instruction. The correspondingly fair attendance for the winter term was 18 and for the spring term 14. 2 boys were above the age of 18. Of the others registered, 32 were males and 30 females, between the ages of 6 and 18, the average age being 10.66 years.

Those who lived farthest away were frequently the most punctual in attendance. One scholar, who came from far up Lafayette creek, the home of Abram Hill, a venerable Oneida chief and a christian man, lost but one day during the month of December; the highest average of the year, however, was attained during this month. These details indicate that in this school and in other schools there are thoroughly faithful, ambitious, wide-awake, cleanly, well-dressed pupils, seemingly both happy and proud in showing their acquirements before strangers. They are neither bashful nor bold, but self-possessed, obedient, and willing. If the number of similar pupils could be doubled at Onondaga it would revolutionize as many households for the better.

The tabulation of the following data is impracticable owing to the variety of the information obtained:

TONAWANDA SCHOOLS.

SCHOOL No. 1, frame building, cost $287; total annual salaries of teacher and employés, $252; all other expenses, $45; Indian contribution for fires, $10; accommodations for 35 scholars; largest attendance at a single session, 24; 9 males and 16 females attended 1 month or more; 8 males and 15 females are between 6 and 18 years of age; 1 male and 1 female are under 6 years of age; average age of pupils, 10 years; average daily attendance during the year, 9; largest average for a month, 18, in June, 1890. Illness of the teacher and a temporary supply scattered the children. The school is on the north and south road leading to the manual farm building.

SCHOOL No. 2, frame building, similar to No. 1 in cost, equipment, salaries, accommodations, and expenses; largest attendance at a single session, 29; 27 males and 12 females attended 1 month or more; 24 males and 12 females are between the ages of 6 and 18; 1 male is over 18 and 2 girls are under 6 years of age; number of months of school, 9; average age of pupils, 11 years; average attendance during the year, 15; largest average attendance for a month, 21.6, in June, 1890. It is a model school, admirably conducted, situated on the central triangle, where the Baptist and Methodist churches are located.

SCHOOL No. 3, frame building, similar to No. 1 in cost, salaries, etc.; largest number present during the year, 28; 23 males and 19 females attended 1 month or more; 1 girl under 6 years of age; average age of pupils, 10 years and 8 months; school maintained for 9 months, with an average daily attendance of 10, the average during September being 12.75, the highest for the school year. Mr. Charles Parker, the teacher, exhibited marked enthusiasm in his work, as well as pride in the progress of his pupils. The school is on the north crossroad.

ALLEGANY SCHOOLS.

The 6 schools upon the Allegany reservation are similar, each costing the state $322.33. Indian contributions for fires, $6.25; salaries, $276.50; all other expenses, $52.08; repairs during the year, $26.22 for each school building.

SCHOOL No. 1, which had 2 lady teachers during the year, is at the fork of the road, west of the Allegany river, nearly opposite the old mission house, in a pagan district; estimated accommodations for 50; largest number present during the year, including some white children, 23; 4 males and 2 females attended 1 month or more during the year; 1 male under 6 years of age, 3 males and 2 females between 6 and 18 years of age; average age of pupils, 11.33 years; average attendance during the year, 4; largest average attendance any month, 5, in October, 1890. Edmond Bone, jr., the grandson of William Bone, who claims to be the only living Seneca of full blood, missed school only 22 times during the year.

SCHOOL No. 2 has accommodations for 50; largest number present, 26; 18 males and 12 females attended 1 month or more during the year; 2 of the females were under the age of 6 years; average age of pupils, 10 years; average attendance during the year, 9.5; largest attendance any month, 16, in May, 1890.

SCHOOL No. 3 has accommodations for 50; largest number present during the year, 40; 4 males and 9 females, all between the ages of 6 and 18, attended 1 month or more during the year; average age, 10.33 years; average attendance, 13.66; largest average attendance any month, 15, in December. Cornelius Fatty, son of George Fatty, was absent only 11 days in the year.

SCHOOL No. 4 has accommodations for 45; largest number present during the year, 21; 16 males and 10 females attended 1 month or more; 2 females under 6 years of age; average age, 9.5 years; average attendance during the year, 13.5, in December, 1889. John Plummer, son of Nathaniel Plummer (Deer tribe), attended school every day, viz, 172 days during the year, and during 22 terms, or 7.33 years, missed school but 1 day when well (and that at the request of his father) and 3 weeks when sick. Special schedule 60 (Allegany) is that of the family of Stephen John, of the Plover clan, and a school trustee. His 3 children attended 156, 157, and 158 out of a possible 172 days. The school is near the Presbyterian church.

SCHOOL No. 5 abandoned.

SCHOOL No. 6 has accommodations for 50; largest number present, 23; 13 males and 11 females attended 1 month or more; 3 males and 4 females under the age of 6; 10 males and 7 females between 6 and 18 years of age; average age, 8 years; average attendance, 13; largest average attendance during any month, 14.5, for the month of June, 1890. This is the school at Carrollton, a strong pagan district; but Howard Redeye, age 11, son of Sackett Redeye (Plover), attended school 163 out of a possible 166 days, and 2 other pagan children attended 159 and 160 days, respectively.

SCHOOL No. 7 has accommodations for 45; located near Quaker bridge and Friends' schoolhouse; largest number present during the year, 27; 12 males and 10 females attended 1 month or more during the year; 3 males and 2 females under the age of 6; 9 males and 2 females between 6 and 18 years of age; average age of pupils, 9 years; average attendance during the year, 8; largest attendance during 1 month, 10, in October, 1889.

CATTARAUGUS SCHOOLS.

The 10 schools upon the Cattaraugus reservation are similar in design, cost, and accessories to those of Allegany, and with the same superintendent, Mr. Joseph E. Hazzard, of Randolph, Cattaraugus county. He writes frankly that he "can not secure competent teachers at the rates authorized". The result has been that young and immature persons from his own neighborhood have undertaken this work, some of them as their initial training in the school-teacher's profession. The best educated parents complain. The attendance fell off at the fall term, 1890, and the work of training the Indian youth is not wisely and smoothly developed. The new teacher at Newtown, the most populous pagan center, is experienced, and will succeed. In every instance the compensation is inadequate. An examination which will admit a young man or a young woman to the privilege of teaching a primary school of white children, unaccompanied by tact, experience, and interest in this special work, is not the true credential to success. Something more than a certificate is both necessary and just. Competent Indian teachers are available, and their exclusion is impolitic and wrong. When one very young beginner excuses the absence of his school register, which provides for record of visiting parents and strangers, as well as of school attendance and recitations, on the ground that "it might get dirty", and a young lady excuses the absence of her register because "she never had any", it is not strange that parents say, "these teachers don't care for anything but their money; the children will do about as well at home". This very common complaint, justly conceived, should be without sufficient cause in this and other respects. No people notice more quickly discrimination against them.

SCHOOL No. 1, conducted by Miss Anna Warner, the most western school, is near the town of Irving. Visitations by the teacher to parents and children when absence becomes noticeable, and original ways of entertaining the pupils, such as the occasional use of the magic lantern, indicate the spirit which can make Indian schools successful and Indian parents sympathetic and supporting; and yet even this school proves the necessity of some method to induce more regular attendance. Accommodations are estimated for 50; highest attendance during the year, 21; 10 males and 12 females attended 1 month or more; under 6 years of age, 1 male and 1 female; between the ages of 6 and 18, 1 male and 1 female; average attendance during the year, 7.1; largest attendance during any one month, 10.75, in September, 1889; special attendance, Kittie M. Silverheels, 160 out of a possible 181 days.

SCHOOL No. 2 has accommodations for 40; largest attendance any one time, 12; attended 1 month or more, 5 males and 3 females; under 6 years, 1 female; between the ages of 6 and 18, 5 males and 2 females; average age, 10 years; largest average attendance during the year, 6.66; largest average attendance during any one month, 8, in April, 1890. This school is taught by a young man. Special attendance, Jacob Pierce, jr., and brothers, 170, 170, and 163 out of a possible 171 days.

SCHOOL No. 3 has accommodations for 50; largest attendance, 30; 16 males and 13 females attended 1 month or more during the year; under 6 years of age, 1; between the ages of 6 and 18, 16 males and 12 females; average age of pupils, 10.5 years; average attendance during the year, 15; largest average attendance during any one month, 16, in May, 1890; location, nearly opposite the Presbyterian church; special attendance, Flora Patterson, 158 out of a possible 178 days.

SCHOOL No. 4. The Thomas Orphan Asylum practically answers for this number.

SCHOOL No. 5 has accommodations for 40; largest attendance during the year, 18; 10 males and 11 females attended 1 month or more during the year; 1 male is under the age of 6, and 9 males and 11 females are between the ages of 6 and 18; average age, 10.33 years; average attendance during the year, 9; largest average attendance any one month, 9.5, in September, 1889. This school is central, near the Methodist church and the courthouse. Special attendance, Ray Crouse, 154 out of a possible 178 days.

SCHOOL No. 6 has accommodations for 40; largest number present at any one time, 25; 14 males and 13 females attended 1 month or more, all between the ages of 6 and 18; average age, 9.5 years; average attendance during the year, 10; largest average attendance during any one month, 12, in June, 1890. This school is on the summit north from the courthouse. Special attendance, Willie Jackson, 156 out of a possible 167 days.

SCHOOL No. 7 is situated in the strongly pagan district of Newtown, in the midst of a large school population. There are accommodations for 50 pupils, and the school is now in charge of Miss Ball, an earnest and experienced teacher. Largest number present at any one time, 45; 28 males and 23 females attended 1 month or more during the year; 3 males were under the age of 6; 25 males and 23 females between the ages of 6 and 18; average age, 9.33 years; average attendance during the year, 24.33; largest average attendance during any one month, 34, in December, 1889; special attendance, Willie Crow, 126 out of a possible 156 days, and George Wilson, jr., 73 days, a full fall term.

SCHOOL No. 8 has accommodations for 40; largest attendance at any one time, 40; 10 males and 7 females attended 1 month or more during the year; 1 male and 1 female are under 6 years of age; 9 males and 6 females are between the ages of 6 and 18; average age, 9 years; average attendance during the year, 6.5; largest attendance any one month, 12, in November, 1889; location, on the "Four-mile level road" to Gowanda.

SCHOOL No. 9 has accommodations for 40; largest attendance at any one time during the year, 20; 12 males and 10 females attended 1 month or more during the year; 2 females under the age of 6; 12 males and 10 females between the ages of 6 and 18; average age of pupils 9.5 years; average attendance during the year, 12.33; the largest average attendance during any one month was in September, 1889; location, on the west road from Versailles to Gowanda.

SCHOOL No. 10 has accommodations for 50; largest attendance during the year, 18; 11 males and 4 females attended 1 month or more during the year, all between the ages of 6 and 18; average age of pupils, 10.5 years; average attendance during the year, 10; largest average attendance during any one month, 12.5, in March, 1890; location, north from Versailles, on the west bank of Cattaraugus creek; Chauncey Parker, teacher; special attendance, John Herbert and Victoris Jimerson, 149 out of a possible 155 days.

SCHOOL No. 11 has accommodations for 50; largest attendance during the year, 25; 12 males and 15 females attended 1 month or more; 1 male is over 18 years of age; 2 males and 2 females are under 6 years of age; 9 males and 13 females are between the ages of 6 and 18 years; average age, 9.66 years; average attendance during the year, 15.66; largest average attendance during any one month, 22.33, in December, 1889; location, on summit west of "One-mile strip"; special attendance, Charlotte David, Letha and Frank Seneca, and Sarah Tallchief, the full fall term of 78 days.

TUSCARORA SCHOOLS.

SCHOOL No. 1, western district, on the crossroad from Frank Mountpleasant's to Captain C. Cusick's farm, on the Mountain road, has accommodations for 35; largest attendance during the year, 32; attendance 1 month or more during the year, 31, viz, males 19 and females 12; under 6 years of age, males 1, females 1; over 18 years of age, 2 males and 2 females; 20 males and 13 females between the ages of 6 and 18 years; average attendance during the year 13.33; largest attendance during any one month, 19, in February, 1890; salaries of teachers and employés, $252; all other expenses, $17.75; value of building, $287.

SCHOOL No. 2, a boarding-school building; accommodations, nominally 35; greatest number present at any one time, 28; attendance 1 month or more during the year, 43, viz, 33 males and 10 females; under 6 years of age, 3 males and 2 females; over 18 years of age, 2 males and 2 females; average age of pupils, 10 years; average attendance during the year, 14; largest average attendance any one month, 17, in February, 1890; salaries, $252; all other expenses, $17.75. Prominent chiefs state that the mission buildings and the necessary assistance are available when the state of New York is prepared to do its part.

STATE SUPERVISION.

Hon. A. S. Draper, superintendent of public instruction for the state of New York, in successive annual reports, as well as in association with the commission appointed by the general assembly of that state, earnestly deplores the condition of the Indian schools, the irregular attendance, and the indifference or opposition of

Eleventh Census: 1890.

Six Nations of New York.

THOMAS ORPHAN ASYLUM.

Cattaraugus Reservation, New York.

New York Engraving & Printing Co.

parents, and states that "this indifference is not chargeable to the character of the schools". The statistics give fuller justice to the Indian than the school register warrants. The fact should be noted that many children do not attend school at all, and many are very irregular in their attendance, after being entered on the school register, and the most laborious and sympathetic efforts of the state and local superintendents, if combined with the efforts of the most capable and self-sacrificing teachers, whether native or English, can not supply the want of some form of compulsory attendance. At the same time the difficulty is not overcome by this conclusion any more than by similar reasoning as to the ignorant classes of people outside the boundaries of the state of New York, and who are equally as hard to approach in the matter of school attendance by constitutional and lawful methods as are the Indians of the Six Nations.

THE THOMAS ORPHAN ASYLUM. (a)

This institution, established in the year 1855 by Mr. Philip E. Thomas, of Baltimore, Maryland, and now generously maintained by the state of New York, is located, as indicated on the map, less than three-quarters of a mile west from the Seneca courthouse, on the main road which leads through the Cattaraugus reservation to Irving. A productive farm, with buildings admirably arranged and suitably heated and ventilated, and with all the accessories of a good boarding school, also a well-arranged hospital and cheerful home, make this a true asylum for the orphan and destitute children of the Six Nations. The names and derivatives of all inmates during the census year are attached to the general schedule of the reservation. During that period 48 boys and 57 girls under the age of 16 enjoyed its instruction and care, with but 2 deaths from the number. The property returns for the year represent the value of farm, buildings, and all properties that make the institution complete as $46,747. The board of trustees, Mr. William C. Bryant, of Buffalo, chairman, are responsible for its general welfare. Elias Johnson, the Tuscarora historian, Nathaniel Kennedy, of Cattaraugus, and David Jimerson, a Tonawanda Seneca, represent the Indians upon the executive board. The superintendent, Mr. J. H. Van Valkenburg, and his wife, after large experience at the state blind asylum, have demonstrated by their management and extension of this great charity the capacity of Indian children for the best development which discriminating forethought and paternal care can realize. The necessary condition that these Indian children can only remain in the asylum until they are 16 removes them from its influence at the very time they are beginning to respond to excellent discipline, regular habits, and careful teaching. They consequently return to their people unfitted for the lives they must lead, and yet unable to sustain the fuller, nobler life of which they have caught a passing glimpse.

Regular hours for study, recreation, and work, with every possible guidance which affection, sympathy, and good judgment can devise, combine in behalf of the orphan inmates to develop the elements of a religious and industrious life. During the year 14 returned to parents or guardians, 2 were sent out to work, and 2 were adopted. Besides the day system of routine duty, the evenings are made cheerful by readings, talks, games, and music until a reasonable retiring hour, and the order, willing obedience, and obliging manners of both boys and girls leave nothing wanting to vindicate the noble purpose of the founder. The girls, who learn to sew, manufactured wearing apparel during the year to the value of $2,515. In addition they make fancy articles, which they are allowed to sell to visitors on their own account, while the boys are no less efficient upon the farm in every form of handiwork adapted to their strength.

The Indian's love for music is systematically developed by superintendent and matron, both being accomplished musicians, and this love for music, with an innate obliging disposition, prompts the cheerful entertainment of interested visitors at all proper times. In addition to their music at home, and their regular service of song at the Presbyterian church on the Sabbath, they are welcome attendants at many public occasions. 767 Indian children have been educated through the agency of the asylum, and to say that a boy or girl "is at the Thomas asylum" is a proverbial assurance of a promising future. In reading, grammar, geography, and history, in deportment, penmanship, drawing, and in their sports, there is a visible pride and interest. The system eliminates tardiness, laziness, and indifference, and establishes systematic habits, industry, and zeal. The studies at the asylum during the year and the number of pupils in each branch, as presented in the following statement, is the best answer to the question, "What can you make of an Indian boy or girl"?

---

a In the summer of 1854 an Indian died on the Cattaraugus reservation, leaving a large family in extreme want. The sympathy which this event occasioned led to inquiries which showed that on that reservation alone there were not less than 50 children in great need of support. The facts coming to the knowledge of Philip E. Thomas, of Baltimore, a Friend, who had in many ways already done much for the Indians, he caused the more destitute to be gathered and kept through the winter at his own expense. This suggested the idea of a permanent asylum. The Seneca nation gave lands, and 2 Seneca brass bands, with a choir of singers, volunteered to give a concert in the city of Buffalo; from these and other sources a beginning was made. The act of incorporation by New York was accompanied by a grant of $2,000 for building, and $10 a year for 2 years for any number of children, not over 50 in all, that might be maintained, besides a pro rata allowance from the general appropriations to asylums. An amendment to the constitution of New York in 1874 forced the issue of abandonment of the Thomas asylum or its transfer to the state. Finally, by act of the legislature passed April 24, 1875, it was transferred to the control of the state of New York. See Executive Document No. 95, Forty-eighth Congress, Second session.

ENGLISH STUDIES.

Advanced reading	35	Advanced arithmetic	30
Intermediate reading	42	Intermediate arithmetic	24
Primary reading	50	Primary arithmetic	36
Advanced spelling	36	Advanced geography	32
Intermediate geography	32	Primary United States history	24
Advanced grammar	29	Advanced United States history	28
Language lessons	44	Advanced physiology	46
Civil government	46	Intermediate physiology	35
Intermediate writing	44	Advanced writing	36
Primary writing	29	Recitation and declamation	123

MUSICAL COURSES.

Instrumental lessons	55	Advanced chorus singing	20
Voice culture and special training	7	Primary chorus singing	36
Intermediate chorus singing	24	Sunday school music	131
Musical notation and singing	80	Anthems and church music	70

There is an active "band of hope" in the school, and the atmosphere of the entire institution is that of a happy family.

SCHOOL WORK OF THE FRIENDS.

William Penn's treaty with the Indians at Shakamaxon "on the 14th day of the 10th month, 1682", laid the foundation for that confidence in the Society of Friends which prompted the great chief Cornplanter to write, in 1791: "Brothers! we have too little wisdom among us, and we can not teach our children that we see their situation requires them to know. We wish them to be taught to read and write, and such other things as you teach your children, especially the love of peace".

Sag-a-ree-sa (The Sword Carrier), a Tuscarora chief, who was present when Timothy Pickering made the Canandaigua treaty of 1794, requested some Friends who accompanied the commissioner from Philadelphia to have some of their people sent to New York as teachers. As secretary of state, Mr. Pickering afterward granted the request. 3 young men began work among the Stockbridge and Oneida Indians in 1796, and 4 visited the Seneca settlement of Cornplanter in 1798. The foundation thus laid was strengthened by the visit of a committee of Friends to all the Six Nations in 1865, and the Friends' school, now in vigorous operation, on the verge of the Allegany reservation, less than a mile from the station at Quaker bridge, on the Allegany river, is the mature fruit of that early conception. It comprises a farm and boarding school, with an attendance of 40 pupils, soon to be increased to 45.

The course of instruction here, more advanced than at the state schools, coupled with the financial benefits enjoyed, is the cause, in part, of the abandonment of the school near the house of Philip Fatty, on the west bank of the Allegany, below West Salamanca, as indicated on the map.

During September, 1890, a committee of Friends from Philadelphia, consisting of George B. Scattergood, Ephraim Smith, Sarah E. Smith, Ann Fry, and Rebecca K. Masters, a minister, visited the school and addressed the Indians in both council house and church. The school, under the superintendence of Friend James Henderson, Rebecca W. Bundy, matron; Elizabeth Conan (in charge of the boys), and Mary Penrose, never enjoyed greater prosperity. Every appointment of good service in playground, schoolroom, dining room, and dormitory, and the good conduct of all the pupils at all hours, evinced the harmonious operation of a generously designed and nobly developed philanthropy.

The annual exhibition proved a substantial test of the loving, faithful work done. The programme of 38 numbers opened with a scripture recitation, followed by the ninety-third psalm, read in unison, and closed with the third chapter of Saint James' epistle. Dialogues, declamations, and class examinations in physiology, arithmetic, geography, and language filled the interval. After listening to the enthusiastic songs of the pupils at the Thomas Orphan Asylum, and witnessing the musical impulse of the Indians generally, the quiet order of the programme at the Friends' school left the impression that one of the quickest avenues to the Indian mind was closed by the sober routine which excluded all song; and yet the tender care, patient labor, and kind discipline were so wholesome and fruitful of good that the missing feature of the programme was in no sense a serious omission. The exhibition room was filled with parents and friends of the homeward-bound youths, and was a fitting memorial day of nearly 100 years of service by the Friends among the Seneca nation.

EDUCATION AND SCHOOLS AT SAINT REGIS.

There are 5 state schools upon this reservation, under the interested personal supervision of Sidney G. Grow, the thoroughly competent state superintendent. The last school building was erected at a cost of $500, and the aggregate value of the 5 buildings is about $1,400. The salaries of the teachers, all females, are $250 each, and the annual incidental expense of each school is $30. The schools are judiciously located, and the deportment and progress of the pupils are commendable.   A new interest has been aroused, as on other reservations, by the various investigations of the conditions and necessities of the Six Nations, and a very decided exhibition of progressive tendencies is noted by citizens who are in daily contact with this people.   The need of education, and especially of a practical business knowledge of the English language, is fully recognized by many, and the schools are beginning to respond to this growing conviction.

SCHOOL No. 1, on the Saint Regis road, north from Hogansburg, shows the following record: Largest attendance any one day, 31; number attending 1 month or more, 25, viz, 12 males and 13 females, all between the ages of 6 and 18; average age, 10 years; average attendance, 13; largest average attendance any single month, 18, in February.   John Lazar (La Salle) and Agnes Torrance did not miss a day.   During a driving snow storm, which lasted from early morning until night, every pupil on the register was present, and also upon the following day, when the mercury dropped 2 degrees below zero.   It had been intimated that visitors might be present about that time, and the ambition of the excellent teacher was aroused, but the response of the pupils was indicative of future possibilities.

SCHOOL No. 2 is 3.33 miles from Hogansburg, on the direct road to Fort Covington.   Largest attendance any one day, 32; number attending 1 month or more, 28, viz, 12 males and 16 females; under the age of 6, males 2 and females 1; between the ages of 6 and 18, males 11 and females 13; average age, 10 years; average attendance, 13; average attendance any single month, 17, in February.   Lewis Herring (Heron) attended every day, and Maggie Gareau (Gorrow) lost but 1 day of the long term.

SCHOOL No. 3 is nearly 2 miles from Hogansburg, on the direct road west to Messina Springs.   Largest attendance any one day, 21; number attending 1 month or more, 24, viz, 11 males and 13 females, all between the ages of 6 and 18; average age, 10 years; average attendance, 15; largest average attendance any single month, 18, in February.   Caroline Billings lost but 1 day.

SCHOOL No. 4 is 2.25 miles northeast from Hogansburg, as indicated on the map.   Largest attendance any one day, 25; number attending 1 month or more, 27, viz, 13 males and 14 females, all between the ages of 6 and 18; average age, 10 years; average attendance, 15; largest average attendance any single month, 18, in February.   Sarah Ranson, Nancy Gareau (Gorrow), Maria Cook, and Angus Cook showed exceptional attendance.

SCHOOL No. 5 is 1.33 miles southwest from Hogansburg, on the new road leading west from the Helena road, at Frank Cook's.   Largest attendance any one day, 21; number attending 1 month or more, 26, viz, 14 males and 12 females, all between the ages of 6 and 18; average age, 10 years; average attendance, 14; largest average attendance any single month, 17, in February; exceptional attendance, Hattie and Thomas Gray and Alexander White, who lost but 1 day of the spring term.

The highest aggregate of attendance any single day in the 5 schools was 130.   The number of those who attended 1 month or more during the school year of 36 weeks was also 130, or about one-third of the 397 of school age (school age in New York ranges from 5 to 21 years).   The data given are in accordance with the census schedules and the school age most common in the United States.

The qualification as to " reading and writing ", which was made in reporting upon the educational progress of the other nations of the Iroquois league, has even greater force among the Saint Regis Indians.   One adult read accurately a long newspaper article, upon the promise of half a dollar, but freely acknowledged that he did not understand the subject-matter of the article.   In penmanship the faculty of copying or drawing and taking mental pictures of characters as so many objectives becomes more delusive when the question is asked, " Can you write English "?   As for penmanship, most adults who can sign their names do it after a mechanical fashion.   The Mohawk dialect of the Iroquois has but 11 letters, A, E, H, I, K, N, O, R, S, T, W.   Striking metaphors and figures of speech, which catch the fancy, are in constant use, and to reach the minds of this people similar means must be employed; hence it is, that Rev. A. A. Wells, the Methodist minister among the Saint Regis Indians, proposes that his granddaughter learn their language, as the best possible preparation for teaching in English.   The objection to Indian teachers is the difficulty of securing those who have thoroughly acquired the English.   The Saint Regis Indians who conduct ordinary conversation in English almost universally hesitate to translate for others when important matters are under consideration although apparently competent to do so.   The white people do not sufficiently insist that Indians who can speak some English should use it habitually.   It is so much less trouble to have an interpreter.   This people do not, as might be expected, understand French; neither do the Canadian Saint Regis Indians.   The New York commission of 1889, in commenting upon the good work accomplished by the jesuit priests, very pertinently said: " The neglect, however, of these missionaries to teach them the English language is a serious misfortune ".   But this is not strange, in view of the fact that the missionaries themselves did not understand the English language, and that Father Mauville, a man of great learning and literary attainment, is still at work perfecting the Iroquois grammar, begun by his predecessors, and is translating the Latin forms and hymns into the Iroquois dialect for church use.   The French could not teach English, and did not teach French. Contact with the Canadian Saint Regis Indians, however social and tribal in its affinities and intercourse, retards, rather than quickens, the American Saint Regis Indians in the acquisition of the English language.   It is true with them, as with the other nations, that this is a prime necessity in their upward progress.

No people are quicker to catch opportunities for easy gain.   A system of rewards, stimulative of effort in the education of their children, if well advised and fostered, would be worth its cost and accomplish lasting good. They need the stimulant of earnest, consistent, painstaking sympathy, and are prepared to respond to it. Superintendent Grow says: " When the commission was here I was almost discouraged.   All was at a low grade. I am surprised at the recent rapid improvement in industrial and all other pursuits, and am especially gratified at the improved condition of the schools and the interest taken by parents in their success ".

Schools Nos. 3 and 5 are in Protestant Indian communities, and Mr. Grow, an enlightened Roman Catholic, with large sympathies and life-long knowledge of this people, has submitted to the Protestant missionary, Mr. Wells, the privilege of suggesting Protestant teachers, of proper capacity, for appointment to those schools. There is wanting nothing in his management to encourage the Saint Regis parents and children in this prime element of their future development.

LANGUAGE.

The passivity of this people is never more apparent than in their indifference to the better use of the English language. It would be expected that Americans visiting Europe would use their native tongue in personal intercourse ; but if they expected to remain abroad they would not fail to perfect themselves in the language of their adopted country. It is not so with the people of the Six Nations. The easiest way of doing anything is their way of doing it. Much of the value of school training is sacrificed by this practice. 10 months of contact with them, living with them, sharing their hospitality, and mingling in all their affairs, serious or social, strengthened the conviction that beyond the range of actual necessity the large majority are unwilling to make the effort, or do not desire to substitute the English for the Indian language. At all times and places where the use of the English is not absolutely indispensable the Indian language is used, but this is not for the purpose of concealing their meaning. The native courtesy toward strangers, offhand kindliness of manner, and good address of this people prevent breaches of companionship ; and yet, even among the nations themselves, the acquirement by one nation of the language of another is rare. Among the Tuscaroras, however mellifluous and musical their dialect, the lips are not used in speaking, and the labials not being pronounced, many intelligent Tuscaroras are unable to converse freely with those of other nations. The constant dependence upon interpreters is a drawback, and represses the desire to understand English. It keeps down the comprehension of ideas, which can not find expression through the Indian vocabulary, and it is simply impossible for the Indian either to appreciate his condition and needs or make substantial progress until he is compelled by necessity to make habitual use of English. The use of an interpreter seems generally to be necessary at the church services to impress a religious sentiment ; but this perfunctory deliverance is unsatisfactory. The minister can not know how far he touches both understanding and heart nor, without knowledge of the Indian language, can he realize the best results. The New York Indians should understand that they must make the acquisition of the English language an essential element in their dealings with the white people.

PART X.

HEALTH AND VITAL STATISTICS.

An examination of the annual reports of the United States agents for many years indicates the classes of diseases heretofore most common among the Six Nations. The reluctance of the Indians to employ physicians springs from want of means, want of easy access to physicians, and, in some measure, to the fact that from time immemorial they have relied much upon the use of medicinal roots and herbs in ordinary ailments. The women are practical nurses, and the offices and appliances of nature require small aid to meet emergencies. This lack of professional treatment and the ignorance of the names of diseases have almost entirely prevented an accurate specification of the causes of death during the census year. The chief diseases reported, other than consumption and kindred lung troubles, of which there are many, have been scrofula and syphilitic ailments in some form. Their relations to the white people have been credited with these to a large extent; but it can not be correctly claimed that pure white and pure Indian blood involves an enfeebled race. Death in infancy, or at an early age, and enfeebled or inefficient maturity belong to a depleted people, who lack the stamina of real constitutional vigor. The natural indolence of the Indian is a part of the antecedent life of his people, which precluded systematic, regular labor. Seasons of half-wild activity in the chase alternate with others of comparative freedom from all active work. Loss of essential vitality does not necessarily ensue. The facts, as disclosed by this enumeration, are suggestive. Catarrhal troubles and diseases of the eye are common with the Tuscaroras, due to exposure, they think, to the lake winds, while at Cattaraugus many attribute their coughs to the harsh winds that sweep up the valley from Lake Erie.

William Bone, of Allegany, claims that he is the only Seneca. It is not certain that any are purely such. The presence of the mustache and beard shows how largely the white element has united with the red, and men like E. M. Poodry, of Tonawanda, and W. C. Hoag, of Allegany, are only two of very many who are of distinct white admixture. This admixture of blood also appears conspicuously among the children without discredit to mental and physical vigor. The mixture of a cultivated and exercised brain with a passive brain or one of narrow and untrained ranges of thought, develops both, and it is an unfortunate but popular error of many to attribute to vice only all Indian approximation to the white man in respect of hair, complexion, and color. The irregularities of early frontier life have left their impress; but all are not heirs of incurable ills. Neither are the Six Nations on the decline. In the Six Nations, from June 30, 1889, to June 30, 1890, the deaths were 161; the births, 185; gain, 24. This includes the Saint Regis Indians.

The Indians of New York invariably trace their stock to that of the predominant female sources, and as remotely as tradition will warrant, notwithstanding there may have been an occasional admixture of white female blood. This last incident is rare, that of Mary Jimerson, the Wyoming captive, being the most conspicuous. It is doubtful if the Mohawks among the Saint Regis, who are the proper representatives of the old Mohawks, are free from admixture with other tribes. Caughnawaga (of Montreal) is properly but another name for Mohawk.

The admixture of French white blood is very marked among the Saint Regis Indians. Other New England captive white people besides the Tarbells, of Groton, Massachusetts, left their impress upon these Indians, and also upon the Oneidas and Onondagas. The grandfather of Mrs. Mountpleasant, of the Senecas, was a French officer. The spirit of each of the Six Nations is adverse to white admixture, and the jealousy of successive generations of "fading" Indians is still very marked among the old pagan element. This is fostered by the fact that children of a white mother, although of half blood, are not within the distribution of annuities, while the children of an Indian having a white father, although of half blood, share the distribution. As a general rule, the Indians themselves do not specially recognize as of exclusively pure Indian origin, with no admixture, those who assert that distinction. Intermarriage between clans, while technically prohibited, does not, as formerly, greatly prevent marriage between the tribes, so that the maternity of the Indian generally determines whether he is to be styled Seneca, Onondaga, or otherwise.

PART XI.

INDIAN NAMES, TRADITIONS, AND REMINISCENCES.

Indian nomenclature almost invariably has a distinct and suggestive meaning, especially in geographical locations, relations, and peculiarities. Only a few of those which relate to the accompanying maps are supplied. The location of Bill Hill's cabin, near the foot of the Onondaga reservation, was called Nan-ta-sa-sis, "going partly round a hill". Tonawanda creek is named from Ta-na-wun-da, meaning "swift water". Oil spring, on the Allegany map, was Te-car-nohs, "dropping oil". The Allegany river was O-hee-yo, "the beautiful river", and the Geneseo was Gen-nis-he-yo, "beautiful valley". Buffalo was Do-sho-weh, "splitting the fork", because near Black Rock (a rocky shore) the waters divided, uniting and dividing again at Date-car-sko-sase, "the highest falls", on the Ne-ah-ga river. The modern Canajoharie was Ga-na-jo-hi-e, "washing the basin"; Chittenango creek, Chu-de-naang, "where the sun shines out"; Oriskany creek, Ole-hisk, "nettles"; Onondaga, O-nun-da-ga-o-no-ga, "on the hills"; Cayuga lake, Gwe-u-gweth, "the lake at the mucky land"; Canandaigua, Ga-nun-da-gwa, "place chosen for a settlement". The Indian meaning for other names finds expression in recognized English substitutes. Thus, "The place of salt" becomes Salina, and "Constant dawn" becomes Aurora. Morgan illustrates the dialectic difference respecting the name for Buffalo as follows: in Seneca, Do-she-weh; in Cayuga, De-o-sho-weh; in Onondaga, De-o-sa-weh; in Oneida, De-ose-lole; in Mohawk, Deo-hose-lole, and in Tuscarora, Ne-o-thro-ra.

Personal names were given from peculiarities or sudden fancies, and upon elevation to chieftainship a new name was given. The celebrated and eloquent Red Jacket, O-te-ti-an-i, "always ready", became Sa-go-ye-wat-ha, "keeper awake". So special uses and qualities or supposed resemblances entered into their nomenclature. Mrs. Sarah L. Lee, of Boston, in her life of Mrs. Erminie Smith, a lifelong friend of the Iroquois, very appropriately applied Chaucer's "day's-eye" (the English daisy) to similar Iroquois forms. "It sheds its blush" describes the watermelon. The white ash was the "bow-tree". The corn, bean, squash, strawberry, and maple were classed as "our life supporters".

At present, through adoption of English customs, the names of Adam, John Adams, Andrew Jackson, Martin Van Buren, Andrew Johnson, Millard Fillmore, "General Scott", Ulysses, Rutherford B., Grover, and Benjamin Harrison have appeared on the Tonawanda list. The name of Washington escapes use. On this same Tonawanda list the Bible names of Abram, Adam, Andrew, Benjamin, Cephas, David, Elijah, Eli, Enos, Elizabeth, Eunice, Esther, Hannah, Isaac, Joshua, Jacob, Jesse, John, Lydia, Mary, Moses, Martha, Noah, Norah, Peter, Reuben, Samson, Samuel, Simon, Simeon, and Stephen are both christian names and surnames, in contrast with those of Big Fire, Blue Sky, Hot Bread, Big Kettle, Black Snake, Silverheels, Spring, Ground, Stone, and Steep Rock on the Allegany reservation and elsewhere. Bone, Blackchief, Bucktooth, Cornfield, Fatty, Hemlock, Halfwhite, Redeye, Logan, Longfinger, Ray, Snow, Twoguns, and Warrior have companionship with Beaver, Crow, Deer, Eel, Fox, and Turkey.

With the exception of old family names of traditional value, names are less frequently given than formerly through some distinct association. Many do not even know their proper Indian name. The tribal relation itself has become so immaterial a matter, through daily association with the white people, that in hundreds of inquiries for "tribe or clan" the first response was good-humored laughter, and often a reference to some one else to give it. Even the most conservative of the old party are losing their relations to the past, except through their religious rites. No single item, apparently of small import, more impressively shows a social transition in progress than this indifference to old names. On the Onondaga school register only 4 ancient Bible names are opposite 29 such names of parent or guardian, and throughout the Six Nations the names of the young children, especially those of the girls, are selected from the more euphonious ones in general use among the white people.

The force of this fact is increased as familiarity with the white people keeps before the more intelligent men and women the names and events of the swiftly passing changes in American society. They are forced to think of and deal with the present, and the superstitions and associations that are only matters of vague tradition gradually die out. The old Indian answer to the inquiry "What's in a name"? no longer implies a peculiarity or quality, but simply identity, and the enforcement of a good English education will turn their traditional legends of names or characteristics into the practical line of dealing with the affairs and surrounding influences of to-day; and yet this change has reasonable limits.

The American people wrong their whole country by the obliteration of Indian names, which made rivers, mountains, and valleys representative of their location, their beauty, and their power. Excepting the aboriginal American, Hebrew history alone, throughout the early ages, thus dignified human qualities and the works of nature. The attempt to obliterate Indian names and to silence Indian tradition is to obliterate landmarks which the American people should be more disposed to rescue and perpetuate. This feature of civilization is neither

CAROLINE G. MOUNTPLEASANT (Ge-keah-saw-sa),
The Peacemaker, Queen of the Senecas—Wolf Clan.

enlightened nor christian. The unity of history is despoiled of its royal prerogative, that of identifying nature in all its forms and man in all his capacities with one superintending Great Spirit over all.

TRADITIONS.

THE ORIGIN OF ALL THINGS.—So many volumes have dealt with the traditions of the Six Nations that only such as have present influence upon the people and blend with government, religion, or social living can be mentioned in this report. In 1825 David Cusick, grandfather of Albert Cusick, of Onondaga, and uncle of Captain Cornelius C. Cusick, of the United States army, published an illustrated pamphlet containing a collection of myths, with the elaborate title, "A tale of the foundation of the Great Island, North America, and the creation of the universe". Its characteristic dealing with the antagonistic forces of "good" and "evil" have value through their harmony with similar ideas presented in the old traditions of the East. Irwakura, chief of the Japanese embassy to America some years since, expressly intimated the conviction that his ancestors and those of the red men were from a common or kindred stock. A mass of Indian school children, interested in their work, certainly present a striking similarity to the Japanese; but nearly all the vague speculations of Indian traditions have been merged in the facts of recorded history. Indian historians only imitate and illustrate the purpose of every other people to associate their ancestors with the original progenitors of the entire human race.

THE QUEEN PEACEMAKER AND THE CITY OF REFUGE.—The Seneca nation, ever the largest, and guarding the western door of the "Long House", which was threatened alike from the north, west, and south, had traditions peculiarly their own, besides those common to the other members of the confederacy. In addition to their success in garden, orchard, and farm products, and housebuilding, their military engineering was considerably in advance of their times. But the original stronghold or fort, Gau-stra-yea, on the mountain ridge, 4 miles east of Lewiston, and located by Elias Johnson as near the "old sawmill", had a peculiar character as the residence of a virgin queen known as the "Peacemaker". When the Iroquois confederacy was first formed the prime factors were mutual protection and domestic peace, and this fort was designed to afford comfort and relieve the distress incident to war. It was a true "city of refuge", to which fugitives from battle, whatever their nationality, might flee for safety and find generous entertainment. Curtains of deerskin separated pursuer and pursued while they were being lodged and fed. Then the curtains were withdrawn, and the hostile parties, at parting, having shared the hospitality of the queen, could neither renew hostility or pursuit without the queen's consent. According to tradition no virgin had for many generations been counted worthy to fill the place or possessed the genius and gifts to honor the position. In 1878 the Tonawanda band proposed to revive the office, and conferred upon Caroline Parker the title. She became the wife of Sachem Chief John Mountpleasant, and the historian justly says: "She ever held open her hospitable house, not only to the Iroquois, but to others of every nation, including the palefaces". She tells pleasantly of her "grandmother's old home, which had 10 fires in it for guests; of the one general meal for the day, for which the wood had to be cut in the ice and the cold, though nobody had to go hungry at other hours", and speaks tenderly of "the shadow which now hovers over her people, as if they alone were to find no 'house of refuge'". She, as well as her brother, anticipates the time when they will share a common citizenship, but deprecates precipitate legislation just at the time when their own people are maturing plans for a better development. This tradition of the "queen peacemaker" is pleasing and in harmony with many of the good qualities belonging to the nation.

MEMORIAL QUALITIES.—The traditions and historical record of the eloquence, patriotism, and domestic virtues of their ancestors are held in higher esteem than those of the field. It was the wisdom of Cornplanter, Governor Blacksnake, the Cayuga chief Logan, Red Jacket, and others which gave them an honored place among the household penates. The teachings of Con-ta-tau-you, Handsome Lake, gained ready lodgment in their hearts, because they embodied a peaceful code, and rebuked violence, intemperance, dishonesty, and lying, which "entangled the feet so that the Indian would fall even upon the level ground".

Known by the name of the "Peace Prophet" (as the brother of Tecumseh had been styled the War Prophet), he so greatly impressed the government with the value of his mission that Hon. H. Dearborn, Secretary of War, in a communication dated March 13, 1802, to Con-ta-tau-you and his brother Senecas, used this language:

If all the red people follow the advice of your friend and teacher, the Handsome Lake, and in future will be sober, industrious, honest, and good, there can be no doubt but that the Great Spirit will take care of you and make you happy. The great council of the sixteen fires and the President of the United States all wish to live with the red men like brothers. * * * For this purpose the great council of the sixteen fires are now considering the propriety of prohibiting the use of spirituous liquors among all their red brethren within the United States. This measure, if carried into effect, will be pleasing in the sight of the Great Being, who delights in the happiness of his common family. Your father, the President, will at all times be your friend, and he will protect you and all his red children from bad people, who would do you or them injury. And he will give you a writing or a paper to assure you that what land you hold can not be taken from you by any person excepting by your consent.

This tribute to Handsome Lake does not stand alone as evidence of qualities especially honored among the Six Nations. The historian Clark, in writing of Os-sa-hin-ta (Captain Frost), who presided over the Onondaga

11

councils from 1830 to 1846, says: " He was distinguished for the nobleness of his character, the peculiar fervidness of his eloquence, and his unimpeachable integrity—qualities which secured for him the unlimited confidence of his nation ". Of Captain Honnos (Oh-he-nu), Abram La Forte (De-hat-ka-tons), Captain Cold (Ut-ha-wah), and others, he says: "All were men whose characters were without reproach, and whose names will live in the unwritten records of the nation so long as a remnant of their perishing institutions is permitted by an allwise Providence to remain ".

Respect for the aged and kindness toward orphans were inculcated in aphorisms of great tenderness and simplicity, like the following :

"It is the will of the Great Spirit that you reverence the aged, even though they be helpless as infants".

"Kindness to the orphan and hospitality to all".

"If you tie up the clothes of an orphan child the Great Spirit will notice it and reward you for it".

"To adopt the orphan and bring him up in virtuous ways is pleasing to the Great Spirit".

"If a stranger wander about your abode, welcome him to your home ; be hospitable toward him ; speak to him with kind words, and forget not always to make mention of the Great Spirit".

The graves of the dead were especially honored. Old Aunt Dinah, who died at the age of 107, on the Onondaga reservation, is kindly remembered by the citizens of Syracuse, as well as by her own people. After the age of 90, she often walked 7 miles to the city and back. A handsome monument has been erected to her memory. Judge A. J. Northrup, who secured a photograph of her family group, gives a reminiscence of her religious experience, very characteristic of her frank simplicity. When asked as to her church relations, she placed her hand upon her head, saying, " I'm 'Piscopal here" ; then, placing her hand upon her heart, she added, " I'm Methodist here ". This confusion was much like that of a converted Seneca at Tonawanda, who wished to be baptized before he died. He had become attached to the Presbyterian minister, but preferred baptism by immersion. The choice was freely granted ; but he declined his friend's kind offer, because he, the Presbyterian minister, had never been immersed, and could not administer the ordinance in that form.

FUNERAL CEREMONIES.—The funeral ceremonies are simple and touching. Among the pagan party, the " dead feast " was long observed ; but public sentiment has nearly ended that observance. There was a 10-day festival, at which the administration upon the effects of the deceased took place, the estate defraying the expenses of the occasion. The precedent or concurrent custom among the white people to have the will made public after the funeral is more formal ; but an examination of the Indian records, taking a transcript in one case, and inquiry among many heads of families of both parties, show that where an explicit will of the deceased was known it was respected as much as among the white people. The excesses once attaching to the " dead feast " have nearly disappeared, and they now in no sense exceed the license and peculiar incidents of a " wake".

The period of 10 days was observed because they allowed that time for the spirit to reach some substantial resting place. The very custom among the white people of burying friends, and especially soldiers, in the best they wore while in life has been from prehistoric times that of the native American. The desecration of a grave was deemed a horrible crime, and upon removal of an established home to another locality the remains of ancestors were often taken with the family. In harmony with this spirit, the hereditary chief, Charlot Victor, of the Flatheads, in Montana, made as the final condition of his signature to an agreement executed in 1889 the assurance that the burial ground of his ancestors should be kept sacred by the United States.

Few scenes are more suggestive of home and christian sympathies than those which occurred after the death of Jacob Pierce, of Cattaraugus, in 1890. The little house at the foot of the hill, at the west end of the " Mile strip", was crowded. The brother, Adam, living in the last house north from Newtown, and 20 other family mourners, accompanied the remains to the Presbyterian church, where a tearful parting took place. Nearly 200 other Indians viewed the face of one of the beloved founders of that christian church, and many followed the remains to the grave. There was no stolidity, indifference, or passive acceptance of the inevitable ; neither was there noisy demonstration, but an effusion of grief, with which the solemnities of the occasion, including prayers, scripture readings, and music, were in keeping.

SUGGESTIVE CHARACTERS.—So many volumes delineate the representative official characters of the Six Nations that only a few of the less publicly honored are noticed, except as they have entered into the body of this report. The memory of Mary Jimerson, taken prisoner at the Wyoming massacre, and who died in 1833, after 80 years of married life among this people, is associated very naturally with her statement that " she never herself received the slightest insult from an Indian, and scarcely knew an instance of infidelity or immorality until the white men introduced spirits among her adopted people ". Her oldest son was one of the victims to strong drink. The incidents of her death, when, as by inspired guidance, the mind grasped the memory of her mother's prayers and blended the morning and evening of life in one closing scene, are worthy of record, and are given in Elias Johnson's tribute to her virtues. Her great-grandson, Theodore F. Jimerson, of Cattaraugus, is an honor to her memory.

Mary Jane Pierce, a daughter of a British officer, came to America in 1825, and settled at Utica, uniting with the First Presbyterian church there. In 1841 she became a missionary to the Indians of the Six Nations. At the treaty ratification in 1841, when Ambrose Spencer and Mr. Hoar were present to see that justice was done the Indians, she became acquainted with Marius Bryant Pierce and was married to him in 1843. He graduated at Dartmouth, studied law at Buffalo, the better to do business for his people, and died in 1874 at the age of 76. The homestead, on the corner of the Brandt and main roads, at Cattaraugus, is for her life use, although she lives in Versailles at present. Her life is thus summed up by herself: "My race had done the red man injustice. I gave my love and life to them". She taught for 14 years at Newtown and Big Flats, and not long since Henry Phillips, 96 years of age, a former pupil, came to see his old teacher before he passed away. She has a daughter, Harriet Pierce, also a teacher of experience, who was educated at Miss Williams' school, Troy, New York, but has been displaced as a teacher among her people.

Old Aunt Cynthia, an Onondaga woman, was a shrewd political manager as well as financier. She lived to be 90 years of age, and at her death left to her favorite nephew, Wilson Reuben, the valuable real estate designated upon the reservation map, and her bank account with the Onondaga county savings bank stood credited with $750.

A few names intimately associated with the development of christianity among these people require mention, because their services are recognized by the Indians themselves as having greatly assisted in their development. The venerable Deacon Samuel Jacobs survives at Tuscarora, reviewing with vivacity and thanksgiving the advancement made during his missionary life and work. Mr. William H. Sage, of Lewiston, has for more than half a century labored with this people. Rev. William Hall (fourscore years of age), at Allegany, gives his recollections of a long life spent among the Senecas. The memory of Rev. Asher Wright and Mrs. Wright, of Buffalo, who founded and for many years managed a sewing or industrial school at Newtown, Cattaraugus, is tenderly cherished by the Indians; and the native missionaries, Henry Silverheels and wife, whose photographs accompany this report, are honored for their holy living and their loving ministrations. The labors of both the native American and the Anglo-American have found their best fruit exactly in proportion as the better culture and education of the latter have reflected the spiritual graces of an inner christian life and offered a safe example for the imitation of the other. Among all the self-sacrificing efforts in the Indians' behalf few have been more beneficial than those of Bishop Hobart, who established the Protestant Episcopal mission at Oneida in 1816. The missionary sent to Oneida was a converted Indian, who had sought an education for the purpose of teaching his own people, and is thus described in Clark's "Onondaga; or, Reminiscenses of earlier and later times", published in 1849: "Eleazur Williams, selected to take charge of this important mission, was the son of Thomas Williams, a distinguished chief of the Saint Regis branch of the Mohawk nation and a descendant of the Rev. John Williams, of Deerfield, Massachusetts, who, with his family and parishioners, was taken captive at the sacking of his native town by the French and Indians in 1704. His labors were successful, and the gospels translated by him are still memorial of those labors". As early as 1764 Samuel Kirkland, of Norwich, Connecticut, left his college studies at Princeton, then noted for its interest in the education of the Indian youths, to devote his life to their service. The names of Kirkland and Williams belong to the surviving traditions of the Oneidas, and the photograph of the Oneida chief, Abram Hill, herewith furnished, is that of a christian who inherits the mercies vouchsafed through their teachings to his people.

Ephraim Webster, a native of New Hampshire, a soldier, and afterward a trader, who was present at the Fort Stanwix treaty of 1784, settled in the Onondaga valley, took part with the Americans and 300 warriors of the Onondagas in the war of 1812, and died at Tuscarora in 1825. He was buried at Onondaga. For many years the Indian agent and interpreter for the Onondagas, he obtained their confidence, and his lease from them of 300 acres of land was confirmed to himself and heirs by the legislature of New York, and is shown on the Onondaga map.

Abram La Forte, father of Daniel and Rev. Thomas La Forte, whose photographs are furnished, was also one of the memorable Onondagas. At one time trusted as a christian, having the promise of great usefulness with his people commensurate with his talents and influence, he relapsed into old customs and opposed the party of progress. The biographical sketch by Clark contains an extract from a letter of La Forte's old teacher, Eleazur Williams, indicating that before his death he returned to his christian faith. These names, whether of old missionaries still surviving or of other workers, are associated with enduring evidence that, if the American people will apply to the facts of this first census of the Six Nations the restorative force of honest, sympathetic, and thoroughly unselfish effort, they can bring into the body politic an element far superior to most foreign importations.

Not less than 30 native Indians, men and women, have been engaged in religious teaching among the Six Nations, and with success. The existing indifference on the part of Indian youths to advanced study is not from want of material, but poverty and want of encouragement from without.

NAMES, TRADITIONS, AND REMINISCENCES OF THE SAINT REGIS INDIANS.

Incidental reference has been made to the principal characters who have figured in the history of the American Saint Regis Indians. Thomas Tarbell (*a*), the only surviving grandson of the elder captive Tarbell, now at the age of 89, retains a fresh recollection of his childhood and the stories of his grandfather's experience. He was baptized on the day of his birth, March 2, 1802, as Tio-na-ta-kew-ente, son of Peter Sa-ti-ga-ren-ton, who was the son of Peter Tarbell. One of the family, living on the summit of the Messina road, was known as "Tarbell on the Hill", giving the name Hill to the next generation. Old Nancy Hill, a pensioner, and 76 years old, thus "lost her real name". Chief Joseph Wood (*b*) lost his name through turning the English meaning of his Indian name into a surname. The first Indian who was persuaded to abandon moccasins slept in the boots he had substituted, and was afterward only known as "Boots", his children perpetuating that name. Another, who was surrendered for adoption on consideration of "a quart of rum", thereby secured to his descendants the name of "Quarts". Louis Gray, the son of Charles Gray, who figured in the war of 1812, gives the story of his grandfather, William Gray, who was captured at the age of 7 in Massachusetts, and at the age of 21 was permitted to visit his native place, but returned to the Indian who had adopted him, to live and die where Hogansburg is now located. Elias Torrance exhibits the silver medal given to his grandfather by George III, displaying the lion and church, in contrast with a cabin and a wolf, without a hint as to the meaning of the design. Louis Sawyer tells the tale, learned from his grandmother, Old Ann, who died at the age of 100, of the early days of Saint Regis. Louis has 3 sons in Minnesota, and a French wife, so that he has much trouble about the time of the annuity payment. He is a Methodist, can read and write, and thinks he pays a penalty for these distinctions. In 1826 Joseph Tarbell went to Europe with a young Frenchman, visited Charles I, also the Pope, and returned with pictures and some money for church use.

The Saint Regis Indians have a strangely mixed ancestry of French pioneers, white captives, and 1 colored man, with well-preserved traditions of all, but with few memorials of their purely Indian history. One wampum, now owned by Margaret Cook, the aged aunt of Running Deer, represents the treaty of George I with the Seven Nations. The king and head chief are represented with joined hands, while on each side is a dog, watchful of danger, and the emblem is supposed to be the pledge: "We will live together or die together. We promise this as long as water runs, the skies do shine, and night brings rest". Hough describes Tirens, one of the sources of the name Torrance, as an Oswegatchie Indian, known as "Peter the Big Speak", because of his bold oratory, as a son of Lesor Tarbell, the younger of the captive brothers. Here again the confusion of names finds its result in the various names culminating in the surname Lazar.

The surroundings of Saint Regis are named with singular fitness to their properties, and yet these, as elsewhere, have gradually lost their title in order to honor some ambitious white man, whose life is crowned with glory if the word "ville" or "burg" can be joined to his name, sacrificing that which the red man so happily fitted to its place.

---

a The recent work of Dr. Samuel A. Green, secretary of the Massachusetts Historical Society, entitled "Groton Spring Indian wars", cites the action of the Massachusetts legislature toward redemption of the Tarbell captives and their sister Sarah, who was subsequently educated at a Montreal convent. It appears that the name "Lesor", now used as a surname, was the familiar name for Eleazur.

b A more striking fact is, that the Indian name for "Wood", which Chief Joseph Wood's father perpetuates as a surname, was an original rendering from English to Iroquois, and, incidentally, back to English, without knowledge of the family up to this day of the reason for either change. The Groton town records, where the family is still largely represented, show that the maiden name of the mother of the captive Tarbell was Elizabeth Wood. Joseph (Tarbell) Wood therefore perpetuates the names of both white ancestors.

GEORGE GEORGE (Skah-lo-hah-dieh),
"Beyond the Sky."
Oneida.

DANIEL GEORGE (Jo-hah-goeh-deh),
"Road Scraper."
Onondaga.

JOHN LOFT (Hea-ren-ho-doh),
"Standing Tree."
Mohawk.

PART XII.

ANNUITIES AND ANNUITY PAYMENTS.

The Six Nations, with the exception of the Saint Regis Indians, who receive no annuities from the United States, draw from the United States and from the state of New York annuities on the basis of past treaties, which secured this fixed income on account of lands sold from time to time, and rights surrendered to other lands which had been claimed by them as parts of their inheritance. They are considerations to the Indians for value received by the United States or the state of New York. This payment is proportionately less in value each year, as the Indian's condition constantly exacts a greater outlay than formerly to meet increased cost of his changed mode of living. The original equivalent of land has been so enhanced in value that the state of New York can well afford to supplement the small resources of the Indian by a reasonable outlay to help him upward in civilized growth. It has done this freely.

The annuities themselves, legally owed and paid without hesitation, bring small returns in visible benefits. The payments by the United States, which are theoretically paid in the early autumn, during the census year were not completed until February, 1891, through delay of the appropriation by Congress for that purpose. They should be paid in the spring, to enable the farmer to purchase seed or implements for his farm.

The various payments during the census year were so similar that reference to one of each, viz, of money at Cattaraugus and goods at Onondaga, will indicate the methods and incidents of all similar payments.

DISTRIBUTION OF ANNUITIES AT THE COURTHOUSE, CATTARAUGUS RESERVATION.

After due notice, the importunate inquiry, extending over months, "When is our annuity money coming"? had its solution. The courthouse of the Seneca nation was crowded with men, women, and children of all ages and conditions. Old Robert Silverheels, a veteran of the war of 1812, past 90 years of age, and entirely dependent upon the charity of his people, emerged from his little cabin to receive his welcome share. Old Solomon O'Bail, grandson of the great Cornplanter, and rapidly reaching his fourscore years, was there. Blind old John Joe, already in his ninth decade, and John Jacket, the tall, bright, and clear-headed representative of the illustrious Red Jacket, awaited their turn. Daniel Twoguns, at the age of 92, who had "so long waited", had but just gone to his rest; but old Joseph Hemlock and wife, each just 80, were there; also Abigail Bennett, at the age of 92, and Mary Snow, but a little younger, watched for the last time the dawning of "annuity day".

The poor, the sick, the wasted, and the cripples came together as at no other time. It was a damp day, yet not cold; but the echoes of many a cough told how surely the dread consumption still retained its grasp on waiting victims. In contrast with the wrinkled and weary faces which eagerly watched the pay table, more than 100 little Indians, from the age of a few weeks upward, were borne, well wrapped, as legal tender for an additional amount, payable to the family which owned them, for every new child is a recipient, the allowance dating before its birth as well as a year after its death, so that during the autumn enumeration there sounded the careful injunction from 5 humble homes: "Write Agent Jackson we've got a new baby. Tell him to mark it down"!

Chester C. Lay, the official interpreter, called the roll. Some responded with a rush; others edged slowly through the crowd at the doors, either extreme calling forth a humorous hit, an outvoiced laugh, or some side remark, audible in the room, all in good humor; but there were those who were hardly able to be present at all, and they silently approached the table, hid away their little treasure, and disappeared.

Those who could write signed the voucher sheet and those who could not made their cross. But there was a second pay table where the Indian man and woman sometimes left the entire sum received from Agent Jackson. It was the table of the merchants, from as far away as Steamburg and Red House, who gave up the orders for goods which had been discounted the year before. This stream also flowed steadily and cheerfully, without higgling or contest, and the payment was spontaneous and prompt, the silent testimony to the honesty of hundreds, who needed the money for approaching winter. But one dispute arose, where an overlined item exceeding the amount named in the order was questioned. When payment was complete a pen was handy, also a new order book in blank, and then was executed in favor of the applicant another assignment in way of trade, but discounting the annuity of 1891.

There were solid men and sensible women who secured their money and went straight back to work or home, and there were many on the courthouse square who settled fraternal debts. For 2 or 3 days also the hard-cider dens at Lawton station and the "Four mile road" replenished their tills, and then the annuity had melted away. Decorum, good order, and cheerfulness had no interruption, and no similar assemblage can ever be witnessed except on annuity day among the Six Nations; no recurring day can ever bring together on earth so many whose years and names tie the census year to the history of 100 years ago.

The agent of the United States for the Six Nations and the New York superintendent of the Saint Regis Indians pay the same gross sum annually whatever the number, dividing accordingly. A scourge of disease would increase either of these distributive payments to each without reduction of the aggregate; hence, the care taken by the Indians to report births and deaths, as the annuity overruns a year, to cover, presumably, cost of sickness and burial.

DISTRIBUTION OF GOODS.

The distribution of the annual quota of goods due from the United States to the Onondagas, closing the series of issues for the year 1890, took place at the council house on the public green at 1 o'clock p. m., February 5, 1891. Congress had postponed this distribution of cotton goods, greatly to the discomfort of the recipients, and here, as on all the reservations during many months, the first inquiry after a brief introduction was, "When shall we get our goods"? It succeeded the inquiry, "When is our annuity coming? We want to get ready for cold weather".

The distribution at Onondaga is a fair representation of similar scenes at the other reservations. Upon due notice by United States Indian Agent T. W. Jackson of the day of his arrival, word was quickly circulated, and at midday men of all ages, and women bearing their children with them, assembled rapidly. They came by the roads and across fields by the most direct routes, and with the utmost propriety seated themselves upon the benches ranged against the walls in the council house, the women occupying one end of the building and the men the other. Very little conversation took place, and the quiet was that of a quaker meeting. In the center lay the bales of muslin, and Orris Farmer, one of the wealthiest of headmen, stood, knife in hand, ready to open them at proper announcement. Meanwhile the agent and his clerk, Mr. James E. Paxon, of Akron, prepared receipts for signature, and at 1 o'clock Daniel La Forte, who has been both president of the Onondagas and chairman of the Six Nations council, announced the hour for distribution. Several chiefs were summoned to the table to sign the receipts on behalf of the people. These were attested by the clerk and a second white man, and the distribution began. With a rapid dash of hands alternately through the folds of muslin, swift as a weaver's shuttle, there were told off to the Oneidas 11 and to the Onondagas 9 yards. A touch of the knife and a sharp, crisp tear told off 1 share, which was quickly passed to the expectant owner. Now and then the representative of a large family would be half buried under the accumulating load, and rippling, good-natured laughter would disturb the silence. With here and there a bonnet, the greater number of the women sat with heads wrapped in bright shawls, nearly one-half holding children, and as quickly as a share was fully made up the contented owner quietly started homeward with the burden. The same was true of the men. Perfect decorum prevailed and all had contented faces. Old Widow Isaacs, whose cabin is near the council house, and who, at an advanced age, sews as industriously for her good-natured son Billy as if he were only 5 years old instead of 50, kept her place well to the front, intensely interested in all that was going on. The distribution lasted until nearly 5 o'clock, and not a rude word, an impatient gesture, or a wry face disturbed the good order and genial feeling. At one time 80 people occupied each end of the hall, all neatly and modestly dressed, and no gathering of white people under similar circumstances could furnish a better model for good conduct.

The very names contrasted with those of other reservations, Webster, Hill, Thomas, Brown, Jones, Jacobs, and Lyons being English. Old John Adams, of the war of 1812, Abram Hill, the honored Oneida chief, and Chief Theodore Webster, keeper of the wampum, bore their years with dignity, and were among the most interested of those present.

Kind-hearted Billy Isaacs, with a soul proportioned to 250 pounds avoirdupois of body, with eyes full of fun twinkling out of a large and very sober face, said: "This severalty in goods is mighty fine, but I'd like to have my share of land, too; be a citizen; and laws for everybody, too; laws that can be read, and laws made to work; that is what we want".

During the 4 hours occupied in the distribution, although both men and women use tobacco freely, no pipes were lighted, and the floor remained unsoiled to the end.

ANNUITY VALUES.

The annuities, in money and goods, are as follows:

The Senecas receive annually from the United States $16,250 in money, and $500 from the state of New York.

The Onondagas receive from the state of New York, $2,430.

The Cayugas, living among the other nations, receive from the state of New York, $2,300.

The Saint Regis Indians receive from the state of New York, $2,130.67. They do not receive any annuity goods from the United States.

The Six Nations also receive from the United States annually the value of $3,500 in goods. The Tuscaroras and Oneidas receive no money annuities.

PART XIII.

THE SIX NATIONS PROBLEM.

The main conclusions of the New York state commission, that "Indian forms of government are no longer adequate to their changed condition and circumstances, that many Indians see the better way and are restive, while others submit in silence", and that too many partial or conflicting laws are nominally in force, but without coherence and general application, are everywhere manifest.

The alleged absurdity of the Six Nations of New York being a "nation within a nation" does not change the fact or nullify the sequence of actual history. This very fact opens to the Indian and to the white man a way of relief, without the impairment of treaties or the disregard of any rights whatever.

Accepting all that the most technical advocate of the Indians' claim to prolonged independence can advance, a higher and equally consistent principle of international law supplies the wholesome remedy.

As contiguous nations must have political intercourse, and upon a basis of mutual benefit, so there must be, on the part of each, some representative authority to adjust conflicting issues between them. The absence of such authority, and the neglect or refusal of any people to place themselves within the range of mutual consideration of the rights of the citizens of both, is among all nations a casus belli. The remedy may not require arms, but a constraint equivalent to that of arms when actual rupture occurs is legitimate.

The Onondagas of New York furnish an opportunity to illustrate this principle. The state pays an annuity to the Onondagas (a). It has the right to be assured that the payment, designed to be per capita, is, in fact, so made. An act directing that said payments shall be made only to persons who, by an authorized, legal vote of the Indian people, have authority to receipt for the same is but just to the state and its beneficiaries. It simply demands " credentials ". The authority granted by the state to certain white men to lease lands on the reservations, and a recognition of such leases by the Indians as valid, might well be accompanied by the condition that a due proportion of said rental should be applied in maintaining the roads which are in common use and to a proportionate share of the cost of maintaining schools, now wholly supported by the state. On the same principle, acting for both landlord and tenant, it would be competent for the United States, in its indorsement of leases by the Seneca nation of lands in the Allegany valley, to appoint a special commissioner to act as referee or umpire, where equitable terms are not agreed upon, at the releasing in 1892; and even to make the condition that a sufficient portion of the sum realized annually shall be applied to keep in good order the public highways and mail routes, and that for the protection of the people who are entitled to the usufruct of said leases the treasurer of the Seneca nation shall annually publish a statement of the distribution and use of said fund. To facilitate the self-reliance, industry, and confidence which such a system would at once develop, the state and federal courts should be open whenever a natural jurisdiction would inhere, where, in the absence of local protection, evils can be remedied and Indian officials be held to strict account. The state and federal courts should, as the former have in several instances, recognize the "Indian common law title" of occupants of reservation lands where such lands have been improved. They should assure such titles, as well as sales, devises, and descent, through courts of surrogate or other competent tribunals, wherever local Indian officials refuse just recognition of such titles or delay a just administration when conflicts arise.

The obligation of the federal government to pay interest on its debt, on account of lands long since sold, does not prevent its assertion of the obligation on the part of the Indian to do his part in maintaining all those other obligations which he owes to his neighbor in matters of mutual interest. All statutes which offer the Indian a premium for dishonest dealing should be repealed, and the Indian be held to his contracts to the extent of his personal holdings.

The advanced element on every reservation of the Six Nations is ready to come up to this standard, which sacrifices nothing but profitless pride, retained at the expense of social education and physical development.

All state laws which regulate marriage, punish adultery and kindred offenses should be available for the Indian complainant, and none of the Indian estates, once legally recognized as held in practical severalty, should hereafter be cumbered by the claims of illegitimate offspring. The liquor laws should be not only maintained but enforced, with the deliberate purpose on the part of the American people to strengthen the Indian for his own sake and for the sake of the commonwealth into which he must, in due time, be fully adopted.

---

a While this manuscript was in hand a letter from Jaris Pierce (Onondaga) came, inclosing an act pending before the New York legislature, carrying out the governmental reforms suggested in a previous chapter respecting Indian government, and confirming the judgment therein expressed, that the Onondaga Indians themselves were ready to take the initiative in civilized progress.

CITIZENSHIP.

There is no occasion to precipitate the technical, very vague, and very unsubstantial condition of citizenship upon the people of the Six Nations. It would only facilitate, while they are poor, the transfer of their lands to hungry white men without benefit to their people at large. The scheme to force the Seneca nation from their existing form of self-government, however feeble that government may be, is simply a mode by which the Senecas, thus being without a representative, can be forced into the courts by action for " partition " and the elimination of their titles as " tenants in common" for the benefit of the white people.

Universal distrust of the New York Indians and almost utter ignorance of the strong undercurrent of improvement will make the actual facts of their true condition as to property, health, long life, and gradual increase upon a sound basis a surprise to many besides the enumerator.

When the usual accompaniments of small incomes in rural districts, together with musical instruments, sewing machines, sewing circles, and social gatherings, were found to have gained rapidly, so that the so-called pagan element had all it could do to hold its own, and when public opinion had already suppressed the gross forms of the old superstition, and the question of future citizenship was boldly, calmly, and reasonably discussed, there was disclosed the fact that patient sympathy from without, instead of active antagonism, had become sound policy.

The Six Nations will make better citizens by a still longer struggle among themselves, if supported generously and charitably by those who are their true friends. They need supporting laws, but not to be rooted up and left to wilt away. They need, most of all, some enforcement of school attendance. The state of New York, itself lacking law for the compulsory attendance of white children, can not consistently come to the Indians' relief. Church organizations already in the field should redouble their labors, restore the industrial school at Newtown, on the Cattaraugus reservation, and realize that they can do better work than ever before. Every church mission on the reservation can stimulate the political transformation if a united, liberal, and harmonious effort be made. This is especially true of the Allegany reservation, where the scattered population, peculiarly related to the white people, needs more of reconstructive work than most others. The Indians need the encouragement of a friendly regenerating force. Then they will gradually gain self-reliance and the ambition that commands respect and success.

THE TITLES TO INDIAN LANDS.

Independent of the pre-emption lien of the Ogden Land Company upon the lands of the Seneca nation, and absolutely as respects the Onondaga, Tonawanda, and Tuscarora Senecas, the Indians already hold their lands substantially in severalty. The theory advanced by many that these lands are so absolutely held in common that the people have no stimulus to improve them is founded upon an erroneous idea of law and fact. The same principle that underlies the English and therefore the American common law obtains here. It has been settled among the Six Nations beyond question that occupation, building upon, and improvement of land by consent of the authorities representing the whole people confer a title, practically in fee simple, excepting that it is inalienable to a foreigner; but it may be conveyed or devised within the nation, and that it is inheritable by the immediate and natural heirs in absence of a will, and that as a system, however crude in form, the distribution of land in case of death almost invariably follows its natural and just direction. The exceptions are not greater than in contests among the white people.

It is equally true that when a party without land applies to the authorities for the formal allotment of land for improvement and cultivation permission to so select and improve land is almost always given. The national title has itself been a guarantee to each individual occupant that this perfect title in the nation is his to control as if he held a deed therefor, and that his use and disposal of said land can not be disturbed. It is also true that there is public domain enough on each reservation to give to every family seeking it all the land needed, and that the disinclination to work, to improve land, and secure support therefrom is the only barrier to a rightful possession and use of said land. It is also a fact that this tenure is so fully recognized that no body of chiefs or ruling representatives of the Six Nations dare assert any right to disturb that tenure or prevent its sale or devise by the tenant, and that every case, so far as known, reported as a violation of this right by the peacemaker courts or by other authority upon the settlement of an estate or dispute as to adjoining boundaries or conflicting titles, has been adjusted upon evidence, and not upon any assumption that the title was disposable at the choice of said court or chiefs. The judges and chiefs on each reservation unequivocally disclaim such alleged authority, and any assertion of the right would be ignored or resisted. Neither is there any existing usage, method, or power by which an assumption of authority so sweeping could be enforced.

An act of Congress or an act of the general assembly of the state of New York which affirmed such titles would simply modernize in form that established, unwritten law of Indian custom which has the same sanction as the original English title in fee simple, while neither an act of Congress nor an act of the general assembly of the state of New York can reach and disturb the Indian title in severalty as thus established and enjoyed.

LEASES OF SIX NATIONS LANDS.

On each of the reservations, as embodied in the report of the special agent, individual Indians hire white men to work their lands for a cash rental or upon shares, the white people rarely occupying the soil for homes. Nearly 100 white persons occupy Indian lands in the vicinity of Red House, on the Allegany reservation. The names of all are given in the general schedule.

On April 14, 1890, the following official announcement was made by the Seneca nation, but its arbitrary and illegal penalties barred any practical enforcement:

LAWS OF THE SENECA NATION.

[Passed April 14, 1890.]

Pursuant to the resolution of the Seneca nation in council dated this aforesaid, your committee respectfully report the following, viz :

Whereas the laws of the United States forbid the occupancy of any other persons than Indians upon any Indian lands; therefore be it—

Resolved, That any Indian or Indians violating the above-mentioned law, outside of the village boundaries, shall be subject to a punishment by confiscation of the land so leased by the council; and, further, that the said Indian or Indians so violating shall be deprived of his annuity for the term of 10 years; and, furthermore, that he shall be deprived of the privileges of voting at any elections or holding any office in the gift of the people of the Seneca nation.

The "village boundaries" referred to indicate the corporations of Carrollton, Salamanca, West Salamanca, Vandalia, Great Valley, and Red House, which were surveyed and located by Commissioners Scattergood, Manly, and Shanklin under act of Congress approved February 19, 1875. This was a ratification of certain antecedent leases which the supreme court of New York had held to be illegal, and these leases, which will mature in 1892, except those to railroads, were provisionally extended by act passed by the Fifty-first Congress, upon mutual agreement of the parties, "for a period not exceeding 99 years from their expiration, May, 1892". The Oil Spring reservation, which is already on a long lease, is not occupied by Indians.

The income from the corporation lands, which is paid directly to the treasurer of the Seneca nation, supports the peacemaker court and maintains such other executive functions as are within the purview of the national council. The present amount is not far from $9,000 per annum, and the ground rent in many cases is only nominal, that of the principal hotel being but $30 per annum, and others, as a rule, proportionately small.

The Onondaga nation also receives into its treasury rental from stone quarries (only 3 quarries being operated in 1890) at the rate of $200 per derrick, as detailed in the special agent's report.

PARTITION.

The demand made by white citizens, as citizens or as legislators, state or national, is based upon the idea, before intimated, that in case the Indians of the Six Nations should abandon their tribal or national systems all lands owned under an original general title, theoretically in common, would call for proceedings in partition, as in the case of an estate where no provision had been made by a decedent for a distribution among joint heirs. Independent of previously matured rights through purchase, gift, or settlement, this claim has no legal basis, unless it first be made to appear that existing individual holdings are at the expense of rightful copartners in interest, who, without their choice and adversely to their rights, are deprived of their distributive shares in a common inheritance.

The immemorial recognition of the right of any family to enter upon the public domain and occupy land, equally open to all, and only improved by the industrious, disqualifies the assenting, passive tenant from claiming any benefits from the industry of the diligent. The indolent Indian alone is responsible for the neglect to avail himself of that which is free to all.

THE NATURAL DISTRIBUTION.

The claim by some that the lands of the Six Nations shall be divided per capita or per stirpes, in severalty, is a form of communism, ignoring all the just equivalent of honest industry and asserting a prerogative of authority over property and fruitful labor that no government in contact with the civilized world at present would dare assert, much less attempt to exercise.

There is not the faintest similarity between Indian occupation of any western reservation and the titles of the Six Nations to their lands. The United States and the state of New York, without anticipating the paramount authority of the federal courts, have the physical power to ignore treaties and contracts for which an adequate consideration has been paid; but nothing less than a casus belli, when all treaties end with conflict and might establishes its false code of right in a new adjustment of relations between the parties, can furnish an excuse for such legislation.

SOCIAL ADJUSTMENTS.

Given a state of facts which warrants a partition of the Indian lands, share and share alike, at any fixed date, and effect the partition; then project the effect forward 1 month, 12 months, 12 years, or a generation, and the argument will be, and is unequivocally announced, that then, or very soon, the Indian property will appear as property of white men, will have been wasted, and only a very few will have preserved their share or have developed and improved it. The result will follow the natural law of industry and idleness, by which invariably only a certain per cent of any people acquire and retain evidence of well-directed industry. Accurate tables have long defined this percentage, so that political economists rarely err in their forecast of the prospectively distributed wealth of different peoples and classes of people.

At present the Six Nations of New York, with their 80,000 acres, are within easy reach, and helpless, with every possible depressive surrounding to destroy hope for the future, if they who have been industrious are to be pooled with the thriftless who never lacked opportunities to acquire land, but improved none.

THE PRESENT STATUS.

Looking backward as far as political economists can forecast the future, then, as now, you see all lands to have been held in common by the various members of the Iroquois league. As at present, the same choice inured to each family to select, cultivate, buy, sell, and transmit to posterity whatever the members thereof elected. The result of that choice or want of choice, of industry or idleness, of economy or waste, of good judgment or thriftlessness is visible in farms or weedy patches, in houses or cabins, in education or ignorance, in decency or filth. The natural and, but for the universal law in all generations of men, remarkable fact is plainly evident that the percentage of the relative grades of acquisition or waste of large or medium accumulations, of bare support or of scant support, is almost identical with the average of communities wholly white, and the percentage of absolute suffering from want much less than in very many settlements of white people.

A DISTINCTION.

Even the Indians of the present generation have worked out this practical law of property and industry. The resolution of all products of that industry back to a common level, in the guise of misnamed severalty (in spite of a practically existing severalty), opens up to the white man his chance to reap fruit from the neglected shares of the indolent, and eliminates the Indian as rapidly as possible from all interest as well as pride and title in the inheritance of his fathers. And this is proposed as a solution of the Indian problem in this present year of grace!

CONCLUSION.

In concluding this report of the condition of the Six Nations in 1890 it is natural to add the fact that in addition to a constant reference to the published testimony taken by the New York commission nearly every witness, whether white or Indian, was visited personally, and their interested co-operation greatly aided the special agent in his work.

The burden of the Ogden Land Company's claim must be lifted. Premature sales to the white people must be prevented.

In the closing words of the New York commission, "It can not be expected that the Indians will at once become self-dependent, and that all state aid or protection can be withdrawn. It will still be necessary to help them over 'the first rough places in the white man's road', and to aid them to gain a foothold in their ascent to self-respect and self-support".

Meanwhile their representative men, those who are to deal with the state and nation, must have adequate credentials, and be required to accept as binding upon them every obligation which belongs to contiguous states, and see that the laws, codes, and relationships of the age shall not be abused by any to the injury of others.

REPORT OF ENUMERATOR JACKSON.

Enumerator T. W. Jackson, United States Indian agent for the Six Nations, in his annual report for 1890, says:

LEGISLATION.—A bill was introduced in the New York state legislature in February, 1890, by Mr. Whipple, member of assembly from Cattaraugus county, to authorize the governor to nominate and appoint three commissioners to superintend the survey of all lands within this state now held or occupied by any band or tribe of Indians, and to allot the same in severalty in fee simple to the Indians entitled to the occupancy thereof. Said commissioners were authorized to allot one share to each person and to secure as far as possible to each occupant the land now held and the improvements already made and owned by him and to permit all persons to select for themselves and their families so far as the same is consistent. All land not practical to allot shall be sold for the benefit of the band or tribe. Section 12 provided as follows.

The land belonging to the Seneca Indians lying within the villages of Vandalia, Carrollton, Great Valley, Salamanca, West Salamanca, or Red House, as well as that leased to railroad corporations, may be sold to white people whenever the said Seneca nation can legally sell the same and choose to do so.

Said act also makes all Indians to whom or in whose behalf any allotment of land has been made, and the children of such Indians, citizens of this state from the date of the approval by the governor of the allotments provided for in said act, and every Indian who, by purchase or otherwise, has become or may hereafter become a resident of this state, shall become and is hereby declared to be a citizen of this state, and shall be subject to the civil and criminal laws of the state, and entitled to all the rights, privileges, and protection thereof, except to be exempt from all laws for the collection of debts or taxation, so far as the same may affect the alienation of their lands, provided said land is within the limits of any Indian reservation, until the expiration of 30 years. Said bill also provides that after the allotment is completed it shall be a misdemeanor for any person or persons in this state to institute or continue any custom or organization or to confer any title inconsistent with the laws of this state in the name of tribal custom, usage, or government.

Said act also provides that it shall not apply to any land in the Allegany, Cattaraugus, or Oil Spring reservations now occupied by the Seneca Indians, nor to the lands of the Tuscarora Indians, until all claims of the Ogden company to said lands are extinguished. The Onondaga reservation was excepted from the provision of this bill.

The friends of the Indians criticised very severely the motives of this bill, and claim—

First. That as soon as this bill becomes a law and the tribal relations are broken up all rents and annuities will cease, and that the Ogden Land Company can immediately proceed to enforce their claims upon the reservation lands.

Second. That the bill is drawn more particularly for the benefit of white persons who are living upon leased reservation lands in the villages of Vandalia, Carrollton, Great Valley, Salamanca, West Salamanca, and Red House, and that these lands are not allotable under the bill and are excepted from the provisions that no land shall be alienated for 30 years; and that their claims were well founded may be judged from the following, over the signature of one of the advocates of the bill:

Let us briefly consider what will be the effect on our leaseholders upon the Allegany reservation. Suppose there is no longer a Seneca nation of Indians. Then, of course, there is no council to renew our leases or to receive any annual rents, they having been abolished, wiped out by act of legislature. Now, this same authority, having by a legislative act been abolished, dissolved the nation and its council, it would be incumbent on them to provide for our relief. The Indians and their friends would also demand that something be done. They could not take our lands and allot them among the tribe. They could no longer be leased. We are as secure in our titles as are the people of Dayton or any other town to theirs.

The bill passed both branches of the legislature, but in the face of these serious objections and many others the governor allowed the bill to die by refusing to sign it.

In my opinion, the proper way to civilize the Indians of New York is to secure a division of their lands in severalty, and place them in full citizenship; but there are many questions and difficulties to be overcome before this can be done without injury to the rights of the Indians. The first and most important thing to be settled is the right of the Ogden Land Company, and the next the lease problem in the villages of Vandalia, Carrollton, Great Valley, Salamanca, West Salamanca, and Red House. These are momentous questions, and to be settled fairly requires the best assistance on behalf of the Indian that can be furnished by the government for their protection.

As stated in my special report upon the subject of leases in these villages, there are many abuses existing in consequence of these, for many of which the Indians are alone to blame. Corruption in its worst form has existed in their councils; and for a small sum of money leaseholders have been known to enter the council and have their annual rent reduced one-half. Many of the complaints made to me by the Indians of their trouble with white intruders I find, upon investigation, to have been brought about by the Indians themselves. For a trifling sum they allow some low white man to occupy their land, and then, after seeing the poor bargain they have made, seek to have him removed by the agent or nation. I find that, after going to an immense amount of trouble and expense in getting one or two intruders removed from the reservation, the council or individual Indians will turn around and, in one-tenth of the time required to remove them, will let on twice as many more. These things make it quite discouraging for the agent.

This state of facts applies more to the Allegany and Cattaraugus reservations than to any of the others, scarcely any complaints coming from any of the reservations in regard to intruders except the Allegany.

SANITARY.—The sanitary condition of the Indians during the past year has been very good. On account of the mildness of the winter they were not compelled to keep housed up, and the most of the time were able to be around, exercising ; and this, in my opinion, does away with a large amount of sickness. If it were one continual summer the Indians of western New York would be able to live better, but our winters are too much for them. Scanty clothing, scanty food, and unclean living make the lot of our Indians a hard one during the cold weather.

AGRICULTURE.—The crops of the Indians upon the reservations in western New York are, I think, fully up to the average. In consequence of the agitation among the Indians in regard to the bill in the legislature for the division of their lands in severalty, there have been few improvements made during the past year. This unsettled condition of these Indians is a great hindrance to their advancement toward civilization. They are expecting at any time some new steps will be taken to change their condition, and they are consequently loath to make extended improvements, either in building or clearing up their land, as they are afraid the benefit will be reaped either by the whites or other Indians.

WHISKY.—There has been very much trouble upon the Allegany reservation during the past year (prior to June 30, 1890) on account of the sale of whisky to the Indians. At Red House drunken rows have been frequent, and fights between white men and Indians in several instances have resulted in serious injuries to the Indians. All efforts to secure conviction of the guilty parties have proved unavailing on account of the refusal of the Indians to tell where they got their whisky. Early in the spring the commissioner of internal revenue was notified by the authorities at Washington not to issue stamps to persons who were to sell liquors on the Indian reservations, and stamps were refused to the dealers residing in the villages upon the Allegany reservation. Pending an appeal by the dealers to the authorities at Washington, some were given authority to sell until the matter was decided. After considerable delay the opinion of the Attorney General upon the question was received, deciding that the government had no authority to issue licenses to sell liquors upon the reservations, and consequently the sale of liquors in the villages upon the reservation has been stopped altogether. This action on the part of the officials at Washington has caused great consternation among the local liquor dealers.

All of which is respectfully submitted.

T. W. JACKSON,
United States Indian Agent.

INDEX TO THE SIX NATIONS OF NEW YORK.